LOVE, LIPSTICK AND LIES

Katie Price

CENTURY

Published by Century 2013

2 4 6 8 10 9 7 5 3 1

First published in Great Britain in 2013 by
Century
Random House, 20 Vauxhall Bridge Road,
London SW1V 2SA

www.randomhouse.co.uk

Addresses for companies within The Random House Group Limited can
be found at: www.randomhouse.co.uk

The Random House Group Limited Reg. No. 954009

A CIP catalogue record for this book
is available from the British Library

HB ISBN 9781780891385
TPB ISBN 9781780891392

The Random House Group Limited supports the Forest Stewardship
Council® (FSC®), the leading international forest-certification organisation.
Our books carrying the FSC label are printed on FSC®-certified paper.
FSC is the only forest-certification scheme supported by the
leading environmental organisations, including Greenpeace.
Our paper procurement policy can be found at:
www.randomhouse.co.uk/environment

Printed and bound by CPI Group (UK) Ltd, Croydon, CR0 4YY

CONTENTS

INTRODUCTION

I can't believe that we're on the fifth instalment of my autobiography. As usual with me, the three years since my last book, *You Only Live Once,* have been a roller-coaster ride. There's always drama with a capital D in my life. Always.

Now I'm older, wiser, with two marriages behind me and on to marriage number three. They say third time lucky, don't they? And I'm keeping everything crossed that three is a magic number. But I have such a good feeling about my husband Kieran. I've kissed a lot of frogs. Here's hoping that he's my prince. It certainly feels as if he is.

I've always said I am who I am. It doesn't matter what anyone says to me, no one can manufacture me, no one can change who I am. I'm not like those celebrities who put on an act of having a perfect life, and never put a foot wrong. I'm not polished. I'm human and flawed. I've got character and personality. I'm like Marmite: you either love me or loathe me. Frankie Boyle 'joked': 'Ah, Katie Price. A bit of a Marmite figure. Half the country hates her, and the other half thinks she belongs on the end of a knife.' Not that I care what the haters think. I can't be any different from who I am. I don't put on an act for the cameras and the press. There isn't the celebrity Katie Price and the other Katie Price. I am always me.

Whatever anyone says about me, whatever criticisms they throw at me, I'm proud of what I have achieved. Top of the list: my children. They make everything worthwhile, and everything I do, I do it for them. I'm like a proud lioness and they are my cubs. I will always protect and defend them. They are my life.

I'm also proud of what I've achieved in my career. I started as a glamour model and Page 3 girl at the age of seventeen, and from there I've gone on to have my own TV series, sell over three and a half million copies of my autobiographies, novels and children's books, I've got my own business empire with KP Equestrian, KP Rocks, my perfumes, lingerie, swimwear, range of hair products – and I'm always thinking of more! I'm financially secure; I can support my family and give them a brilliant life-style. I'm living proof that you can make something of yourself if you try hard enough.

So here goes...the next instalment.

CHAPTER 1

THE REBOUND MARRIAGE

There is only one word to describe my second marriage, to Alex Reid, and that's rebound. I'm aware it sounds harsh but it's true. I never should have rushed into marrying him. We all make mistakes and that was one big one…However, in my own defence, I met Alex in July 2009, at the absolute worst time of my life. I needed someone to protect me and Alex seemed to fit the bill. If I'm honest, it could have been any man, within reason, who was kind, attractive, and looked strong enough to protect me. I was desperate for some kind of security because my world had just fallen apart.

Earlier that year, in May, Peter Andre, my then husband, had walked out on me just a month after I'd suffered a miscarriage. I was still reeling from the devastating loss of our baby. I knew that our marriage had been on the rocks for a while, but I never thought he would leave me. I was heartbroken.

When I met Pete on *I'm a Celebrity...Get Me Out of Here!* in 2004, I fell head over heels in love with him and believed he felt the same about me. Celebrities often go on that kind of show and put on an act; some of them might fake a romance to get the viewers interested in them. I can honestly say that didn't happen with Pete and me. What we had was real – certainly as far as I was concerned. I thought I had found 'the one', the man who completed me, the man I wanted to spend the rest of my life with. Fast-forward five years and we'd had two children together, first Junior and then Princess, and along with my son Harvey, I thought we had a secure, happy family, something which I have always wanted. But that happy family was destroyed when Pete walked out, telling me it was over in a phone call. To this day he has never properly spoken to me about why he left so I could never get any closure on our marriage, though he would often drop hints in the magazine interviews he subsequently gave that there was a dark secret behind our divorce. There was no dark secret. I think he was swayed into leaving me.

From the moment he left in May 2009 (less than two months after I had given my then manager Claire Powell notice that I did not want her to continue acting for me), I was hounded by the press. The tabloids and magazines wrote terrible stories about me, while Pete was held up as some kind of saint, the perfect father, and a victim. I was back to being called Jordan and blamed for the break up of our marriage. There seemed to be no sympathy for me at all. Someone even came up with the Team Pete/ Team Katie idea, and some so-called celebs were quoted as saying that they were on Team Pete. No one seemed to realise that this wasn't about taking sides. It wasn't a game. It was about a family that had broken up, and at the heart of it were our children.

As far as I know, never once, when all the lies were printed about me, did Pete ever defend me and say, 'Hang on. These stories aren't true! I don't want a bad word said against the mother of my children. We may have had our differences but she's a good mum.' Instead it felt to me as if he was building up his own career and image by trashing mine. This may sound like sour grapes but it is true. Within a matter of weeks Pete was promoting his new album. I've always wondered how he would have promoted it if we hadn't split up, especially given the lyrics of some of the songs on it, which were published in various magazines with the suggestion that they were about me.

Worse than any of that, I also had to face up to a new life where I wouldn't have Princess and Junior living with me all the time because they would be spending time with their father. I missed them so badly when they were away, it was like a physical pain. They were both so little. My babies. Princess was only one and a half and Junior was four. They needed to be with their mum. I had felt under pressure to agree to joint custody, even though I thought the children should spend most of their time with me. Pete had walked out, and yet it felt as if I was the one being punished.

There was no one to stand up for me. In March I had given Claire Powell notice that I was going to leave her, but indicated that I would consider a new way of working with her if that were possible. For a long time I hadn't been happy with the way she had managed me. Her style had become too controlling and I never felt that I had any freedom. It was all work, work, work, every aspect of my life and my marriage filmed or photographed or discussed in interviews. I swear the constant filming was one of the reasons our marriage broke up. Pete and I never had any time or space to ourselves.

According to our contract she was supposed to represent me until June, but from the moment Pete walked out on me in May I didn't feel Claire was there for me at all, and as far as I know she never tried to put a stop to any of the untrue stories that were published about me as she would have done before he left. When I asked her why she was not protecting me and asked her to do something, she actually told me, via a letter to my lawyer, that she would do so only if I signed a new contract with her for a further five years, on terms that were disadvantageous to me. I felt that this was taking advantage of the situation and could not understand how she thought she was going to be able to represent both me and Pete going forward. That seemed to me to be impossible. When my lawyer went through the contract he confirmed that there was no way I could agree to the terms she had proposed.

I had thought that she was more than a manager; I had thought she was my friend. But, looking back, it seems she was primarily in it for the money. I'd lost my husband, and then two more friends – Jamelah Asmar and Michelle Clack – decided to cut off all contact with me, and instead side with Pete. Later, Michelle, who was someone I counted as one of my best and oldest friends, sold a story blaming me for the break up of the marriage, and Jamelah attempted to do the same, though the *News of the World* did not publish it. I felt betrayed by people I had trusted and incredibly alone at that time.

And then I met Alex. He was this big, strong man, well over six foot, handsome in a kind of beaten-up way, and I was instantly drawn to him. I felt as if he could be my knight in shining armour and protect me. I needed that. As well as the emotional pain I was in, I felt physically under attack as newspaper *paparazzi* pursued me everywhere and camped outside my front gate. Often I would resort to hiding in the boot of the car, under a blanket while whoever was driving me would wind down their window and say to the waiting paps, 'Have a look inside, she's not here.' Anything to avoid them. But I didn't always have a driver and there were times when I felt like a hunted animal, as the paps chased me whenever I drove anywhere, often making me fearful for my safety. They played a dangerous cat-

and-mouse game where one of their cars would go behind me, one in front, and I would be stuck in the middle. For years I'd had a premonition that I would die in a car accident and that feeling intensified during this time. I was haunted by thoughts that I would die and my children would be left without their mother.

But turning to Alex wasn't just about the press attention and the negative stories; it was about feeling that someone cared about me and would stick by me no matter what. After the split with Pete I felt that no man would ever want me again after they had read all the terrible lies about me printed by the press. My reputation had been completely trashed. It felt like a huge deal that Alex still wanted to be with me, and didn't take any notice of what had been written. It felt as if it was the two of us against the rest of the world because as soon as the press found out that I was with Alex, they raked together all the dirt they possibly could on him as well. I felt protected by him, and also protective of him. At the time I believed I was in love with him, but I think I was more like a drowning woman reaching out for help. I desperately needed someone to save me, and Alex was there.

Our relationship very quickly became serious and he moved in. I'm the kind of person who thinks you only live once and that you should live your life the way you want to. It doesn't matter what anyone else thinks, it's about being true to yourself. After all, there are no rules that say you have to wait a certain length of time before you can fall in love with someone else after a marriage ends. There were some people who thought I had moved on too quickly after Pete left me. But he had made it brutally clear that our marriage was over. What was I supposed to do? Sit around and wait for his permission to see someone else?

In Alex I thought that I had found a man I could be happy with. There weren't the competing egos that there had been in my relationship with Pete when we spent so much time working together. Alex seemed to have many good qualities; he was charming, kind and warm, a big softie really, as well as a gentleman. I liked the fact that he had his own career as a professional fighter, and trained every day. We could also go out together and have fun, because he didn't have a problem with me having a drink in the way Pete always had. I felt he looked after me; I felt safe in his arms, as if everything was going to be all right; that I could get through it this time. He looked after me in other ways as well, always trying to get me to eat healthily and to train at the gym. Most important of all, he was good with my kids. However, none of these things lasted...

From the start none of my family and friends were happy about my relationship with Alex. They didn't trust his motives and tried to warn me about him, telling me that they were sure he was only with me because he wanted to be famous and that I shouldn't trust him. And I'd say, 'No, you're all wrong. He genuinely wants to be with *me*. He knows that I don't want another "Katie and

Peter" relationship. He knows I don't want our personal life splashed across the papers. He loves *me*.' I refused to listen to anyone. Now I wish I had...It would have saved me a whole lot of heartache and money.

They say love is blind, don't they? I certainly was. Alex always said that he wasn't after fame, but I should have read the signs. Of course he wanted fame! He'd tried to make it as an actor but had failed; he'd tried to be a model without success. He was a thirty-four-year-old man who still lived at home with his parents. He was signing on, teaching kickboxing and working as a personal trainer. He must have thought he was made for life when he met me.

But my friends and family had another big reason to be wary of him. This outwardly masculine cage fighter had an alter ego, Roxanne. In private Alex liked to dress up as a woman. I found out when my personal trainer, Sol, who also knew Alex and had introduced us, asked me if I had seen him dressed up as a woman yet. He said it in such a jokey way that even though I was surprised by the revelation, as anyone would be, I thought it must all be for a laugh.

I immediately asked Alex if this was true and he admitted it straight out. He told me that he had dressed up as a woman for fun. He seemed to underplay the whole thing, as if it wasn't really that important, nothing serious – and definitely nothing to worry about.

Even with him making light of it like this, everyone else around me was taken aback. But not me. Instead I was curious to find out more. I am very open-minded and don't like to be too quick to judge anyone. As long as it was something that was kept well away from my children, I felt I could accept it. After all, Alex had accepted me for myself and had rescued me at a time when I was at rock bottom.

Writing about him now makes me wish I could re-wind time and cut Alex Reid out of my life because I had absolutely no idea what I was letting myself in for. By the time we split up, just over a year and a half later, his sleazy, sordid behaviour had left me feeling disturbed, vulnerable and frightened. It would take me a long time to recover from my rebound marriage to a man with such serious issues.

I admit that once I found out about Alex's secret I was the one who pursued the subject. I wanted to find out more. I was intrigued. When I'm with someone I don't want there to be any secrets, I want everything out in the open. Once I knew that Alex dressed up as a woman he referred to as Roxanne, I wanted to see what it was all about. It was hard for me to imagine what this very masculine man would look like as a woman. He was a professional cage fighter, and that seemed to be the most macho, aggressive sport where fighters have to be incredibly tough. Cage fighting is a full-contact combat sport where two men fight using Mixed Martial Arts. It is raw and brutal, nothing seems to be banned except biting, and you can kick and punch your opponent pretty much everywhere except in the nuts. I had watched videos of Alex fighting and I'd seen other cage fights so I knew all about it.

One night when we were on our own, and were getting a little drunk on cocktails of vodka, Malibu and Coke that we later called the Roxanne, I said, 'Come on then. Show me Roxanne. Let me dress you up and put make up on you.' Alex refused at first, and seemed taken aback that I would even ask. But I persisted; I am very persuasive when I want to be, and in the end he agreed.

As I went through different outfits in my dressing room, trying to find the right wig, underwear and dress for Roxanne, I had no idea what I was unleashing by allowing Alex to be her with me. If I had I would have stopped there and then. Actually I would have finished with him and run a mile. But I didn't know. I thought it was a bit of harmless fun, though in time I would learn I could not have been more wrong. So there I was, carefully putting red lipstick on him, checking that I had done his make up how he liked it. And the response I got back from him was overwhelming. He told me that he loved me, that I was the best girl ever, that I was his perfect woman. I don't think he could believe that I accepted this side of him. But I did then because I had no idea what it really meant.

I wasn't disturbed that first time by his cross-dressing because I had been the one to initiate it. I was a little shocked by his appearance, as anyone would be seeing their macho boyfriend in lingerie and make up! But because I felt in control, I thought everything was fine.

I felt as if I was sharing something with Alex, and that there was a bond of trust and respect between us. We talked all the time as I helped him get made up, bantering away with each other.

But after that first time, it soon became clear that there was a sexual side to his cross-dressing. He admitted that he dressed up as Roxanne for sexual thrills. From his description it sounded as if he didn't do it very often. I respected Alex for being honest with me. I was sure a lot of men would have tried to hide something like this. It's okay, I thought, it's something he does in private; he's sexually adventurous, and uninhibited, and so am I. Naively, I didn't think it could hurt me. What I didn't know was that by accepting this side of Alex, I had opened up Pandora's box. We were going to end up with three people in our relationship – me, Alex and Roxanne – and I definitely hadn't signed up for her. The truth was I didn't know what I was letting myself in for back then. I had no idea of the extent of Alex's secret life. I thought it was only a very small part of him. Little did I know that it would take over and ultimately destroy our marriage.

Most couples get up to some role-play in the bedroom, don't they? That's what I thought we were doing when Alex dressed up as Roxanne and I joined him in the bedroom. I thought it was something to make our sex life more adventurous, give it a little extra spice, and that it would happen only very occasionally. I've always been up for a bit of experimentation. I felt I could handle it;

that I was fully in control, the one saying, 'If you want to dress up, you can.' And that if and when I wanted him to stop, he would. I didn't find out until much later that he wouldn't. I didn't know what appalling scenes I would later be confronted with as Alex lost himself in the depraved world of Roxanne and turned my bedroom into a sex dungeon with porn playing, sex toys everywhere, and in the midst of it all a desperate man, with dead eyes, about as far away from the charming, kind Alex I had met as you could possibly imagine.

From the moment we had first got together we'd had a good sex life. I had actually broken my own rule and slept with him on our first date, that's how strong the attraction had been...or maybe how desperate I was to find a man at that time! And I won't deny that I enjoyed the first few experiences when he showed me Roxanne. It gave me a kind of weird excitement to be doing something different, to act more like a man in the bedroom. As I've already said, I'm up for experimenting, when it feels safe and I can trust my partner. I really didn't think it would happen very often; I felt as if we were just fooling around role-playing, and that this was all Alex would ever expect me to do. But even so I can remember thinking: This isn't normal. Do I really want my boyfriend to look like this? To act like this?

I'd say for the first year of our relationship, the Roxanne side didn't happen very often at all and the rest of the time we had normal sex. But to Alex it must have been like an awakening. As our relationship went on, he would want me to do more and more extreme things to him...Looking back, I wonder if those first few times with me were enough for him or whether he had to dress up as Roxanne more than he let on.

*   *   *

I knew it wouldn't be long before the press found out about Roxanne, and I dropped my own hint that I already knew and didn't care when I named my newest horse Jordan's Cross Dresser in August. (He is now called Wallace II.) By October all the tabloids were on to the story. I felt protective of Alex and wanted to show that I stood by him so I arranged for him to do an interview and shoot with *OK!* magazine, and managed to negotiate a nice fat fee for him. In the interview he talked about his cross-dressing and how he felt he had nothing to hide, nothing to prove to anyone, and nothing to be ashamed of. And back then I didn't think he had anything to be ashamed of either because he still hadn't revealed the dark, disturbing side of his life.

Then I decided that we could really put on a show to prove to everyone that I knew about Alex's cross-dressing and it didn't bother me, with the launch of my style book *Standing Out.* In an eye-catching press call, I was joined by Alex, as well as my brother and my friends Andrew and Phil, dressed in exact copies of four of my most famous outfits. Alex was in a gold swimsuit, like the one I had worn when I dressed up as Xena: Warrior Princess on a trip to Ibiza. It was our way of saying 'Up yours!' to anyone who thought there was something wrong with what Alex did. It was meant to be very tongue-in-cheek and light-hearted. It certainly grabbed the press's attention and I received great coverage for my new book.

But that day was the first inkling I had that maybe it wasn't just a bit of fun for Alex. He had been drinking heavily as he prepared for the press call, and by the time we were photographed he was drunk. Afterwards we all went for a meal and then to the theatre, but Alex didn't seem to want to be there. I suddenly clicked that he wanted to go back to the hotel and dress up again.

That night we had sex with him being Roxanne. We both drank a lot and I remember waking up in the morning and feeling really hungover, with all these images in my head of what we had done. When I look back, it seems that I always had to have a drink in order to deal with him being Roxanne; I was never completely sober during those encounters. I wasn't at all sure if I liked what had just happened. It was a relief to get up and go out into the world to do the press interviews for my book. I pushed the events of the night to the back of my mind. Maybe it had happened because he was so drunk and stressed about all the press coverage he had been getting, I told myself. Negative press coverage had become a painful fact of life for me, but for Alex it was something new. It must have been tough on him.

A few weeks later we went to the BloodLust Ball at Hampton Court House, just after Hallowe'en. Everyone dresses outrageously for this event and we were no exception. I went as a very kinky Catwoman in a black PVC corset with red leopard-print stockings and matching gloves, mask and a tail. Alex dressed up as a woman, in a fishnet top, bra, g-string and patent leather boots.

Although by now I had seen him dressed up as Roxanne several times, it was still a shock to see him out in public like that, even at a fancy dress ball. I had to remind myself that underneath all the make up, he was still my boyfriend. But I was starting to see that he didn't just put on the clothes and make up, he seemed to become a different person too. I would notice it in his eyes first; there would be a different look in them, a vacant expression. The same thing happened when he was preparing to fight, as if he was going into a different zone, turning into Alex the fighter. Here it was like a switch clicking him from Alex to Roxanne, and a complete change would come over him. He spoke in a softer, quieter voice. His whole personality altered, and he was shy and quiet whereas usually he was confident and outgoing. That night it was as if I wasn't with Alex, I was with Roxanne. It unsettled me; this was something I hadn't been prepared for. Alex dressing up in lingerie and wearing make up and wanting to have sex like that was one thing, but this whole personality change was creepy. However, I reassured myself that the moment he took off the make up and outfit he would be back to being the Alex I loved. Looking back, I can only say that I had become very good at convincing myself that everything would be all right because I so wanted things to work out between us.

I ended up leaving the ball before him and he travelled home later with two of my friends. Diana does the publicity for my books, and Gary has been my make-up artist for years. They thought he was behaving really oddly and couldn't talk to him at all. Apparently they heard a funny noise coming from the back seat where he was sitting and were shocked to find him doing something of a sexual nature in the taxi, completely oblivious to them being there. I know! When they told me back at the house, I think I underplayed it, explained it away as him being drunk. It was only later as I was having serious concerns about Alex that I thought back to what they had told me, and how early on it had revealed the seedy, disturbing side of his cross-dressing.

CHAPTER 2

SECOND TIME UNLUCKY

A whirlwind three months after we had met, Alex proposed to me and I said yes. I still thought that his cross-dressing was something that I was in control of and, as I've said, it rarely happened before we were married in 2010. But even without Roxanne we had problems...

In November 2009 I appeared for the second time on *I'm a Celebrity...Get Me Out of Here!* I had agreed to go on the reality show again because I wanted people to see that I was a completely different woman from the heartless bitch the press had portrayed me as for the past six months. The first time I had gone on the show in 2004 I'm sure many people thought that I was just a glamour-girl bimbo, who got her tits out for a living, and spent all her time plastered in make up, falling pissed out of night clubs. But they changed their opinion when they saw what I was like in the jungle. I'd like to think that they saw the real me then; that I came across as down-to-earth, ready to take on any of the challenges, however disgusting and frightening; and that I was a woman capable of falling deeply in love.

But the second trip to the jungle was not a positive experience for me. I hope I showed the real me again, but I felt powerless to reverse the negative coverage of me in the press. The public voted for me to do every single bush-tucker trial, and it did get to me. It felt as if the viewers really wanted to give me a bad time, that they actually enjoyed seeing me scared and vulnerable.

It was the tasks involving water that terrified me the most as I've had a fear of being out of my depth ever since I was a teenager and had a panic attack while I was swimming and actually thought I was going to drown. Heights terrify me as well. Somehow I endured the tasks involving water, though I had a panic attack after one of these and had to say the words 'I'm a Celebrity . . . Get Me Out of Here!' in order to be rescued. I made it through the Hell Hole Challenge, which involved climbing a sixty-foot wall and sticking my hand into holes where there were spiders, snakes and rats. I put my face into a tank full of slime and stinking mealworm larvae to collect the stars with my teeth; I had thousands of cockroaches poured on to my head and into my jacket and boots; I did all the disgusting eating tasks, munching on grubs and cockroaches, though I spat out the fish eye and drew the line at chewing down a kangaroo's testicle!

I felt drained by these daily ordeals, as if the public were bent on torturing and punishing me. Of course I'd expected to do some bush-tucker trials when I went in, but had never imagined it would be so relentless. By the time I was voted to do the seventh trial in a row I couldn't take any more. I walked off the show. I'm usually up for anything but I don't think I was physically or mentally prepared for doing so many gruelling tasks on top of a year where my marriage had ended and I'd endured such a public mauling by the press.

I was looking forward to being reunited with Alex in Australia and my kids in the UK. I certainly needed one of Alex's cuddles after what I'd been through. But he wasn't there to meet me. Instead I was met by my good friend Michelle Heaton, who told me that it appeared Alex had been selling stories while I was away and, to cap it all, there had been a front-page story in one tabloid that he was flying out to Australia to propose to me. I had told Alex categorically that I didn't want him to talk about me in the press, that we would be finished if he ever did. I felt as if he had completely betrayed my trust. On top of everything else... *this*. I didn't know how much more I could take.

'We're over,' I told him on the phone. I didn't want to hear anything he had to say; I was so angry and hurt. When I was interviewed by Ant and Dec on ITV, I told them that Alex and I were no longer together. But later

I agreed to meet up with him. Alex denied selling any stories, talked me round, and charmed me. I wanted to believe him; I thought I loved him. I didn't want our relationship to be over so I accepted his explanation. No one around me believed him, though. They all thought I was crazy to take him back. I know what I'm like, and when I'm in a relationship I want it to work; I try my hardest to make it work. I always want to believe in that fairy-tale, happy-ever-after ending, and when there are problems I try and find excuses for situations. And when there's been a problem, afterwards I think, Oh, it's all right now. Things will get better. That's definitely what I thought back then with Alex. Things will get better. And they did for a while...for a few months after that we had great times.

*   *   *

Although I had made it clear from the start with Alex that I didn't want a relationship with someone in the public eye, he kept pushing me, saying he wanted to do an interview or go on such and such a show. As much as I didn't want him to, I knew I couldn't stop him. I warned him that if he started doing interviews with the press then they would be on his case even more than they already were. But then he was offered the chance to appear on *Celebrity Big Brother*. The press had written so much rubbish about our relationship, and about us, that I thought it would be good for the public to see what Alex was really like. I knew that he wouldn't dress up as Roxanne on-screen and thought that he would come across really well. So my management negotiated a good deal for him to appear on the show – around a hundred and fifty grand.

Sure enough, Alex impressed everyone with his appearance. He came across as a genuinely lovely guy. Everyone on the show got on with him, and the public obviously liked him because they voted for him to win – the same public who had booed him when he had gone into the house. I missed him so much it was ridiculous! I pined for him so badly, I would be glued to the TV in the evenings and couldn't go to sleep until I knew he was tucked up in bed. I realised then that I definitely wanted to marry him, and as soon as I possibly could.

When he came out of the house he was greeted by a cheering crowd. 'I'm a man in love!' he told them. 'I love Katie Price!' The cheers changed to boos when he mentioned my name, the press had done such a good job of making me out to be a bitch, but Alex stood up for me, told them to stop because they didn't know me. I was really touched by his support – my fighter, fighting for me. I'd already had the ordeal of being booed at the National Television Awards earlier that month, and however brave a face you put on, it's a deeply horrible experience. I'd love to know why the people who booed thought it was okay to do that to someone they didn't even know. It was just like being bullied at school. And as Alex said, these people didn't even know me. Whenever I meet new people they always say that I'm very different from the way they expect; usually they comment on how down-to-earth and nice I am, after the press have made me out to be a heartless, publicity-seeking cow.

A few days after Alex was crowned the winner of *Celebrity Big Brother* we flew to Las Vegas and got married. It was a real spur-of-the-moment decision, and it felt really romantic and special. I was excited about our future together. The photographs of the wedding were lovely; we looked so happy together.

Now that we were married the time felt right for me to have another baby. We had been trying for several months, in fact, and I was starting to feel concerned that I hadn't become pregnant yet. At that time, I still had no idea how significant a part his cross-dressing and wanting sex as Roxanne played in Alex's life. The year before, I'd suffered a miscarriage, which as any woman knows who's been through one is heartbreaking. I kept worrying that there might be something wrong with me as I hadn't fallen pregnant since, though I'd never had a problem conceiving before. By April I was so worried that we sought medical advice.

After we'd both had a series of tests it was decided that we needed fertility treatment, something called ICSI. It's used where a man has a low sperm count or where the sperm have low motility (are poor swimmers). Basically the best sperm are selected and then injected into the egg. I would have to take hormones to stimulate egg production, and that meant that I would have to give myself daily injections and would have to inject myself in the stomach. I have a life-long phobia of needles and, while I can inject my son Harvey with the daily growth-hormone drugs he needs with no problem at all, I absolutely hate being injected myself. I don't think Alex quite understood how I felt and what a big deal this was to me. But I put that down to him being a man. I don't think many of them understand the emotions women experience when they are trying to get pregnant, or even while the pregnancy is progressing. The significance of it all doesn't seem to hit most men until they are presented with a real-life baby.

* * *

A week or so later we went to Egypt on holiday, along with my friend Polly and her husband Andrew, who was also my riding instructor, my son Harvey, and Polly and Andrew's two children. I had been good friends with the couple (and I still am) since I decided that I wanted to take up dressage in 2008, and we had stayed friends throughout my traumatic break up with Pete, when the newspapers were full of speculation about why my marriage had broken up, and were persistently trying to link me to Andrew. They had tracked him and Polly down in Spain where they were on holiday, and contacted Polly's friends on Facebook and tried to dig up dirt on the two of them, and on me, but of course there was nothing to find out.

The doctor thought that our Egypt trip in April was

perfect timing as then we would be relaxed during the treatment to follow. As things turned out, that wasn't the case. This was partly due to the volcano erupting in Iceland that caused all flights to be grounded, which resulted in me getting back late for the next stage of my treatment. Anyone who has ever had fertility treatment will appreciate exactly how stressed I was about the delay. If we didn't get back by a certain date then we would have to stop that course of treatment and start again in two months' time. Not only is it a very emotional thing to undertake, it's also very expensive, and I was paying for the treatment. Alex didn't pay for any of it.

And, as if an unexpected volcanic eruption wasn't enough of a problem, there were other things that were starting to worry me. It was in Egypt that Alex's obsession with training started to grate on me. I appreciated how committed he was to his sport, but he went to the gym every single morning. I did think he could have eased off a little as this was supposed to be a holiday. I felt it was fortunate that I had Polly and Andrew with me otherwise I could have been pretty lonely.

Worse was to come. One day we were all having lunch when out of the blue he asked, 'So how much are you worth then?'

WTF! Why was he asking me this?

For a minute I didn't think I could have heard him right, it was so unexpected and so inappropriate.

'Go on then, tell me, how much are you worth?'

No one I had ever had a relationship with before had asked me this question, not even Pete and we had been together for five years.

I looked over at Andrew and Polly, who seemed to be as shocked as I felt.

I took a deep breath and replied, 'That's my business. I'm not telling you.'

Alex frowned, and looked pissed off. 'Yeah, but I'm your husband, you should be able to tell me. You *should* tell me.'

I shook my head. 'Well, I'm not going to.'

'I can't believe you won't tell me! Come on, I know the Beckhams are worth millions. So what are you worth?'

God! Didn't he get the message? 'I'm not telling you, and I'm not discussing this any further.' I thought that would be the end of it, but when we went back to our suite Alex was sulky and said, 'I find it really offensive that you won't tell me.'

He found it offensive!

'Look, even Pete didn't ask me that. I don't want to talk about it. It shouldn't matter anyway. I thought you were with me because of me, not because of how much money I have?'

But he wouldn't let it drop. 'If we're together, we should know everything about each other. We shouldn't have any secrets. I'm really pissed off that you won't share this with me.'

We had only been married three months and maybe it was because we were newly married that he thought he should know everything, but I felt annoyed that he should ask this and expect to be told. I've never asked any of the men I've been with about how much money they have, including Alex. When I met him it didn't concern me that he didn't have any money because I fell for him, not his bank balance. And just as well as there was bugger all in it!

I would never dream of asking anyone that question. Why should it matter? I think it's downright rude. I've often been asked how much money I earn in press interviews, and have never discussed it; it's no one's business but mine.

I pushed this disagreement to the back of my mind but it did start off a niggle of doubt about whether I had done the right thing in marrying Alex so quickly, and about his true motives for marrying me. I'd thought it was for love. But were my friends right? Was it all about the money for him? I tried to tell myself that it couldn't be. He had signed a pre-nup just before we got married in Vegas, and had always said he didn't want any of my money.

But a similar thing was to happen later in the year when we invited friends round to the house for a barbecue. We were all in the back garden, enjoying ourselves, when Alex started acting almost as if he was lord of the manor, pointing out the boundaries.

I sensed my friends looking at me as if to say, OMG! It was my house and my garden and my boundaries! It was nothing to do with him; none of it belonged to him. Again I had this uneasy feeling about Alex and money. Again I pushed it to the back of my mind.

But back to April... When we returned to the UK it was time to harvest my eggs and inject them with the specially selected sperm. Three days later I had to return to the clinic to have the embryos implanted – an important and significant moment in the treatment as I think anyone would understand. Anyone apparently except Alex, who said, 'If you want me to come with you, I'll come. If not I'll go training.'

Training? At a time like this? How insensitive was that! I was probably my own worst enemy because instead of saying, 'Yes, please come with me,' I told him it was up to him. If he didn't want to come, then he didn't have to. Though I did point out that if I were a man in this situation, I would be there for my partner.

Alex chose to go training. I was really upset. In spite of what I had said to him, it should have been obvious that I wanted him to be with me. I've always done these tests on the men in my life; I think it must be down to the insecurity I've felt with them. I remember how they react and store it up for future use, as if to say to myself: See, you knew that was going to happen, you knew you couldn't trust him... This had been my little test for Alex, to find out if he would put me before his training and support me. Because he hadn't, I did start to doubt him. If he didn't even want to see our embryos being implanted, what would he be like if I actually had a baby? Would he give me the support I needed then?

I knew that at least one member of his family wasn't happy with him about this. They made it clear to him when they found out, and he called me to apologise, telling me that he hadn't realised it was such a big deal. Now I can't help thinking that if he had been paying for the treatment, he would have been there...sorry, can't help having a dig. So, yes, he should have come with me. However, I know that I don't like to show it when I'm feeling vulnerable or when something is really bothering me. I will deny it and make out that I'm fine. I've always done it, even though so often it has led to me being hurt.

A few days later the press reported that I had been having fertility treatment. I was deeply distressed that they had got hold of this fact, which was so personal and so private. I felt as if they were always digging away at me. I actually broke down in front of Alex and my mum one morning in early May.

Now don't get me wrong, I know that I have engaged with the press and enjoyed the benefits of doing so. I am not a hypocrite and know I have to take the rough with the smooth. But the whole way they had treated me around that time, and frequently run negative and untrue stories, was taking its toll on me. It was all rough and no smooth at all. Pete had walked out on me and I was hounded by the press for an entire year. And now here I was, waiting to find out if I was pregnant and *still* under attack. I felt so vulnerable; I didn't know how much more I could take. And then I started experiencing stomach cramps and bleeding. The treatment hadn't worked. I wasn't pregnant. I was really upset. It was a tough time. And then I did feel that Alex was supportive. Again, I had the feeling it was us against the rest of the world. I needed him by my side.

And still the fall-out from my first marriage wouldn't go away. There was so much stress. Both Pete and Claire Powell sued me for comments I had made very early on after the breakup of the marriage. I was already at rock bottom because of the battering I had received from the press; this almost made me feel as if I couldn't go on. It's no exaggeration to say I felt suicidal, and it was only my children and the support of my family and friends that got me through. Instead of fighting Pete in court, I settled with him. I didn't have the strength for a battle at that time.

He was a good father figure to Harvey while we were married. The issue with Pete seeing Harvey after the break-up was not about that. There has to be a fully trained special needs nanny to accompany my son on any visit. His medical condition simply requires it. My mother and I have interviewed and identified suitable candidates and given Pete the details. It seems the nannies have not worked out for him and nothing has happened to resolve the situation. The longer it has gone on, the less Harvey wants to go and see Pete. Now, you mention Pete's name and Harvey kicks off because he doesn't want to go there for the weekend. It is a shame that this is the situation as Pete was good for him.

And even when my ex-husband wasn't threatening or taking legal action, there was a constant stream of negative comments about me from him, or his 'friends', in his magazine column or the tabloids. This was particularly upsetting when it was anything to do with our children. For instance, he had a go at me in the media at the beginning of 2010 when the press picked up on a picture of Princess that my sister had on Facebook. She didn't realise that it could be seen by everyone.

In the photo Princess was wearing make up and fake lashes. The picture had been taken when I had been shooting my style book and Princess had wanted to dress up like Mummy; she was playing, nothing more than that. She was the one who stuck on the lashes and put the make up on herself. She was only doing what so many other little girls do. We were actually still married when that picture was taken and Pete didn't have a problem with it then. Instead, I remember he laughed and said how cute she looked. I'd even done an *OK!* shoot with Princess when Pete was there, with me putting make up on her, as a bit of fun, and he didn't complain then either, because he knew our daughter liked playing with it. Then, when we split, suddenly Princess messing about with make up is not okay and Pete's on GMTV talking about it, followed by child psychologists commenting, and I get slated by the media.

He also criticised me publicly in his column for using straighteners on Princess's hair. Usually I straighten it simply by brushing it out with a bristle brush. I had corkscrew-curly hair just like her when I was growing up and before I discovered extensions, so I'm something of an expert in straightening curly hair with a brush! It really wasn't a big deal. I'm not trying to make her grow up more quickly, or turn her into one of those children who take part in American-style beauty pageants. And it certainly isn't as if she plays with make up all the time; she's just as happy playing outside, collecting eggs from our chickens and going for a ride on her pony.

Pete didn't need to express his concern by writing about it in a magazine and talking about it on TV; he could have spoken to me and we could have sorted it out between ourselves, like grown ups. But no. It felt as if yet again he was portraying himself as the perfect dad, and me as the bad mother. I hated that because it wasn't true.

On another occasion, in April 2010, an hour after Princess had arrived back at Pete's house after being with me, my lawyer phoned because they had received a letter from Pete's lawyer saying that they were concerned about marks they had found on her. This was a new low. Immediately I phoned Pete and said, 'What are you talking about?'

He told me that she had a black eye and bruises.

'Pete, she was playing around with make up this afternoon! It's probably smudged mascara!'

I was so outraged that he could be suggesting that Princess could have come to any harm with me, I called the police myself.

'You need to go and check on my daughter,' I told them. 'My ex is saying that she has bruises on her, and there is no way that she does. I want to clear my name. I'm not having it said that I have harmed my little girl, when there is no way that I have.'

Child Protection Officers went that day and checked Princess, and of course they found nothing wrong. They said it was perfectly normal for a young child to have a couple of bruises on her legs from playing, and there was nothing visible on her face at all. I hadn't wanted to go to the extreme of involving the police, but I feared if I didn't a story would have been leaked to the press that Princess had left my care with bruises on her. As it was, one did appear in the tabloid press, and let me tell you, that didn't come from me...I'm not accusing Pete, and he did say that he wasn't accusing me either, but sometimes it's very difficult trying to live normally when someone sells a story like this to the press. The story appeared in the *News of the World* saying that this incident was caused over some smudged mascara. Pete then came out in his *New!* magazine column a few days later, saying that the bruises were not smudged mascara and how upset he was. Astonishingly, the *Daily Star* (published by the same organisation that publishes Pete's column) featured a front-page story that screamed 'Jordan baby's bruised face and body: Andre shock at injured tot'. The story claimed that Princess had been covered in a 'bizarre' set of bruises, and there were pictures of a 'concerned' and 'devoted' Pete – together with an invitation to read his new magazine article. That story was written by one Gemma Wheatley – more about her later, she now works for Pete and Claire Powell – though the *Daily Star* later admitted that it was untrue.

*   *   *

Having Alex by my side helped me through those tough times, when I felt everything I did was picked apart and criticised. But since we had got married in Vegas there were things that had started to concern me about him. For instance, there were several more times when he'd wanted to dress up as Roxanne. It wasn't so much the dressing up that was disturbing; it was his behaviour at those times. I could always tell when he wanted to dress up: there'd be that vacant look in his eyes that I've already mentioned. It was really starting to unsettle me; I thought he maybe needed help in dealing with this side of him, which no longer felt like a bit of fun.

I asked him why he wanted to dress up, so many times, but he couldn't explain it. Whether it was a release from stress after his fights, or a way of dealing with his emotions, I have no idea.

We watched a couple of documentaries about couples where the man liked to dress up as a woman, and the women would talk about how they felt. They all sounded exactly like I had at the beginning of my relationship with Alex, when I'd said that I supported him. And it was as if the documentary was saying that you could be a cross-dresser and still have a happy marriage. But these men were different from Alex; they would wear women's clothes but still be themselves. There was no personality change, and it didn't seem to be a sexual thing for them.

I felt the sex we had when Alex was being Roxanne was becoming more extreme. I would be the one doing things to him, things that I wasn't sure I wanted to do, things that I found increasingly weird and disturbing. It wasn't as if Alex ever sat down and said, 'Right, now I want you to do this to me...' They just happened, over time. I ended up doing things I wish I had not done because I wanted to please him; I'm always a pleaser in any relationship. And then, as I'd done it once, he expected it to happen again, and that's what he always wanted, whereas once would have been enough for me. More than enough...

I've tried a few things in my time, but I'd never before f***** a man dressed up as a woman who happened to be my husband. I felt as if I was crossing a line, going to a dark place where there were no boundaries, where there was no normal. It felt seedy and dirty. It frightened me. I realised that each time we had sex with Alex being Roxanne he wanted me to do something else, or the sex lasted longer. There was none of that banter we'd had the first few times, and it definitely wasn't a laugh. I kept thinking, Kate, what are you doing? This is not normal. But still I went along with it. I wanted to make him happy. It will be all right, I would tell myself. We can sort this out. You may wonder why I didn't get out then, but I genuinely thought I loved him and was still reeling from the end of my first marriage. I needed this relationship to work.

But looking back, it was as if my marrying Alex had made him feel secure enough to unleash the side of him which usually he kept well hidden. I still didn't really know what I had let myself in for, but even though there were some doubts in my mind about him by then I went ahead with planning our wedding blessing in July. I wanted to believe that we could have a future together.

CHAPTER 3

BEAUTY AND THE BEAST

On the morning of the wedding blessing my mum remembers seeing me in my bedroom, just before we left for the church, standing in my wedding dress. And there was something about the expression on my face apparently that made her wonder if I was going to turn up at the ceremony or if I was going to back out. She has that special intuition only mums have, knowing deep down when something isn't right. In fact, my feeling was that I might as well go ahead with the blessing because we were already married, but I wasn't happy about it. I felt that Alex was not the man I had first met. There was a shadow over our relationship.

I remember him being quite emotional during our wedding blessing and later during the speeches, when he declared his love for me, telling everyone that he was like an oyster: rugged on the outside while inside there was a pearl in his heart, and I was that pearl. Did I feel that he was my pearl? I can't say that I did, but I was happy to be surrounded by my friends and family all day.

But later that night I didn't want to go to bed with Alex. Instead I stayed up with my friends, dancing and drinking and enjoying the party. Wasn't that a sign that there was something wrong? Shouldn't I have wanted to be with my husband on this day that was supposed to be about celebrating our life together?

We went to Thailand for our honeymoon, though maybe 'honeymoon' wasn't the right description because we had the film crew with us, from my production company, making a three-part special about our wedding for ITV2. And thank God we did, because I had a better time talking to them than I did to Alex...

First we flew to Bangkok and went to some of the eye-opening shows there. It was meant to be a laugh, though I found Alex's behaviour a little strange. He kept looking at all the men who were dressed as women, the ladyboys, and flirting with them. To be honest, I found that quite disturbing. He also bought himself, or rather Roxanne, some g-strings made specially for men, so that they can tuck everything away. I can't say that I felt comfortable with that either. It was like Roxanne was spilling out into the rest of our marriage, and I didn't want her to. It didn't feel as if the Roxanne side of him was private any more because he was becoming so blatant about it.

I remembered the first time I had made Alex up, and how accepting I had been of his female persona. I didn't feel like that now. I was starting to dread him wanting to dress up because I knew what it would mean. And yet I still tried to put on a brave face about it. Just before our wedding blessing we had both appeared on *Alan Carr: Chatty Man*, and I had tried to joke about Alex's cross-dressing, because I wanted to show that I stood by him, saying, 'You know what happens in fairytales when the clock strikes twelve, Cinderella disappears and out comes Roxanne.' But how I wished it wasn't so . . .

After Bangkok we left for the tropical island of Koh Phangan. It was a beautiful location and I had hoped that we would have a relaxing time there together. But Alex was in training for a big fight he was due to have at the end of September, and yet again when we were away he didn't want to interrupt his training. He didn't want to drink; all he wanted to do was work out and find someone to help him train. I felt quite pissed off. I understood that he needed to train because he had a fight coming up, but surely he could have missed a couple of days on our honeymoon?

There was one funny moment when we went on an elephant ride and some people passed us and shouted out, 'Oh, look, it's Peter Andre and Katie Price!' I think I thought it was funnier than Alex did, and was almost tempted to shout back, 'No, I'm on to the next one!'

But I was annoyed too because even at this remote location the paps tracked us down and photographed us sunbathing on our private balcony. Sometimes I felt I could never escape from them. Earlier in the month they had almost wrecked our wedding blessing when they had surrounded the 80s-style A-Team van I'd arrived at the church in. It was supposed to be pap-proof but they started rocking it and ripped off the screens that were covering the back window. One man managed to wrench open the back door and shove his camera in, trying to get a shot. He whacked my PA in the face, not caring that he had hurt her; someone else tried to open the front door. I was in the van under siege for about ten minutes while my security team wrestled the paps away. I remember feeling so overwhelmed with anger and frustration that I cried. They were treating me like an animal; in fact, worse than an animal.

Once again, I don't want to appear hypocritical. I accept that I have engaged with the press in the past, but does that mean I should have to accept abuse and being put in danger by them? It's not all of them, of course. The old-school photographers are great and you build a relationship with them over time, but with digital technology any idiot with a camera can be a pap these days and some of them have no scruples.

My security team had put up a screen, between the van and the church, to keep the paps at bay, but as I was hurried in some of them charged at it, ripping it down. Even when we'd managed to make it inside we weren't safe. Some paps forced open the door, nearly knocking down one of the church wardens.

And now here they were again, on this idyllic island in the middle of nowhere. I fucking hated them! How the hell did they know we were there? Someone must have tipped them off. Now I have a suspicion it might have been Alex.

* * *

Back home again I felt our relationship start to deteriorate and very quickly go downhill. From being pleased that Alex was a professional fighter, I started to see what a selfish, self-absorbed life that was. It seemed to take up his entire time. He went training every single morning, came home, ate – a lot – and took all these different supplements, then wanted to sleep. Hmm, that wasn't what I had signed up for...I'd started to find him boring, no fun to be with any more. I understood that he had to step up his training when he had a fight coming up, that he had to lose weight and eat properly, and it was bound to take up a lot of time. But he was always obsessed, even when he wasn't preparing for a fight. I thought he should still have been up for doing fun things, but he wasn't.

And then my then nanny discovered that Alex had been taking Harvey's growth-hormone drugs and injecting them into himself. She told me that the doctor had phoned to check because we seemed to be ordering more than usual and he was concerned. With a sinking heart I realised that there was only one person who would do that, and that person was my husband. When

I confronted Alex he admitted it. My nanny Jo was there to witness the scene.

'Why would you do that!' I exclaimed, furious that he had been helping himself to my son's medicine. It was crucial for Harvey's health.

'I thought you could just order more supplies, I didn't realise it was a problem,' was his reply. He didn't seem bothered at all. I couldn't believe his attitude.

Jo and I ended up having to lock the medicine away. I just didn't trust Alex not to take it again. Really, I think he crossed the line then and I should have told him to get out of my house and out of my life. I felt that he was only ever thinking of himself, in his own selfish world. I am not sure that I felt the same way about him again after that.

And then there was the money thing. Even though he had earned some good money through his involvement with me, Alex hardly paid for anything and that really started to annoy me. I felt he was tight-fisted and it seemed to me that he would only ever spend money on himself. He bought himself a pink sex machine. Without going into details, it had a metal frame that moved which you could put different attachments on and...well, you can guess the rest. The cleaner found it under our bed and moved it into my downstairs gym without realising what it was! It was one of the very few things Alex bought, though he did buy me a diamond necklace that he gave me on the day of our wedding blessing.

I felt as if I was the man in the relationship, going out and earning the money, treating Alex with gifts. I paid for all the holidays, all the meals out, basically everything we did. I started to think, Here we go again…I'd had relationships like this in the past, before I was married to Pete. They had never ended well.

I sometimes feel that because I have money, the men I've been involved with have taken advantage and thought, Oh, it's okay, I can have a lazy day. I don't have to work. Kate will pay, she'll sort this out. The same goes for organising things for us to do, having a bit of get up and go. I wanted Alex to say, 'Right, this weekend I'm taking you and the kids away camping.' Or to Center Parcs. Anything really, just so long as it wasn't always about me organising every single thing. He had been great with the kids at the beginning of our relationship, but as the months went by he did less and less with them. I also felt he was becoming lazy around the house. Because I have a housekeeper, Alex seemed to think that he didn't have to lift a finger.

I'm the kind of girl who falls in love with someone and just wants to be with them – it doesn't matter what their background is or what they do. But I've worked hard for what I've got, and when I'd come home tired after work and find Alex crashed out on the sofa, or sitting at the table eating, and he'd say he didn't want to do anything that night, it would put my back up. And I would think: Well, I don't want to do anything with you either! And so the rot quickly set in.

I started to feel that he was becoming obsessed with being a celebrity. I was proud of him for winning *Celebrity Big Brother* and I had got him a TV series of his own through my production company, looking at different martial arts. He also had a weekly column in a celebrity magazine – and all those things he only got because of me. But still that didn't seem to be enough for him. He wanted to do more magazine and press interviews. I was always wary about him doing them because I didn't want him to talk about our relationship and me. I'd had all that with my first marriage, and look where that ended up...I hated the idea of anyone using my name to get famous because if they did that I would never know if they really loved me for myself, or if they just loved the idea of being with me because of what it brought them.

One of Alex's friends became his manager and he was someone I did not like. Alex also joined an acting agency, wanting to get back into that line of work. I thought, Hang on. He's changed from the man I met who was committed only to his sport. Now he wants his own manager, he wants to be in magazines, he wants to be an actor...what's going on? He seemed to be becoming a completely different person from the man I had first met. He insisted that he needed to change his image so he would be taken more seriously in the acting world, and instead of wearing the trendy clothes that I liked he started wearing trench coats and sleeveless jumpers over shirts, trying to cultivate this preppie image. It was so not him, and so not how I like a man to dress. I hated it, to be honest, and thought he looked like a bouncer. And, yes, I did tell him that.

But I could have coped with all the training and the difficulties over money, even with his fame obsession. It was his alter ego Roxanne who ultimately destroyed our marriage. I think because I had been initially accepting of what he did, Alex took advantage and pushed it to the very limit. It was like I gave him an inch and he took a mile. Because I was open-minded, he saw that as a green light to go ahead and do whatever he wanted. As far as I am concerned he completely abused my trust. The first time Alex had shown me Roxanne, he hadn't been like that at all, he had still been himself; otherwise I wouldn't have wanted to be with him, no question.

After our wedding blessing in July, things took a very sinister turn. I felt as if Roxanne was taking over my husband. It was no longer something he did every now and then, once in a blue moon; it seemed more and more frequent, and was deeply disturbing to me. I came to absolutely dread the whole becoming Roxanne ritual.

'Please don't do it,' I would beg him. *'Please.'* But it was as if he couldn't stop. He was driven to do it.

I knew the whole routine by heart. It started with Alex getting that vacant, glazed look in his eyes. He seemed to love the ritual. In fact, he told me that he loved the preparation most of all and took his time, spending over two hours getting ready to be Roxanne. He would begin at night, while I was pottering round the house or watching TV. I hated it. By now I knew that once he had changed into her, he would be like that all night.

The picture of Alex dressed up in kinky black underwear, which was taken when we were at the BloodLust ball, is a good example of his getting-ready routine. He would always begin by having a bath and shaving his whole body. Next came make up, and he'd want red fake nails, red lipstick, fake lashes, the works. All the time he'd be planning what he was going to wear. He'd always want fishnets and suspenders, plus a tight little dress. He would parade around the room staring into the mirror, change the dress, change the wig, until he had found the combination he liked. He would always put on vibrating nipple clamps, which is why he hasn't got any nipples left. Awful, I know, but that's the truth as I mentioned when I went on *The Graham Norton Show*.

And once he was fully transformed into Roxanne he was lost to me. He loved doing all this so much…too much. More than anything else, it seemed, and he didn't care what I thought or how it made me feel. I felt that I was nothing to him at those times. Alex had retreated into his own little world where no one else could reach him.

'Alex, Alex! Stop it!' I would plead with him, but there was no response. I would click my fingers in front of his face and he wouldn't even register me doing it. It was frightening to see him so withdrawn.

And he wanted me to do more and more extreme

things to him. Think of the most disturbing porn you could imagine, and times that by ten, and only then are you getting close to what I witnessed and what Alex wanted me to join in with. I couldn't believe some of the things that he wanted me to do to him and, looking back, I can't believe that I did them. But it had been a gradual progression, a slippery slope, and now I was in a room with a man I didn't even know, doing things that weren't normal. This wasn't role play, this wasn't experimental, this was sick. I didn't want this in my life. I felt that what he was making me do, and what I had to see him doing to himself, wasn't human. It was damaging, shocking, obscene. I know many people reading this will think, Well, why the hell didn't you get out of that relationship? Chuck Alex out of the house? But it's never that easy once you are married. Trust me, I tried my best a few months later when I knew I couldn't go on...and then it took weeks to get him to go.

One night we went to a party my friends Nick and Royston were having at their house. Alex disappeared upstairs for ages and I had no idea what he was up to. But then it all became horribly clear when he reappeared dressed up as Roxanne in a pink wig, a little black dress, fishnet tights and high heels. I was shocked and embarrassed that he was doing this in public, at my friends' house, surrounded by people we didn't know. Disgust and anger raged through me as he tottered towards me. Inside I was thinking, What the hell am I doing with him? I can do better than this! And the cheek of him, doing this out in public! It really was as if he had no respect for me. I felt completely humiliated.

I could see how shocked everyone was by his transformation and finally realised that I had been deceiving myself in thinking that I could handle this. Alex's behaviour was by now seriously disturbing. When he was out of earshot my friends crowded round me and all said things along the lines of, 'Kate, what the fuck are you doing with him?' Yet even though I privately agreed with them, I felt I had no choice but to be the supportive wife, and pretend that I was okay with it, when inside it was eating away at me like poison.

There were these gorgeous waiters at the party, working for Butlers in the Buff, where employees just wear an apron, a bow tie and a smile! Ironically it was something my third husband Kieran used to do... And I thought, Look at them, so sexy and ripped and clean-cut, and look at the state of my husband. Alex was by then fully in Roxanne mode, and had become really shy and quiet as he always did, and wouldn't talk to anyone except me, so it wasn't even as if we could have a laugh with him. I felt completely let down. I didn't see how he could care about my feelings.

Apparently he had planned all along to cross-dress that night and had brought his bag of Roxanne tricks with him. At the party he had asked my friend Dawn to do his make up for him. She had agreed, thinking it was all a joke, not realising that for Alex this was serious and he was transforming into Roxanne. Round and round in my head went the thoughts: *I don't want this any more. What the fuck am I going to do now?* Once again I felt very alone and very vulnerable. I had married this man, he was in my life, but he had serious issues. Again I begged him to stop and to get help. Again he promised that he would, but he didn't.

* * *

In September Alex had arranged the biggest fight of his career. It was to be against Tom Watson, a really successful boxing champion. I had arranged the financial side for him, plus a percentage of the ticket sales, which was a bit different from the few hundred pounds he used to get for a fight. It's amazing what happens when you go out with the Pricey...

I went along to support him and it was so hard for me to watch as Alex got punched, beaten and kicked. I've never seen another man able to take the punches and blows that Alex could. It was incredible the way he would pull himself up from the ground and carry on fighting. When he fought he had that same vacant look in his eyes he would get when he was being Roxanne. It was like he was in a different zone, one where he didn't feel pain.

He fought hard but lost. Afterwards he was in a terrible state, with a battered and bruised face, a split lip and a black eye. But there was no opportunity for me to comfort him because as soon as we got home he went straight upstairs to the bedroom. He had that vacant look in his eyes again and I knew what that meant...

What was going on with him? Was being Roxanne the reward he gave himself for fighting? Did he even *want* to be a fighter? Or was he punishing himself for wanting to cross-dress every time he put up his fists? I now think that his fights were very traumatic for Alex and that they went against his true nature. He fought to prove that he was manly, but he dreaded them too. I think he was being tormented and torn apart by his own conflicting feelings. He desperately needed help, that was certain, and our short-lived marriage was falling apart.

By now I hated everything about him dressing as Roxanne. After first thinking it was something new and adventurous, I had come to view it as seedy, disgusting and vile. His cross-dressing compulsion had completely taken over the Alex I'd believed I knew. And I thought, This is taking me down a road I absolutely don't want to go down. I told him how I felt, broke down in tears more than once as, again and again, I begged him to stop. But I couldn't seem to get through to him, and he couldn't seem to stop.

The worst moment came when I was away on a book signing tour in the autumn and couldn't get hold of Alex by phone. I had a sickening feeling that I knew exactly why. When I finally got through to him, I said, 'What are you doing? Are you being Roxanne?'

'Yes,' came his reply in that disturbingly quiet voice he spoke in when he was cross-dressing.

'I'm coming home now. You've got to take it all off and stop!' I shouted.

The thought of going back to find him in that state repelled me. I was frightened by the thought of being alone with him if he was going to be Roxanne, because that meant he would be completely unreachable, in a trance, in his own world. Desperate for some support, I phoned my friends Jane and Derek and asked them to come over with me. I couldn't do this alone. Thank God, they immediately agreed to. I needed my friends.

When I arrived home there was no sign of Alex downstairs. Oh, God, that meant he was still in the bedroom, which meant he was still being Roxanne. I felt sick with dread as I walked up the stairs. I couldn't believe that this was happening, that this was what had become of our marriage. Trying to stay strong, I opened the door. The room stank of cigarette smoke, booze and sex.

Inside I was confronted with the most shocking sight. Our bedroom had been turned into a sex dungeon. My husband, dressed up in stockings, suspenders, heels, make up and a wig, had tied a strap-on dildo to my dressing table. I won't describe exactly what he was doing – I'll leave it to your imagination. What I will say is that it was the worst thing I have ever seen.

I can hardly tell you how disgusted I felt. It was gross, vile behaviour. It was like he was degrading himself and me. Sex toys were scattered all over the bed. He was so out of it, and so lost he didn't even look up as I walked in, but carried on with what he was doing. I stormed over to him.

'Stop doing that!' I screamed. 'Get that shit off…now!'

Finally he looked at me, that horrible vacant expression in his eyes, a prisoner in his warped Roxanne world.

'I'm going downstairs, and when I come back, you'd better have taken all this off!' I shouted.

But it took more shouting, screaming and pleading from me before he stopped and switched back to being Alex.

I couldn't stand any more of this. Yet again I begged him to stop the cross-dressing, told him that it was destroying our marriage. I said he had to get help and see a therapist, and he promised he would. I said I would help him and pay for therapy. But nothing made any difference. When he finally went it was no help at all. Alex didn't change his behaviour in the least.

I was so disturbed by what was going on that I confided in his mum. It was Bonfire Night and I was having a party for friends and family. It was not news to her as she knew all about Alex's cross-dressing. When I had first met him he was living at home and I'd always felt like a teenager when I went round to his parents' place. 'He's got to stop it!' I told her. 'I can't handle it any more, it's taking over our marriage.' Looking back, it seems weird to have had to ask my own mother-in-law to talk to her son about his cross-dressing. But that's how desperate I was.

She agreed she would say something, and after she had, Alex promised to calm down that side of his life but he just couldn't. And meanwhile our marriage was breaking down. I didn't want to be part of his seedy world.

I was feeling stressed out, constantly on edge, constantly dreading that he would switch to being Roxanne.

It was such a shame because I wanted our marriage to work. I'm someone who doesn't want to give up on anything and will always try my hardest, but the Roxanne thing was something I couldn't handle. It disturbed me, and it dominated our marriage. Because Alex took it to such an extreme level it destroyed my trust in him. He overstepped all the boundaries. I don't mind experimenting as a couple, but if you do, it should be something you try jointly. As I said earlier, with Alex it reached a point where he didn't seem to care if I was there or not; in fact, I think he preferred it when I wasn't.

I wish that, right at the start, when we'd first met, Alex had told me the extent of his cross-dressing and what a major part of his life it was. I would still probably have been attracted to him, because I did like him a lot, and I would have experimented, maybe once, just because I have that thrill-seeking side to me, but I would also have been very wary. I would never have let him move in with me, and I definitely wouldn't have married him. The whole cross-dressing scene was not something I wanted to be involved in. I wanted a family life, with more children, and I didn't want to take on someone with all the problems Alex seemed to have. I couldn't help wondering where it was going to end. To be fair to him, he was never Roxanne when the kids were in the house – that made it easier to deal with at first, but not for long.

We started arguing more and more. Instead of looking forward to seeing him when I got back from work, I would dread it. On top of the Roxanne thing I felt that Alex had changed from the easy-going guy I had first met. He became very moody. If I had people over he would lie sprawled out on the sofa, not bothering to socialise. It felt a bit as if he was saying, Now I'm married to her, I don't have to make any effort. I can do what I want. All I can say is that when I first met him he was a real charmer; I thought he was a gentleman, felt protected by him, but I was wrong. So, so, so, so wrong. What was it with me and those types? Dwight had been a charmer, and Alex had been a charmer. Pete hadn't needed to be a charmer because it was love at first sight, on both sides – or so at least I believe.

Around December 2010 things got so bad that I knew I couldn't go on like this. We had been married for less than a year, and I had tried my best, but I knew in my heart we had to split. As if that wasn't enough, at the beginning of the month, that so-called comedian Boyle made his vile comment about Harvey, which deeply upset me. I had the worst Christmas ever. Pete had Junior and Princess that year, and I always hated not having them with me for the holiday. Christmas has been a difficult time for me since my first marriage ended. I always feel sad then because I wish that Pete and I could be friends and celebrate the holiday together with the children.

The atmosphere between Alex and me was awful. I

couldn't bear to be around him. I didn't feel that spark for him any more. It felt so fake, opening the presents he'd bought me, because inside I was thinking: I don't want to be with you.

I told him after Christmas that our marriage was on the rocks and he looked at me with his puppy-dog eyes and got all emotional, saying, 'No, we can work it out! We're strong, we can get through this. We're meant to be together.'

I thought, We're fucking not, not after everything you've put me through! I knew I wanted to be free from him and from the side of his life that he didn't seem able to control. But because I wanted to feel that I had tried everything, I arranged for us to go to the Maldives at the end of December. Usually I paid for all our holidays, but this time I asked Alex to go halves with me. I thought, No way am I paying for a luxury holiday when I don't even think I want to be with you anymore!

On previous visits to the Maldives I've usually stayed in a luxurious waterside villa with the most incredible view of the ocean. I went there on honeymoon with Pete, and then later on my own with the kids. As I was so unhappy with Alex it didn't seem right to stay somewhere like that, nor did I want to pay for it. So we booked into a regular villa. It was still lovely but you didn't get the VIP treatment.

The Maldives is supposed to be a romantic place, but as soon as we arrived I realised that I didn't have any romantic feelings left towards my husband. It was a terrible holiday. Alex went training and I had various treatments at the spa. When you're really into your partner, it's great being on holiday as you love time alone with them. But I could tell I was definitely off Alex as I couldn't bear it when it was just the two of us. All I wanted to do was socialise with the other couples we met. Alex complained that he never got to be alone with me, but really I had nothing to say to him. I knew he was never going to be able to give up the cross-dressing and what he wanted to do in the bedroom, and for me that was a deal-breaker. We had no future together.

There was speculation in the press that we were finished. Alex was desperate to prove that we weren't and wanted to send the press photographs of us together. Not wanting another row, I went along with it and we sent my manager some pictures, which he then released to the press. I don't think they fooled anyone. It was over.

On New Year's Eve we went to a party and Alex got drunk. Instead of going back to the villa with him, I let someone else take him back while I carried on partying. I didn't care any more. When you go somewhere like the Maldives, you see all these other couples, who are so obviously in love, and I remember thinking: I wish that was me…because I wasn't in love any more. No, I was desperate for an exit from a marriage which had become hell for me.

CHAPTER 4

IT'S OVER

Back in the UK I told Alex it was over, that I couldn't be with him. He cried and seemed devastated. I'd like to think that was because he was sad about the marriage breaking up, but I can't help wondering if it was because he was going to lose a life-style...

I sat down with him and asked if he would write a press statement with me. I even suggested that we should enter into an agreement whereby we both kept the details of our married life together confidential. After what had happened when Pete left me, I wanted us to put up a united front to the press – and I wanted to stop him from selling any stories.

But Alex wouldn't agree. I gave him a little more time, but then a photograph appeared in the press of him posing for a photograph with my son Junior at the

Alex and me preparing
a big nosh up in my
pink horsebox, early on
in our relationship…
when I thought I was
happy, but was on the
rebound big time…

Still can't believe I married him…at least he didn't wear that on our wedding day…with Alex and Nick Malenko.

Roxanne gets an outing with me and my good friend Nick Malenko. I'm looking good, not sure about the bloke in the middle…

Out for lunch with
my three cubs:
Harvey, Princess and
Junior. My kids are
everything to me.

The kids love *Peppa
Pig* so couldn't resist
taking them to the
theme park.

Harvey and me.

Me and my Princess.

A night out with the girls! Michelle and Jane.

Working the camera. And smoulder…

Opposite top: A blonder me, out with Derek and Jane.

Opposite bottom: Me, Melodie, Jane and my younger sister, Sophie – having a ladies' night in…in my horse box!

My friend Derek, Leo and me. Don't think Leo realises that he's telling every one to f off!

gym inside a Mixed Martial Arts fighting cage. I was absolutely furious. Alex knew that I had decided to withdraw my children from the public eye, and there he was, bigging up his relationship with my son. I don't know if he sold the picture (he said he had not), but he certainly posed for it, and he must have known what would happen. That really was the final straw.

On 19 January 2011 I issued a press statement outlining my reasons for ending the marriage. In it I admitted that I had married Alex too quickly and that it had been a mistake. But I also said that Alex had changed from the man I fell in love with, that he had 'issues' and I had tried to help him with them, but they had put too much of a strain on our relationship. (I meant Roxanne, of course.) And I said he had become fascinated by life in the media and that his desire to promote himself caused problems within our marriage. I said that I had hoped that we could end our relationship amicably and without a war of words in the press. That Alex had always liked to portray himself as being honourable and I hoped he behaved like that now. But it seemed there was little chance of that in the weeks and months that followed.

Even though I had made it crystal clear that our marriage was over, incredibly Alex refused to move out of the house! Instead he moved into an upstairs bedroom, with all his stuff, and locked the door.

'I know you've been advised by your lawyer to stay here because they've told you that you'll get more money out of me that way, but you will never get a fucking penny!' I shouted at him, disgusted by his behaviour.

'You're not welcome here! Don't touch any of my things...don't eat any of my food...get out of my house!' I added. I was so angry that he was still on my property and not man enough to leave.

Then I tried to appeal to his better nature. 'For God's sake, my children are here! I don't want them seeing any of this. Please go!' But he still refused. In fact, he didn't reply; he didn't seem to care that he was causing so much distress.

At the same time Scotland Yard paid me a visit and told me that a gang of criminals had targeted me and were planning to steal my jewellery and kidnap me! I mean, WTF! More drama! Sometimes I think that if my life was a film, everyone would think it was well OTT because so many extreme things have happened to me. Apparently the police had good intelligence that a criminal gang planned to break into my house when I wasn't there. Then, when I arrived home, they planned to tie me up and force me at knife point to tell them where my jewellery was. The detectives told me to make sure that I had memorised the code to my safe, which didn't exactly inspire confidence. 'If you know who this gang is, why can't you arrest them!' I exclaimed. I mean, this wasn't the first kidnap threat I'd had, but it was no less frightening.

'We can't arrest them until they make a move,' came the far from reassuring reply.

Genuinely fearful for my safety and that of my children, I brought in my own security. They stayed in the house and patrolled the grounds, and one guard slept outside my bedroom door. Alex wanted to know what was going on, but the police had told me not to tell anyone. He thought I had called in the police to prevent him from coming into the house. *I wish.* In the end I had to tell him about the threat to me as he kept on asking me.

'I'll protect you,' he told me. But the time for that had long-since passed.

'I don't need you to do that! I need you to go! Get out of my house!' I replied. But he still refused.

One night I was out with Gary my make-up artist friend when a detective called me and told me not to go home as they suspected the gang were on their way to my house. The police were following them. I don't exactly know what happened next, but apparently the police lost the car at a petrol station. I stayed at Gary's and the following morning the police called to say that they had new information: the gang had dropped their plan to kidnap me. Maybe they realised that they had been rumbled.

Alex and I did spend one last night together. He had asked me to go away with him and I'd agreed. I didn't want us to break up on bad terms, because of what had happened with Pete and me. I thought, Alex has got his issues, but if I'm nice to him, he'll be nice back. I couldn't cope with any more stress. We went to Alexander House, a nearby spa hotel, somewhere I knew well. We had argued so bitterly in the weeks before that it might seem strange we could think of spending time together, but as far as I was concerned we were meeting as friends. As I tweeted then: 'Me and Alex are not back together but are still good friends: it's called being grown up and adult.' But while we were sitting in the corner of the restaurant having lunch, I heard a familiar click, click, click, and instantly I knew it was a pap. And sure enough, a photographer had run into the restaurant to snatch a shot of us, and then legged it.

'Look! A fucking pap!' I shouted, and told Alex to chase the press pest, which he did. Didn't catch him, though.

But how did any pap know that we were there, eating in the restaurant at that particular moment? It seemed too much of a coincidence to me. It had been one of our favourite spa hotels when we were together, and we had never been bothered there before. Again, I had a suspicion that Alex had tipped the press off...I asked him, and he denied it.

'Well, it's very weird that they knew we were going to be here, at this exact moment,' I replied, thoroughly pissed off. Alex didn't want us to split up and I couldn't help thinking that he would be glad of any pictures coming out that seemed to show we were still together, even though that was a million miles from the truth.

Finally he got the message that I wanted him gone, and moved out. What a relief! But I'm afraid that there was no chance we could stay friends in the weeks that followed. Alex didn't stay silent; instead he sold a string of stories to the press about how heartbroken he was, and what it was like being married to me. It seemed he had to comment on every single thing I did. It was pathetic, and every single one of those stories was a fresh reminder to me of why I was right to get rid of him. Many of the things that were written were out and out rubbish. As usual, someone I had been close to was making themselves look better by painting me as the villain. And what made me laugh was, if I really was as bad as they made out, why had they ever stayed with me in the first place?

I wanted to get divorced as quickly as possible. But of course that didn't happen because Alex was after my money and it would take nearly a year and a half for things to be resolved legally.

Alex went on to have a relationship with Chantelle Houghton. She was exactly the sort he would go for because he loves that glamour-girl look. All I wanted to do was ring Chantelle and warn her about him. She had mentioned in an interview that she already knew about Alex dressing up as Roxanne and that she was fine with it, that he had told her it was all a joke. And I thought: You have no idea what you are getting into. I wanted to say, Don't even touch him with a barge pole. Trust me!

But I was wary of getting in touch because I didn't know how she would react. There had been a time when she was handled by my former manager, Claire Powell, after I had split up with Pete, and she had been friends with my ex-husband. I imagined that they would have portrayed me as a bad person and I thought she probably wouldn't listen to me or even like me.

She quickly fell pregnant. I wasn't at all jealous, even though I wanted another child; instead I was worried for Chantelle. She hardly knew Alex at that point and didn't know what was coming her way. People think a baby will make a couple happier, but that's only if they are okay in the first place. A baby can put a strain on any relationship, and I didn't think that Alex would be able to cope. Sure enough, their relationship didn't last. When Chantelle was eight months pregnant she came home and discovered that Alex had turned their bedroom into a dungeon, with sex toys scattered everywhere and porn playing on the TV. He was in full Roxanne mode, in stockings, suspenders, a red wig and heels. In spite of her begging him to stop, *The Sun* reported his sex binge lasted four days. It was all horribly familiar to me.

And then Chantelle and I did get in touch with each other, a kind of support group for survivors of a relationship with Alex Reid. I felt very sorry for her and think she was relieved to speak to me because I knew exactly how she felt. She was reassured to know that you could get through it and be happy again.

Being married to Alex left its mark on me. I had to see my therapist to try and process all the Roxanne shit, because it really had messed with my head and disturbed me.

I used to think Alex was handsome and had a nice smile...and I did love his legs! But when I look at him now all I can see is Roxanne, a really ugly woman in make up. Alex is naturally so masculine that when he dresses as a woman he looks particularly awful. I no longer see him as the fun guy I first met. Instead I see dirty, seedy Roxanne. I see someone with a lot of problems, which need to be sorted out.

In my last book I talked about how I felt Alex accepted me for what I was, and he did, but I met him at a time when I was emotionally vulnerable because my marriage had just ended badly. I needed to be with someone. There were some good times, but they were outweighed by the many bad times...I can't really see anything positive about our marriage, it's like there's a dark cloud hanging over that time. Yet when I think of my first marriage, however bitter things have become between Pete and me, I still feel that there was an emotional bond, and I think of the children we had together and the family times we shared.

I bitterly regret marrying Alex. Falling in love so quickly felt like fun at first. I enjoyed being spontaneous and impulsive. But ultimately it was a destructive impulse because it cost me a lot, emotionally and financially, and Alex embarrassed me by selling stories about me. And yet it had felt so good when we first met.

Afterwards I realised I must learn to follow my head, not my heart...but I couldn't help wanting more of that fairy-tale, whirlwind romance. If I'm into someone, I'm into them. I find it hard to hold back. But after Alex I would definitely have to be more cautious.

CHAPTER 5

HOLA!

Oh my God! The sheer relief when Alex finally moved out. I wouldn't have to witness any more of his disturbing behaviour. I don't think I fully appreciated then just how much of an impact it had had on me, on my self-esteem and on my confidence with men. I had married him on the rebound and we were only together some fifteen months, but it took me a hell of a lot longer to recover from the experience. I had trusted a man and paid a high price for it.

I didn't have a single regret about leaving him. I would still get texts from him, asking me if I missed his cuddles, and I'd reply that I did, because I hoped if we could be nice to each other, it might stop him from selling more stories. And, I'm not going to lie, in spite of everything I *did* miss his cuddles…he was nice to cuddle, when he wasn't being Roxanne! But there's a difference between missing someone and wanting to get back with them, and I knew I was *never* going to get back with Alex. At that time I thought I wanted to be single for a while; I'd had it with men and relationships for now. Or so I thought. It just shows how wrong you can be, as I was about to find out on a certain night in LA . . .

I'd flown out to the States in February 2011 for a week of business meetings and shoots. The highlights of the week were going to be Elton John's high-profile AIDS Foundation Oscars party and my shoot, the following day, for the American edition of *OK!* It was a huge coup, as not many Brits ever get to be on the cover, and it was a first for me. I had brought a mini-entourage: my best friends Gary and Phil, my brother Dan, Harvey and his nanny.

We had arranged for my son to go to some classes at the school he had attended in 2008 when I was over there with Pete, filming our reality show. Harvey had absolutely loved his time there and had made the most amazing progress. But I'm afraid that had been the only good thing to come out of my three-month stay in LA, which had been easily one of the most miserable and lonely times of my life. I wasn't getting on with Pete then and didn't know what was going wrong with our marriage. He was very distant with me, off recording his music all the time, and when we were together we would only argue. I'd felt cut off from my friends and family in the UK, stuck out in Malibu which is some distance from the parts of LA I know and like, such as Beverly Hills. Yes, we were in a mansion with a pool. But when you're unhappy and you know things aren't going well, it doesn't matter where you are. All the glamour and glitz in the world won't make up for that.

But it seemed a long time ago now and I didn't feel weighed down by sad memories. I was looking forward to spending a week in LA. I love the busy vibe it has, the shops, the restaurants, and of course the weather! It was bloody freezing back in the UK, but here the sun was shining.

But one thing I don't like about LA is the way the paps behave sometimes. From the moment we were walking through arrivals at LAX they were on our case, big time, thrusting their cameras in our faces, desperate to get their shots, not caring how aggressive and intimidating they were being. And while I'm used to it by now, after eighteen years in the business, it doesn't mean I enjoy it or think it's right that photographers behave like that. I can deal with it, but I really don't like it when I'm with my children. Harvey in particular is incredibly sensitive to noise. But the fact that I was with my disabled son made no difference to the paps, who only cared about getting their money shot.

Thankfully once we were in the hotel we could relax and recover from the flight. Usually I stay at the Beverly Wilshire, near Rodeo Drive, the luxury hotel where *Pretty Woman* was filmed. This time we were staying at a different hotel on Sunset Boulevard. After an evening of chilling out, the next day we got down to work, having meetings with a production company to discuss various ideas for reality shows and formatted shows for me. Over the next few days it was manic as I did a series of interviews with online gossip magazines, a photo shoot, and went to the *OK!* party. Oh, plus, I managed to squeeze in some shopping of course, hitting The Grove and The Beverly Center – two fantastic retail wonderlands! And I had to pop into my all-time favourite lingerie store, Trashy Lingerie. I love my underwear. It's a bit of an obsession with me. In 2012 I even had a tattoo of a garter done on my thigh. I've got quite a few tattoos by now but that one hurt the most because it took the longest to do, and it isn't even finished. It hurt even more than the cheeky pink love heart I've got on my bits!

Best of all, Harvey had a brilliant time at the Junior Blind of America School. To my amazement, even though it was over three years ago, he clearly remembered the school and exactly where his classroom had been, as well as all the teacher's names. He even remembered the morning ritual where all the children sit round in a circle and sing a good morning song while playing a drum. He's definitely got a better memory than me!

*   *   *

In Oscars week, it's *all* about what you look like on the red carpet. The world's media are watching, filming, commenting, criticising. Not that I cared what anyone thought of what I was wearing. I've been slated in the 'What Were You Thinking?' pages of celeb mags, and worst-dressed lists, often enough not to give a shit. It was more how *I* felt about how I looked that mattered to me – and I was starting to have doubts about my choice of outfit for Elton's party.

I had planned to wear a long white crocheted dress. It was a designer number by Pucci that I'd thought would look striking. It probably did flash a bit (okay, a lot) of flesh, but that's me... I always want to stand out at those kinds of events, which is easier said than done in Hollywood as everyone else is trying to do just that. This was a big red-carpet event, FFS! And I wanted to look the business. I'd hated the dress I'd worn the previous year to the same party: an electric blue sequined gown decorated with two huge corsages. Everyone else had loved it but I didn't think it was me at all and had felt uncomfortable in it all night. It felt too sophisticated and grown-up. Maybe when I'm older I'll appreciate it. Put it this way, it's the kind of dress my mum loves to see me in. But I reckon I've still got *it*, and while I have... well, I'm going to flaunt it. I decided I needed a dress with the wow factor.

As we were in LA that shouldn't be too difficult, I thought. During Oscars week they have these events called 'gifting suites', where designers display their dresses and accessories for celebrities to borrow. I went looking with a stylist I knew and between us we found a dress that I liked. It was a black sequined halterneck, showing off plenty of cleavage, with a short puffball-style skirt so my legs were out too. That so-called style 'rule' where you show either cleavage or legs... *please,* it's not for me. I needed the dress to do most of the work as I was not at all happy about my hair, which still hadn't recovered from a botched bleach job in December. I had gone from brunette to blonde and had new extensions that cost me a fortune, plus I had flown out to LA to have it done. But back in the UK, to my horror, my hair began breaking and the extensions pulled it out from the root. It had cost me another fortune to rectify the damage, and it took ages for the remaining hair to recover. In the meantime I had these honey-brown extensions that I didn't like, although everyone else thought they looked fine.

But apart from the hair, I felt I was good to hit the red carpet. I'd had my teeth polished, to achieve the ultimate Hollywood smile; I was tanned and I'd had Botox. On my face that is – I hadn't gone to the extreme of having it injected into my armpits to stop any sweating, as apparently so many actors do before they hit the red carpet. Hold the front page! Shock, horror... leading actress shows off sweat rings as she waves to the crowd. Actually it probably *would* make the front page. When Julia Roberts revealed a less than fuzz-free armpit at a film premiere the tabloids went mental.

Day four of our whirlwind trip saw Gary and me getting ready for the Oscars party. This would be the third year I'd been to Elton's extravaganza. The first time I had gone with Pete. It hadn't been a good experience. We weren't getting on well, and he had his eye on me all night, making sure I didn't have anything to drink. It wasn't as if I was going to get wasted and make a show of myself. I simply wanted a glass of champagne, like every other person there... but, oh, no, that wasn't good enough for Pete, who always hated me having anything to drink and always had a go at me if I did. Now that was something I *didn't* miss from my first marriage... The second year I went on my own and met up with my good friend Tanya. To be honest, though, I couldn't wait to leave. I went back to the hotel, took off the blue dress and put on my trackies to order room service of chips and hot chocolate. Bliss. This time it was going to be Gary and me, partners in crime. Or, as he joked, a pair of Californian twins with our 'blonde hair, black outfits, white teeth and orange tans'.

'Cheeky bastard!' I shot back, laughing. 'You can speak for yourself with the orange part. I'm a perfect bronze... it's you who's overdone it.'

'Pot – kettle,' muttered Gary.

I've been up countless red carpets but I still get nervous beforehand. So does Gary. In fact, we were both panicking and winding ourselves up as we were driven to the Pacific Design Center on Melrose Avenue, where the party was being held. Would we get in once we had walked up the red carpet, or would we be turned away and have to do the walk of shame in front of the world's media? It was completely illogical as I knew we were both on the guest list and I had the invitation in my hand! But in any case, I don't like being on red carpets because you know you will be photographed from every conceivable angle – and some of them are far from flattering.

'Here goes,' said Gary as the car pulled up at the kerb. And then our driver was opening the door for us. It was now or never.

But we made it up the carpet, posed for the photographers, flashed our perfect smiles and were allowed in.

We both needed a drink after that and headed straight for the bar area where we ordered our vodka and Cokes. We were happily people watching and star spotting (Heidi Klum, Seal, Kim Kardashian, Paul Rudd, Sharon and Kelly Osbourne for starters) when we both noticed an incredibly handsome guy in a tuxedo walk past. He looked straight at me.

'Fucking hell!' I exclaimed, grabbing Gary's arm. 'How good-looking is he!'

'Absolutely gorgeous,' Gary agreed.

'Do you reckon he's gay?'

'Yeah, I'm pretty sure,' he replied. Of course we found out later that Gary's gaydar was completely off. It was a case of wishful thinking...But at that moment I thought, Oh, well, he's probably right. The guy's far too good-looking to be straight. Just my luck. Then I thought, Kate, don't even go on the manhunt. Just relax, enjoy the party.

We downed a couple more drinks and then had to take our seats for dinner, during which we watched the Oscars live on a big screen. Our table included editors from American *OK!* magazine and the Hollywood actress Tori Spelling and her husband. But I couldn't get that good-looking guy out of my head and kept scanning the room, hoping to get another glimpse of him. And then I saw him walk by our table, and we both locked eyes, and…wow! I felt a spark of instantaneous attraction. He was so fucking fit! Tall, well over six foot, broad-shouldered, with what looked like a muscular body, boyishly handsome face, dark chocolate-brown eyes – possibly Spanish or Latin American. I couldn't keep my eyes off him. And there I was, saying I was off men…Never say never.

Lots of people are restrained at these kind of celeb events, pacing themselves with the amount they drink, sipping mineral water so they don't end up doing anything they'll regret or get photographed looking shit-faced as they stumble out of the party. Lots of people…but it probably won't surprise you that I am not one of them. I was out to have a good time and I was getting happily pissed. So after dinner, the events of that night are all a bit of a blur. I remember talking to Jamie Foxx, the Hollywood actor, and he was chatting away to me. But as for what he said, I have absolutely no idea.

At one point I went off to the ladies' and when I came out I saw Gary standing with the handsome guy. Well, hello! It was like one of those moments when everything and everyone else seems to fade into the background. All I focused on was him and that gorgeous face of his. Yes, I could still focus, just about.

'*Hola,*' he said to me when I joined them.

Ah, so not English then. And, as I very quickly discovered, not able to speak English either. Not a single word. Gary and I worked out that he spoke Spanish, for all the good that was going to do us as neither of us could speak a word. Yet even from this brief encounter I could sense that there was great chemistry between the mystery man and me. And all the time I was thinking, OMG! He is so gorgeous!

At one point a woman joined us and was able to translate our conversations and at first I thought he must be with her, but he wasn't. Incredible as it seemed, he was single. We found out he was called Leandro. We spent the rest of the night together, taking photographs of each other and ourselves together. Once the Oscars ceremony was over there was apparently some amazing entertainment, with Elton John performing with Florence Welch, but I only had eyes for Leandro...or Leo as I decided to call him, as it was much easier to say. I felt like pinching myself, hardly able to believe that this man was interested in me! Me, a mum of three over thirty. I wouldn't in my wildest dreams have imagined someone like him giving me a second glance. And yet here he was, gazing deep into my eyes. I hadn't planned to go out and meet someone. It had just happened.

Gary wanted to go on to a gay club and I said, 'We have to take that guy Leo with us!' I wasn't leaving him behind. So then Gary and I had to mime that we wanted to leave to go dancing, for Leo's benefit. Acting may not be our strong point, but he willingly came with us. I'm not sure if he had any idea where we were taking him.

It was a cool night outside and Leo was a perfect gentleman and put his coat round my shoulders. Later we discovered that someone had taken a picture of us and, while I hate being photographed in public, this one was really sweet and showed Leo with his arm round me, all protective and reassuring. A proper romantic gesture.

I should have gone straight back to my hotel room, like a good girl, and had a large glass of water and a couple of painkillers and gone to bed as I had the all-important shoot for *OK!* USA the following day. Should have. Didn't. We spent the next few hours going wild at the gay club, dancing and drinking and having a fantastic time. Fucking hell! I thought to myself, as I danced with Leo. How did I manage to pull *him*?

Our flirtation didn't end at the club. Leo came back to my hotel suite with me.

Here you go, you dirty stop out! I thought as we tumbled on to the bed together, kissing passionately. And I knew full well it wasn't going to end with a kiss. I knew I was going to have sex with him. I was probably never going to see him again, he didn't know who I was. So what if he didn't speak English, he was so fit! Why would I turn him down? I was single. I'd just come out of a dysfunctional relationship that had really messed with my head. Fuck it! I'll do it! I decided. And do it we did. All night, or rather what remained of the night. And, believe me, the fact that we couldn't speak the same language didn't matter one bit. The language of lurve and all that...

* * *

I think I had an hour's sleep. Somehow I dragged myself out of bed the following morning even though I would rather have stayed right there with Leo. He looked every bit as good in the morning as he had the night before. I'm not sure if the same could be said about me. I felt wrecked, but also blissed out. It had been quite a night.

There's only one cure for a hangover. Food. A lot of models starve themselves before a shoot, take diuretics and God knows what, but that's never been my style, hungover or not. The very first photographer who took pictures of me during my Page 3 days, a lovely guy called Beverley Goodway, who sadly died a year ago, used to think it was hilarious that before we started the shoot, without fail, I would have two jacket potatoes with beans and cheese. I'd always be starving after driving up from Brighton to the London studio. I got very good at breathing in, put it that way. There is a real art to making sure you don't show too much ribcage.

Leo and I went out for breakfast with the gang at a nearby café. Because of the language barrier it was like playing a game of charades as we tried to work out what Leo did. He mimed something that looked like a plane and from that we came to the conclusion that maybe he was a pilot. Or I hoped pilot rather than cabin crew, though to be honest I didn't care. I've never minded what the men I fancy do, so long as they do something! Later, we found out that he was trying to tell us that he was getting a friend's private plane back to Miami. There was no chance we were ever going to get *that* from his mime. I couldn't resist taking a picture of us together and putting it straight on Twitter. I think I must still have been drunk because I never usually do that kind of thing. We swapped numbers and then he was gone and we had to head to the Hollywood Hills for my shoot with *OK!*

All I can say is, thank God for cosmetics. I was knackered and shagged out. Literally. Leo had been a very energetic and passionate lover. I needed Gary to work his magic, pile on the slap (a technical term) and make me beautiful! After a good two hours, he had transformed me from hungover, dirty stop out to swan. You would never know to look at me that I'd only had an hour's sleep, or what I had been up to all night.

The shoot was at a stunning modern house in Beverly Hills, with an infinity pool and breathtaking views of the whole of LA. But all I could think about was Leo. Please let him text me or call me, I thought, checking my phone at every available opportunity during the eighteen costume changes. I even broke my own rule and texted him first, saying, *Hi, it's Kate. Hope you had a good flight and to hear from you soon.* That sounded so polite and formal after our wild night of passion. What I wanted to say was, *Text me! I can't stop thinking about you!* I kept looking at the picture I'd taken of him. He was so gorgeous! I *really* wanted to see him again. I didn't know anything about him, not what he did for a living nor how old he was. Nothing apart from his name, Leandro. Nor did he know anything about me. He definitely didn't seem to know that I was famous back in the UK, which was all to the good.

My plan to stay single was in shreds. I was head over heels in lust with a man who couldn't speak English, but the chemistry was so strong I couldn't resist it. Believe me, I know it sounds nuts after being with someone only a matter of hours, but it was true. Of course at that stage it was a purely physical attraction because I couldn't really tell what his personality was like. He certainly looked the part. It was only much, much later, when his English had improved, that he turned out to be the biggest prick of all the men I have ever been with!

CHAPTER 6

I HAVE TO SEE HIM AGAIN!

It's hard, because of how my relationship with Leo turned out, to look back on that time in February 2011 and be objective. I do feel a great deal of bitterness about the things he said and did when we split up, which made me question if he had ever been genuine...But if I keep all that out of my head, the fact was that the start of our relationship was very romantic. There we were, two strangers who had fallen for each other straight away. It seemed like fate.

But the fact we didn't speak the same language was not going to make this relationship easy. My friend Lisa, who lives out in LA, set up a translator for me on my phone so that when Leo texted me I was able to copy and paste the text and then translate it. From then on he and I texted each other all the time. I found out that he was a model and TV presenter, and he was Argentinian. He gave the impression that he was very well known in his own country. Okay, so it wasn't great that he lived on a different continent and didn't speak English, but it seemed a positive sign that he at least came from the same industry as me and that he was famous. As I've already said, one of the many things that drove Alex and me apart was his thirst for celebrity. But Leo was already famous. He wouldn't have to use me or my name to promote himself, I thought. That would be a first.

I don't think you can help your feelings or who you fall for. I knew it was under two months since I had split from Alex, though the truth was our relationship had been over a long time before that. And I knew other people would think I should wait a while before having another relationship. But my feelings for Leo were overwhelming and they felt right to me. I had asked him if he had Googled me, thinking, Please don't because the pictures are shit and the stories about me even worse...It would be enough to put anyone off. He said that he hadn't. Looking back, I think it's almost certain that he would have. It's human nature, isn't it? I had Googled him and seen all his modelling pictures, which were stunning.

My head was telling me that I shouldn't jump into another relationship so soon after my marriage break up, but my heart was telling me the opposite. Me being me, my heart won. And so six days after we had met, I asked Leo to come over to England and see me. He wasn't filming and it seemed like an ideal opportunity for us to get to know each other better. As he was packing for the trip I knew that he had a friend with him who spoke English and I texted him, via her, to explain that I had two other children besides Harvey. I laid it all out for him. At the time I was naïve and thought nothing of him coming to see me after we had spent only one night together. But looking back, I wonder whether he had already done his research on me and discovered that I was well known and had money. Why else would a young man who was that good-looking and eligible fly to another country to be with an older woman, with three kids, when he could easily get any beautiful young model? But maybe I had been amazing on that one night...!

I was on a shoot when Leo arrived at Heathrow and so I arranged for Rob my driver to pick him up, along with Phil, and bring him to me. I was so excited about seeing Leo again! I rushed to the car once I had finished work, and as soon as I saw him I felt that spark of attraction, that chemistry. It completely overtook the language barrier. It was such an intense feeling.

Rob drove us back to Gary and Phil's flat in central London. We had paps following the car and I was furious that they had tracked us down. I couldn't understand how they knew where we were. Once we were safely inside the flat Leo took out his laptop and pretended that he had to do some work for a few minutes. Then he showed me that he had translated the words of a Spanish love song into English, explaining that they summed up how he felt about me. At the time I thought that was so romantic. My interpretation looking back? That he was a proper charmer and very calculating...He knew exactly how to push my buttons. But okay, back to how I felt then. The gesture impressed me.

He had also brought me some presents: a set of silver stirrups, kind of Western-style, that they ride with in Argentina, chocolates and a poncho. It reminded me a little bit of when you have a foreign student to stay and they bring you gifts from their country! I didn't attempt to explain that to him via Google Translate. God knows what would have come out. I think I wore the poncho once – not really my thing. When we split, I sold it on eBay. But at least he made the effort, I thought. Still, I couldn't help wondering how he knew I was into riding. I hadn't told him. Now I can only think he *had* done his research on me.

He was such a contrast to Alex, so masculine and so clean-cut and such a gentleman. And making love with him was so refreshing, because it was so normal... Imagine standing in a hurricane, in Force-12 winds – that was what sex had felt like with Alex towards the end. Then imagine lying in a field full of daisies in warm sunshine – that was what sex with Leo felt like. No wonder I fell for him.

The press attention was insane though. We couldn't go anywhere without being pursued by the paps, which was not an ideal start to a relationship. It didn't seem to faze Leo though, he seemed to enjoy it. I know I always get criticised for introducing my boyfriends to my children too quickly, but Leo stayed with Gary and Phil up in London when I had the children, and with me only when they were with their dad. In spite of the language barrier, Gary and Phil had already given Leo their seal of approval, and my other friends and family who met him really liked him as well. Even when there is a language problem you can still get a good sense of what someone is like and Leo had lovely manners when he was introduced to people, was a real gentleman. He seemed charming and outgoing.

Most importantly of all, when he finally met Junior and Princess he was good with them. He was good with Harvey too. I've said it before: any man who wants to be with me, first and foremost has to be good with my children. If they're not interested, then it doesn't matter how much I like them, they are never going to be part of my life. All I want, and all I have ever wanted, is to create a secure, happy family unit.

Leo also had a playful side and liked bantering with me and teasing me, though of course we were limited by the language barrier. He seemed easygoing and up for a laugh. You have to have that in a relationship, I think. It felt right to be with him, and I believed it would be amazing, if only we could speak the same language. Back then I was optimistic and thought that when he learned English our relationship would have a brilliant future.

Leo also shared my love of riding – the first man I had ever had a relationship with to do that. I soon learned that it was not a good idea to let him loose on my very expensive dressage horses, though, as he had a ride on Wallace, one of my favourites, and let's just say it didn't go well. Dressage horses are so finely tuned and used to responding to certain very specific commands. Leo was a confident rider, who had been riding all his life, but he was more used to galloping across the plains, or whatever they have in Argentina. It was a miracle Wallace didn't buck him off.

I got the impression Leo was quite posh and came from a good family and again I hoped that he hadn't Googled me or he might be in for a bit of a surprise on that score...Such a lot of shocking stuff has been written about me over the years, a hell of a lot of which is completely made up shit, but once it's on the web, it's out there for everyone to read.

Leo was easily the best-looking guy I had ever been with. He was a beautiful man and dressed really well, in just the style I liked, young and on trend. But it wasn't just about his looks. It was how he made me feel...and he made me feel so good. He was always hugging and kissing me, which I love, and paying me attention. I think I really needed that after what I'd been through with Alex. I know I'm insecure and want to be loved, but at the same time I can be a nightmare because I'm fiercely independent. What can I say? I'm a complex woman! A typical Gemini.

One weekend during Leo's visit I decided we should all get away to the country, ideally in the middle of nowhere, a place the paps couldn't track us down. I booked a log cabin for myself, Leo and my gay Mafia – Gary, Phil, Royston and Nick – along with my sister and her boyfriend. 'One lady and four campers,' I joked to Gary, not forgetting my gorgeous, fit, new boyfriend. I think Gary was expecting some kind of glamorous spa retreat, which was so typical of him. He's such a neat freak and hates getting dirty. I love being in the countryside, but my friends are city types – it made me crack up as we all stumbled around in the woods, in the pitch dark, trying to locate the cabin. We were winding each other up, saying it was like *The Blair Witch Project*, but the fact was you could hear traffic in the distance. We were not starring in our own horror movie.

We had a great time. It was still hard trying to have a conversation with Leo, and we had to rely on Google Translate, which didn't always get the meaning across, but I did feel this intense bond between us. We were very physical with each other, and not just in the bedroom. I think we were like that to compensate for the fact we couldn't tell each other how we felt.

But throughout his visit, I had this nagging feeling of sadness as I knew he would be flying back to Argentina very soon and then we would be apart. I tried to tell myself that it would be good if we didn't live together straight away, as I had done in past relationships, especially with Alex, which had left me feeling suffocated because he was always in the house. But it didn't work. I knew I would be desolate when Leo left. And so when he invited me to go to Argentina, I had to go. He told me that he wanted to introduce me to his family, a very big deal apparently because I would be only the second girl he had ever done that with. Great, I thought, he's as serious about me as I am about him. I loved that we were so open with each other about our feelings. No playing games, which I hate because they do your head in when you're constantly questioning if the man likes you. I suppose the language barrier meant there could be no games between us. It was either all or nothing.

I had only just started filming my TV reality show, *Katie,* for Sky. After my experience with Pete, when we were filmed all the time and no aspect of our marriage seemed to be off limits, which had really affected our relationship, I had vowed that I would keep my significant other off camera. But if I did this with Leo, I wouldn't be able to see him, as he would be in Argentina and I would be in the UK. And I was really falling for him. He seemed almost too good to be true. My friends and family always say that I need someone strong because I can be bossy and I'm very independent. I don't need to rely on anyone else to support me because if I want something, I can just get it myself, which I know can be hard to take for the men in my life. They need to earn my respect and not let me walk all over them, because if I can, I will. I always like to push it and see how far

I can go. Right from the start Leo kept me in check and I didn't feel I had the upper hand at all. In fact, he was the one who bossed *me* around and put me in my place. It amazed my friends, because if he asked me to do something and I didn't get round to it, he would keep asking until I did.

He was also very sociable back then and liked going out, meeting up with friends and having a few drinks, though never getting drunk. And he had his own career. He might have looked like a pretty boy but he was very intelligent. Sometimes I found it hard to believe he was only twenty-five as he seemed to have an old head on young shoulders. At last, I thought, I've found my equal, my match. My friends all advised me to be cautious about rushing in however. As Gary said, 'Leo will be different in Argentina because he'll be with his mates. And it will either be really good and what you're into, or he might turn out to be a kid. He is only twenty-five, don't forget.' But I still had a good feeling about him.

* * *

Because of last-minute issues with my divorce I was actually going to make two trips to Argentina, one for just three days and another lasting just over two weeks, after the Easter holidays.

When I landed in Buenos Aires the first time Leo was there waiting for me in Arrivals, looking as gorgeous as ever. I had almost forgotten how tall he was, how broad-shouldered. It felt so romantic as he swept me up in his arms. 'Hello, Baby,' he said, kissing me. And then he whisked me back to his apartment where we made up for being apart...

He had given me the impression that he had a large place, but it was actually quite small. It was a typical boy's pad, full of his skateboarding and snowboarding gear. But I thought it was sweet. And, in a romantic gesture, Leo had arranged candles round the tiny bath, which I could just about fit my big toe in.

The next day he took me out for lunch, at some lovely restaurant just outside the city, and insisted on paying. It might not sound that unusual to you, but believe me it was unusual for me back then. I was used to paying for everything when I went out, but every girl likes to be treated, don't they? I still tried to pay, but Leo wouldn't hear of it. Then he'd organised a boat for us to travel back to Buenos Aires. I was feeling really looked after. Yes, we had the camera crew with us, but to be honest I'm so used to being filmed, and I got on so well with the crew, that it didn't feel like an intrusion, more like part of the furniture.

The next thing Leo had planned was a party to introduce me to his friends. He held it on the roof terrace of his apartment, by the pool. He had invited nearly thirty people and I was so impressed by how calm and organised he was. True, he had friends helping him make all the salads in the kitchen while he grilled the meat on the massive barbecue outside. But if it had been me, I'd have been flapping about and running late. Not

Leo. He had everything under control, which was just as well really as I went to have a rest and ended up falling asleep. I arrived at the party after the first guests. Oops! I did offer to help, but he replied, 'No, no, you chill.' And so I did. It wasn't that easy as not many of his friends spoke English, but they were all lovely to me. I have to say, though, Argentinian girls are very pretty...far too pretty for my liking. Talk about competition!

Towards the end, when I'd had a couple of glasses of wine, I wanted to liven things up a little and get everyone dancing, but that was because it was hard work trying to communicate and dancing is the universal language, isn't it? Overall it had been a good night and it only increased my respect for Leo, who had been such a great host.

The following day we escaped to the beach again for our last day in Argentina and I asked our Spanish-speaking cameraman to tell Leo that I'd fallen deeply for him. I thought he was the perfect package. I hadn't felt this happy for a long time. Because of what happened later when we split, looking back I wonder if the way Leo treated me then was all part of a plan to reel me in, that he didn't ever love me but only wanted a famous partner...I really hope not.

Then it was back to the UK together. Friends asked how on earth we could have a relationship when we didn't even speak the same language, but somehow we managed to communicate. In fact, if there was a translator then it became a problem – we liked working things out for ourselves. And on the plus side it meant that we could never argue! Oh, yes, he did try and teach me the odd word or phrase in Spanish: *Hola, gracias, ¿Cómo está?* Most important of all, *Te quiero*: I love you. Did I love him already? I think it was more like lust, which I have to say can feel like love. Our relationship seemed so romantic and fairy-tale-like, probably even more so because of what had gone before it...which, believe me, had never been like a fairy tale. More like a horror story towards the end.

I wanted to throw a party for Leo when we were back. He had been so generous to me when I was out in Argentina and I wanted to show him some hospitality Pricey-style. A barbecue seemed like a perfect idea. There was just one problem...my barbecue had completely rusted as I had left it out on the patio throughout the winter. There was no way *that* was ever going to grill a sausage again. Pete had taken my other barbecue when we split.

I had to have one! From what I could gather, barbecuing food was an important tradition in Argentina as they seemed to be big meat eaters. Leo had a huge built-in grill on his terrace, where he could cook whole sides of beef. He was quite a man's man and really into building things and DIY. If you needed something fixing he would do it. The complete opposite to Pete who never did anything like that when we were together. Anyway Leo got it into his head that he was going to build me a barbecue outside from scratch and we spent quite a while in B&Q trying to track down what he needed.

Oh, the glamour of my life! In the end, after a tortuous twenty minutes, we ended up buying two barbecues in kit form, which had been my suggestion all along.

I'm not sure if I was quite so good a host as Leo. By now my friends are used to my style of entertaining, where it's all a bit last-minute, but I get there in the end and there is always plenty of food. Too much of it sometimes. I love to feed my friends until they're so stuffed they're only fit for collapsing in the cinema room and watching a movie and us all chilling out together. I love a full house. Leo expertly put together the barbecues and very sweetly involved Harvey in their construction. And even though the party was meant to be for him, Leo ended up grilling all the food. I got the impression that he would rather do that...especially when he saw the state of my mashed potato. Usually it's the business. This time it was both runny and lumpy. But, hey, I have many other good qualities.

CHAPTER 7

REALITY KATIE

As well as being a model, author and businesswoman, I also have a TV career. I have made three documentaries about my life with the filmmaker Richard Macer, and then in 2004 came the first series of the long-running reality show that I made with Pete. After we split I had my own series, *What Katie Did Next,* and filmed a three-part special on my wedding to Alex Reid, *Katie and Alex: For Better, For Worse.*

After my first marriage broke up and I still wanted to make reality shows, I formed my own production company, Pricey Media. My reality shows had all been made for ITV2 and I'd always enjoyed a very good relationship with everyone at the channel. The production company for these shows was Can TV, which was run by Neville Hendricks, partner (business, and for a while personal) of Claire Powell, who ran my former management company. He had been instrumental in creating the 'reality-show' style, and was continuing to make shows with Pete. But in March 2010 I was offered a deal with Sky Living TV to make two series of my show for them, as well as some factual entertainment series. The offer was too good to turn down, we are talking megabucks, and I signed up with Sky. But then the executives I had made the deal with left the channel, and the people who took over didn't seem so interested in promoting my shows.

Once I was making my own reality series, I had some decisions to make. First of all I decided that I no longer wanted my children to be filmed for the show or to appear in any of my photo shoots. I wanted to withdraw them from the public eye and allow them to have as normal a childhood as possible. The series I had filmed with Pete had always included a lot of footage of us with our children, even the moments up to Junior's and Princess's births, but after we broke up I realised that wasn't appropriate any more. There was some pressure on me for them to be included, but they were at an age by then when they were becoming aware of the cameras and what they meant. They had enough to cope with as their parents had recently split up. I wanted to protect them and give them some time to grow up like normal kids. I think I also wanted to prove that I don't need to have my children in my reality show or in shoots to promote myself.

I took advice on whether or not I should have Harvey in my series, from his teachers and from other parents of disabled children. Harvey's not aware of being filmed but that does not make it right in itself. What I do feel is that he is an inspiration, and the experts and my family agreed that it was good to keep him in my series, as it helped raise awareness about bringing up kids with disabilities and hopefully inspired other families. I know from the response that I received from viewers of the show that they really appreciated this. I think we have to include the disabled more in the everyday life of our country. As we saw from the Paralympics, those who cope with disabilities are inspirational, talented, and have huge amounts to offer. As a society we are perhaps a little reluctant to realise that, until important events like the Paralympics demonstrate it to us. I did, however, make sure Harvey was not in the show all the time.

I asked Pete to do the same, and keep Princess and Junior out of his series and shoots, but he refused. His argument seemed to be that it had never bothered me when we were married so why should it now? And that the kids loved doing it. (Of course they did, they're kids!)

It was true that when I was married to him, and we were managed by Claire Powell, I felt as if we were in this bubble where our whole lives were about being filmed and photographed. It became normal to us. We were in *OK!*, week in and week out, and no one was saying that this was wrong. But it all became too much for me. When my marriage broke up and the bubble burst, I had a reality check. That was not how I was going to live my life any more, and I was disappointed when Pete carried on involving the kids in his series and shoots. He didn't seem to understand my reasoning, and some people in the media claimed I was only doing it to have a go at him. They claimed my position was hypocritical, and that it was a pointless stance given that Pete would continue to have them in his show anyway. But I knew I was right, and when the kids are with me there are no photo shoots, and there's no filming. They can just enjoy being with me, their mum. If that makes me a hypocrite then fine, but I actually think it would be more wrong of me to have realised that the kids should not be exposed as much as they were being and then do nothing about it. I am nothing if not a trier!

Pete has continued to do numerous photo shoots with Junior and Princess for *OK!,* and I would love to know if he has put the money he's earned in trust for them. As far as I'm concerned, they are entitled to it. I actually wrote on Twitter that my kids must have a big bank balance now because of all the work they had done with their dad. To be honest, I am disappointed that he has continued to do all those shoots with them, but he is still with the same management and still in the same 'bubble'. When he walked out on me the press were convinced that he was the victim, that he was the perfect father and I was a bitch and a bad mother.

I have no idea what he thinks about this but he has never, to my knowledge, said anything to the press to contradict this impression. There was even a shoot of him going strawberry picking with the kids. *Seriously?* He never did anything like that with them when we were together. He was always far more interested in working on his music. The one good thing to have come out of our marriage breaking up is that he does far more things with the kids nowadays. But I wish less of it was filmed or photographed, and I think one day he will see that what I am trying to do in removing them from the public eye is the right thing to do.

I don't watch his reality series but friends tell me how much of it involves the children and I don't like that at all. When they were very little it didn't seem to be such an issue, but as they are getting older of course they are aware of being filmed and it has an effect on them. It's got to the point where Junior says, 'I'm famous!' And I have to gently say, 'No, you're not, it's your mummy and daddy who work in the media.' Or I hear him say to people, 'My dad's Peter Andre!' and that worries me. If you look at the kids of some Hollywood actors, they are often in trouble because they've lived off the back of their parents' fame and haven't achieved anything for themselves. I don't want my fame to affect my children's lives. I want them to be treated just like any other kids, and I don't want their friends to be friends with them just because of who their parents are.

I hate thinking that when they go to Pete's house they

will be filmed. It should just be about them spending time with their dad, doing normal things. But it seems I'm not going to get my way about this and I am worried about the possible effect on them.

*   *   *

The other big decision I made was that I didn't want the men in my life to feature in my series. After filming with Pete and then Alex, I wanted my relationships to remain private. However, this didn't quite go to plan...I had just begun filming my new series, *Katie,* when I met Leo. And in spite of my recent resolution, he ended up being in the series because that was the only way I could get to see him, otherwise he would have been in Argentina and I would have remained in the UK filming. Maybe having him in the series gave him the false expectation that his life would always be like this, I don't know. But that's exactly why I *really* am never going to do it again!

I know I've complained in the past about filming taking over my life, but that was when I was with Pete and then it really was too full on. I came to dread hearing the doorbell ring, knowing that it would be the film crew. The experience of filming was so much better when it was with my own production company, Pricey Media, because I felt I had more control. Though I have to say, filming the second series was pretty full on as it lasted over seven or so months. The director seemed to like including interviews with my family, and they loved it when my mum or brother criticised me and said they were going to have a go at me for something. For example, they included a scene with my mum commenting on the way I dress, saying that she had always had a battle with me about the way I looked. And how she would like me to wear a sensible outfit on a night out, instead of showing off my boobs and backside!

'You're thirty-three!' she exclaimed. 'What are you trying to prove!'

'Am I supposed to go out dressed like a nun?' I retorted, getting the last word in as usual.

I guess the director wanted the extra drama – as if there wasn't enough in my life! You know that with the Pricey something surprising is always going to happen . . .

Also, they kept saying that they wanted to see the real Katie, reveal a softer side to me.

Well, I had to put them straight there. 'You're not going to see me crying on TV unless I'm genuinely upset about something! I can't turn it on and off like that.' It was as if they constantly wanted to wring more emotion out of me, to drum up more sympathy. But I thought that could turn out to be a depressing show and that was the last thing I wanted to make! And, as I've said so many times before, I can only be myself. I don't put on an act for the cameras. The series was supposed to be capturing the reality of my life, warts and all. And I think that's exactly what viewers got.

You may be surprised to hear me say this, given how successful my reality shows have been, and how many of them I have made, but I have to say I think reality TV has had its day. There are just too many shows out there now, and I think the public sees them as a bit fake and staged. But I was one of the first to get in there and my show was never scripted. What you saw was *my* reality. Once my series was on Sky its viewing figures were often compared with Pete's on ITV2, and this seemed to be yet another way of putting me down because mine were lower. But what people didn't seem to realise when they made this comparison was that ITV2 is a free channel, which everyone can get, whereas Sky is pay TV and not everyone has that, so of course my viewing figures would be lower. As I write this, I'm thinking about putting together a series to air on *YouTube*. I reckon that's the way forward.

In 2011 I also filmed a documentary for Sky Living called *Standing Up For Harvey* in the wake of Frankie Boyle's outrageous and sick so-called joke about him, which I will write more about later in this book. It was about speaking out for my son, who can't defend himself, as well as for other people with disabilities, hearing their stories and experiences. I wanted to confront the prejudice that Boyle's comment revealed, and to show what bringing up a disabled child is really like.

The fact that Boyle could make such an insensitive comment showed that he didn't have a clue what life was like for disabled children and those who care for them. My production team invited him to take part in a discussion on the programme, so he could explain why he made that 'joke' and why he thinks it is acceptable to speak about a disabled child in that way. And I wanted an apology. But guess what? We received a point blank refusal. Which I think says everything you need to know about him.

I met representatives from charities, including Mencap which campaigns for people with disabilities, to get their reaction to the Boyle comment. They firmly believed that it was no joke; it was bullying. As Sarah Bernard, Head of Communications at Mencap said, 'Channel 4 claimed to be pushing the boundaries by airing such a comment, but Mencap believes that such jokes can lead to taunting, harassment and bullying of people with disabilities.' There had been a tragic case in 2009 where a mother had committed suicide with her disabled daughter, setting their car alight, because they had suffered years of discriminatory abuse from a gang.

I met up with a group of young people with learning disabilities at a support group run by Mencap, to hear about their experiences. They all talked about how they had been bullied and called names, just because they had a disability. I felt so moved by their stories and how much they had been hurt by the cruelty of some people, it made me even more determined to stand up for the disabled.

I also invited a group of mums with disabled children over to my house, people I had known since Harvey was a baby, to get their views. As one of the mums said: 'I'd like Frankie Boyle to spend a week in our shoes, looking after a child with special needs, and then tell me if he finds a joke like that funny.' And other mums talked about how isolating it can be having a disabled child because, as one said, 'People don't accept different and challenging behaviours, they think that it's because the children are naughty or that we're bad parents, and it has nothing to do with that. It's because the child has a disability.'

I absolutely loved making the documentary. For a start it was on a subject that was close to my heart, and it was great feeling that I had helped to give a voice to disabled people who all too often don't have one at all. In fact, I'd love to make more documentaries like that, ones that are serious but also entertaining. Because Harvey is autistic, I would find it really inspiring to make a programme about what it is like to bring up a child with autism and to find out more about the condition.

I had an amazing response from viewers after the programme, with a stream of emails, tweets and letters. Some people saw me for the first time as a mum, and saw a different side to me. I'm really proud of the documentary. It was repeated on Sky and they said it was one of the highest-rated shows they'd ever had.

One more thought on Boyle. I see he sued the *Daily Mirror* over an article that he felt described him as racist, and won. I am sure he is not a racist and can see why he would be upset by being called one. But why then does he think it's okay to be discriminatory about the disabled? Why would people thinking that of him not upset him just as much? Years ago comedians who made jokes now accepted as racist were given air time on TV, but society has moved on and there are now strict laws in place to deal with racial discrimination. I don't think the disabled enjoy the same protection, when of course they should. I believe in years to come those who make Boyle-style jokes about the disabled will be viewed in the same way as those dinosaurs who made racist jokes years ago.

*   *   *

I'm always up for doing things for charity on TV, and in March 2011 I was in *Let's Dance for Comic Relief*. I had to dress up as Freddie Mercury in his iconic video to 'I Want to Break Free', where he is in drag as a kinky housewife. So I was going to be a woman, dressed up as a man, dressed up as a woman... To be honest the costume was the least of my worries. Everyone who knows me, knows that I can't dance.

We had one week to rehearse and I was working myself up into a complete state because I couldn't do the moves! And I was going to be on live TV! I can go on live TV and talk about myself, but dance? The choreographer kept telling me to be more exaggerated about my moves and really perform. Easier said than done to someone with two left feet...

I did look hilarious in the costume, wearing a bouffant black wig, moustache, full make up, fake body hair and a PVC skirt and pink top. I didn't care that I looked like a complete twat. The lovely Graham Norton, who was one of the judges, said after my performance, 'I love you, Katie Price, that was just fearless.' Somehow I managed to get a place in the final, but then I was knocked out. The whole experience was really good fun and it was brilliant to help raise money for charity. I especially enjoyed doing the little sketch before my routine where I took the piss out of myself for having so many products out in my name. See? I really don't take myself too seriously.

CHAPTER 8

ARGENTINA AGAIN

On 17 April Leo and I flew back out to Argentina. I paid for us both to fly first-class. I thought then that he acted as if he was very used to this life-style and seemed to sit back on the flight as if he was a king, expecting to be waited on, but I didn't care because I was so into him.

On this visit we were going to meet his parents. I remember how I felt on the plane as we flew out: convinced that Leo and I were good together. I must have been pretty confident about his feelings for me as I changed into the onesie that my brother had bought me for Christmas – though it's true to say I always change into something comfortable for a flight, especially one that's sixteen hours long. It's okay, I changed out of it before we landed, and upped the glamour stakes in a pair of skin-tight leggings and a silver sequined jacket and heels. And of course the celebrity must-have — a huge pair of designer shades so the paps didn't catch me blinking or squinting or generally looking shit.

I had found out that Leo's dad Hector had been a politician, and his mum Mercedes had been a beauty queen. Again, I got the feeling that Leo came from quite a posh family and that the girls he usually went for would be like the ones in *Made In Chelsea*, all born with silver spoons in their mouths and living off Mummy and Daddy. Apparently in Argentina, when the press reported on Leo and me getting together, they seemed to think that I was a posh girl too. Well, they had that a bit wrong, hadn't they? Someone hadn't done their research...

I was really looking forward to meeting them, as well as feeling a little apprehensive because I really wanted them to like me. Leo seemed very close to his parents and I didn't want them to think that I was too old for him, or that because I already had children, he shouldn't get involved with me. Mind you, I had just found out that Leo had a five-year-old daughter himself. He told me that he'd been seeing the mother for two months when he was twenty and then they split up, it hadn't been a serious relationship. Afterwards she'd turned up to see him at his parents' house and told him she was pregnant and that the baby was his. He told her that he wasn't ready to be a dad, and that he was moving to Buenos Aires to pursue a modelling career. He saw the baby girl when she was born but I think at first he didn't have anything to do with her; it was only later that he wanted her to have his surname, and started paying maintenance. I suppose I was glad that he had a child, because then he might be able to understand better what it was like for me being a mum, but I didn't think it sounded great that he hadn't been involved in his daughter's life...However, I put that down to his being too young at the time.

His parents lived in Córdoba, a mountainous region 700 kilometres north-west of Buenos Aires. I was blown away by their place: a ranch in the heart of beautiful countryside, surrounded by fields and mountains and horses. I loved it! Everyone made me feel so welcome, even though neither Leo's parents nor his sisters spoke a word of English...and I really mean not a word. And there was no one to translate on that first meeting as I had wanted it to be private, without the cameras. But I can honestly say it wasn't a problem. I had a really good time. Again I got the feeling that what Leo and I had was special, and that his family was every bit as important to him as mine was to me.

Wow, the life-style there was right up my street! So much of it was spent outdoors. We ate outside, and all Leo's nieces and nephews played round us and then jumped on their ponies and went off for a ride. Later he and I joined them. I felt so free there, I loved being surrounded by so much space, and the scenery was beautiful. I thought how much I would like my kids to visit this place; they would absolutely love the space and being able to play outside. I had felt increasingly hemmed in back in the UK, where although I had a reasonable-sized garden there were no open fields. Whenever we went out of the front gate we ran the risk of being photographed by the paps who lurked in the road, waiting for a chance to snap us. I wanted my children to be able to roam and have adventures in a safe place. Leo's family even had a horse and cart. It all reminded me a bit of *The Waltons,* because the whole place seemed to be set back in time, when there was a slower pace of life. And there wasn't a pap with a long-lens camera in sight! I really felt that I fitted in there. It was just my kind of lifestyle. I am a complete country girl at heart.

The following day I went out for lunch with Leo and his parents. He wanted me to see the scenery round Córdoba and so we booked into a restaurant two hours' drive away. It was a spectacular journey, through fields, hills and mountains. But there was a nasty surprise waiting for us when we arrived at the remote hilltop restaurant that seemed to be in the middle of nowhere. The paps had somehow found out and were waiting for us there. I bloody hate some of them, the worst are real parasites! I'd had three lovely days without them and really didn't want them getting pictures of this private time. And so I got the waiter to take pictures of us all having lunch and immediately posted them on my Twitter page. Screw those paps who were trying to make money out of me. But it had been strange that they had turned up there…someone must have tipped them off. Now I wonder if it might even have been Leo.

I was learning that he was something of a daredevil, an adrenalin junkie. It was a bit like being with Action Man because he always wanted to be out there doing something: riding his quad bike, horse riding, generally testing and pushing himself. He played polo and had been to military school, so he was good at shooting. He went motor-cross riding, had a skateboard with an engine that could go to 40 m.p.h. and would race on it against his friends. He was like a good-looking Jackass! And while I am a bit of a daredevil and thrill-seeker myself, and love all those scary rides at amusement parks, there are some things that I'm genuinely scared of. Heights, for instance. Leo wanted us to go sky-diving.

'Yeah, I'm up for it!' I said, all blasé, like it was no big deal. When I appeared in *I'm a Celebrity…Get Me Out of Here!* I even had it written into my contract that I wouldn't have to parachute out of the helicopter, as the rest of the contestants had to, because I am so scared of heights. But there was something about Leo that made me feel safe and protected and believe that I could do anything.

But when it came to it, I was shitting myself! First of all we had to run through the safety procedures, and all the time in my head I was thinking, I can't do it, I just can't do it. Leo's mum and dad had come to watch us make the jump and that made me feel that I had to do it, to prove myself and not let Leo down. No one could speak English on the plane and I actually thought I was going to have a panic attack. My legs had turned to jelly and I could feel my breathing getting shallower – a sure sign of a panic attack approaching. No one else seemed to realise the state I was in. My instructor tapped me on the shoulder and said cheerfully, 'Okay, one minute.' That is, one minute before I jumped out of a plane at twelve thousand feet…what was I doing here! I must have been stark raving bonkers ever to agree to this, I thought.

'I can't do it,' I exclaimed, 'I just can't.'

'Yes, you can,' Leo told me confidently. I don't think he realised how genuinely petrified I was. And then I was being flung out of the plane, strapped to my instructor and plunging down, down, down, down. It was absolutely terrifying. An experience I never want to repeat. When we landed, the adrenalin was still pumping through me and I remember saying, 'Oh my God, oh my God,' over and over again. I didn't even know what I felt. Relief that I had made it above all. I think I impressed Leo's parents though. But bloody hell, there have to be easier ways! I would rather have taken everyone out for dinner…And that wasn't the end of my extreme sports. On another day we went paragliding off a cliff. I felt physically sick and could hardly bear to look down at the ground, far below us. But I also felt a great sense of achievement. And at the end of the ordeal I had Leo to hug me and tell me that he loved me.

I'm definitely much happier on horseback than

flinging myself out of a plane and there was plenty of riding when we were away. On one ride we met up with this Indian guy who was, I was told, chanting for an eagle to come, and playing panpipes as we rode up the mountain. I've absolutely no idea what was going on. I kept looking at the cameraman and raising my eyebrows, mouthing, 'What the fuck is this?' But Leo told me to 'shush' and that I had to respect the man. Of course that only made me want to laugh more. I'm just not into all that mystical stuff like some people are; I can't lose myself in it. I was all too aware that I was on a ride with a man who seemed to be bonkers, calling out crap. However, when we reached the summit and he was still chanting, the herd of cattle up there suddenly moved and huddled close together. Everyone dismounted and began searching on the ground. Apparently they were looking for an eagle feather. Suddenly there was a shout of excitement and the Indian guy held up a black feather. This was what all the fuss had been about. A black eagle feather is very rare. He insisted on giving it to Leo and me, and told us that it would bring us luck. I thought nothing of it really and when we drove back Leo tucked it behind the passenger mirror. I didn't know then but in a couple of days we would need all the luck in the world...

Another time we went on an amazing horse trek. It was supposed to be a five-hour ride, but it ended up being fourteen hours in the saddle. I have never ridden for that long, ever. It felt like being in a Western as we rode up the mountains on surfaces I didn't think horses could even walk on. The terrain was incredibly stony and steep. It took us five hours to get to the top of the mountain and, while I was relieved finally to dismount, I couldn't help thinking that we were going to have to ride back again... We had a massive barbecue – the Argentinians really do like their meat – and as I watched them laying out chunks of it on the grill, I thought it didn't look very appetising. It definitely wasn't anything like the cuts you buy in Sainsbury's, already neatly chopped up and packaged. Just as well I wasn't a vegetarian! I tucked in when it was served up as I was starving. I'd already seen how Leo and his family would drive out into the countryside in a truck when it was dark and hunt rabbits, which would then be cooked in a stew. This was proper country living.

My daredevil experiences didn't end there as we also went quad-biking for the day with a group of Leo's friends. I hesitated to get on the back of Leo's bike as he was so reckless and fearless. He looked the part though – he had all the gear and his own quad bike. Like I said, bit of an Action Man. I ended up riding with Lulie, a friend of Leo's who was staying with us, as she could speak English and translated for us. She was the woman who had been responsible for getting him his presenter job on the TV show, and with my woman's intuition I reckoned she fancied him. But it wasn't a big deal; besides, I imagined lots of women fancied him. What wasn't to fancy!

Quad biking was brilliant. I've done it lots of times, but this seemed to be especially good. We raced over dirt tracks and through puddles, and I didn't care about getting covered in mud. And it was a good opportunity to meet more of Leo's circle. They were all friendly and the girls were good-looking, but maybe a bit bland compared to me. They didn't seem to have my devil-may-care streak.

It was Valentine's Day the following day and I wanted to buy Leo a card and a present. When we'd finished quad biking I managed to track down a shop — which was quite something as we were in the middle of nowhere — and buy a huge teddy bear, chocolates and a card, and smuggle it all into the boot of the car without Leo seeing. I'm not sure if they celebrate Valentine's Day there in the same way we do in the UK, but I wanted to mark it with Leo, who was giving me such a magical experience in Argentina. We had dinner then got back in the car for the long drive home, exhausted by our active day but feeling thoroughly happy.

CHAPTER 9

MY HERO

It was midnight by the time we set off. The roads were narrow and wound through mountainous terrain. Leo was driving the 4x4. I was glad it was him rather than me, though usually in relationships I'm always the one to drive. Ben and Rupert, two of the camera crew, were asleep in the back and Lulie was translating the conversation for Leo and me. We were talking about how the mother of his daughter had suddenly become difficult and had sold a story on him, perhaps because she had seen pictures of him with me in the press. And we were saying how into each other we were, and how happy we were to be together, when suddenly Lulie cried, 'Watch out!'

Staring through the windscreen, to my horror I saw two horses right in front of us, and car lights coming from the other direction on the narrow road. Leo desperately tried to brake but it was too late, the horses were too close. We ploughed straight into the back of them. They were thrown on to the bonnet, hit the windscreen and bounced off.

It's hard remembering exactly what happened as it was such a shocking experience, but I remember the car skidding for what seemed like a long way. Leo stayed in control and flung his arm out to protect me because I only had the seat belt across my waist, I didn't have it over my chest. If he hadn't done that I would have gone straight into the windscreen, no doubt about it. The airbags had failed to inflate on impact. The car came to a stop and for a moment there was complete silence. I must have shut my eyes. When I opened them I saw that the windscreen had completely caved in. It was only inches away from my face. Leo was facing forward, still clutching the wheel, and looked to be in shock. I reached out to him. 'Are you okay?' I exclaimed, terrified that he was hurt. But he turned to me and seemed to be fine. Then I called out to the others and they were unhurt as well.

We all got out of the car. It was pitch black, and steam was coming off the engine. I could hear this terrible moaning coming from the animal which was lying across the road, a mare. It was a gruesome sight. She'd been terribly injured; her back leg had completely snapped and we could see the bone sticking out. There was blood everywhere. I couldn't believe the poor creature was still alive. I bent down and could see the raw fear in her eyes. I stroked her nose, whispering soothing words, trying to bring her some comfort in her last moments. Mercifully, she soon died. Then I heard a rustling in the bushes by the side of the road and said, 'Oh my God! That's the other horse.'

We found it, a foal, lying off to one side. Like his mother's, his back legs had been terribly injured. He was desperately trying to get up but couldn't. I can't tell you how heartbreaking it was to see this poor animal in such pain, and with such fear in his eyes. I stroked his nose and neck and murmured, 'Okay, boy, okay.' Until he too died. It was like being in a nightmare. The shock, the smell of blood, the darkness. We were all stunned. I remember crying, and I was physically shaking. I couldn't believe that this had happened.

The car that had passed us returned to check how we were. The driver was convinced we had all died in the collision. And as we took in the state of our car we couldn't believe that none of us had been hurt. It was a write-off; the windscreen had caved in and the front end was buckled and mangled. You couldn't imagine how anyone could have walked away unscathed from such a scene. Leo had only been going at thirty miles an hour or so, but the roads round there weren't proper tarmac, they were narrow dirt tracks full of potholes. If he hadn't done such a brilliant job of controlling the car we could have broken through a fence and plunged down a ravine or hit the other vehicle head on.

Later, when I was back in the UK, I showed some pictures of the crash to Adrian, the guy who was doing physio on my knee. He had been a paramedic, and when he saw the car he said that those were the kinds of accidents he would be called to then and all the people involved would have been killed. 'I have no idea how you survived that,' he told me. I have no idea either. It was horrific and I've long had this premonition that I would die in a car accident, so if it was going to happen, that would have been my time... We had all been incredibly lucky. Afterwards Leo mentioned the black eagle feather and said that it had protected us. I don't know about that but something had saved us, that was for sure.

I was devastated that the horses had died. Apparently the mare and her foal had escaped from a nearby farm after someone had left the gate open. Horses are one of my greatest passions, they are such wonderful, beautiful animals, and seeing two die in agony, right in front of me, affected me deeply. When I look at my horses now I sometimes remember what those two looked like when they were dying and it's a disturbing memory.

I was desperate to speak to my children and let them know that I'd had an accident but that I was okay, and tell them how much I loved them. And I wanted to speak to my mum and my brother. When something shocking like that happens you need to speak to your family. But there was barely any signal on my phone and I couldn't get through. Finally I managed to reach Catherine, my

PA, and told her what had happened. She said later that I sounded totally shocked.

Leo was deeply upset when we got back to the ranch, a kind of delayed reaction to what had happened. There is no doubt in my mind that I would have gone through the windscreen and been horrifically injured, or even killed, if he hadn't put out his arm to save me. He was my hero; he had saved my life. It definitely brought us closer. We had survived this shocking ordeal together. A few days later we got matching tattoos done. I had Leo's name and the date we met tattooed on my left calf, and he had my name tattooed on his leg. I'll never learn, will I? By then I'd had the tattoo of Pete's name covered up with a rose design...

After the accident I remember commenting to camera that Leo was perfect and I was still trying to find a fault in him. He ticked all the right boxes with his character and looks, and seemed almost too good to be true. I didn't think that anyone could be that perfect – not only as my boyfriend, but also at everything he did: his job, riding, cooking, DIY...you name it, he could do it. At one point during my visit he picked up a set of panpipes and even knew how to play them! I hate the sound of panpipes, but I was still impressed.

I loved his strong character, though sometimes we did clash because he definitely wanted things done his way. I don't know if that was his Latino temperament, but I didn't mind that – I would far rather be with someone who is a strong character than a doormat. He told me that he had never been out with anyone like me before. It sounded as if he was usually the one in control, and it seemed as if he'd met his match with me.

And I loved it that he wanted to protect and look after me. During my visit he wouldn't let me pay for anything. And let me tell you, that was a complete novelty! However, there was one time when he needed some cash to pay for some accommodation and asked if he could borrow some from me. I ended up giving him around fifteen hundred pounds. He promised to pay me back, but he never did. At the time I thought nothing of it; after all, he had been so generous to me. It was only a few months later that I remembered it and wondered if it had been a sign that Leo wasn't all he said he was. But that was later...Back then I was falling in love with him. I would have done anything for him, and he would have done anything for me.

But there were still two big problems...he lived sixteen hours away by air, and he couldn't speak fluent English. But by this time we were desperate to be together. He was due to start filming in May for his new game show series, and said he would find it hard not to see me. He actually cried when he talked about it, saying, 'I can't be without you.'

I couldn't stay in Argentina with him because of my children. We decided that every month I would fly out to see him and then the following month he would fly to the UK to be with me. It sounded okay in theory, but in my heart I couldn't see it working. Because of my children and my career, I've never wanted to have a long-distance relationship. I don't think they can ever work. And so Leo made the decision to give up his TV presenting job, saying he couldn't bear not to be with me. He was coming to England as soon as he could. We had only known each other for two months but we knew in our hearts that we had to be together. And there is no doubt that surviving the accident gave us an intense bond. But even then I did think it was surprising that he would give up his career to be with me, because I wouldn't give up my career for any man.

*   *   *

The horrific car accident where the horses so tragically died inspired part of the plot for my next novel, *In The Name of Love,* where Charlie, the heroine, has an accident when her horse collides with a car, and she is powerless to save him. From then on she has a phobia about riding and suffers from flashbacks to that terrible day. And then, in an ironic twist of fate, she falls passionately in love with, of all people, a Spanish event rider! Though he speaks far better English than Leo . . . I definitely like to put my characters through it. After all I've been through myself, I want my novels to reflect the drama.

I never write about real people who I've met and had relationships with, but I do draw on my experiences, and on my own feelings, for inspiration. I guess that's one good thing to come out of my tempestuous love life! So, for example, *Angel,* my first novel, is about a beautiful young girl who becomes an incredibly successful glamour model, and is a woman who always follows her heart rather than her head. Ring any bells? One of my other heroines, Sapphire, runs a successful business in Brighton, and has her own share of heartbreak and passion. I wanted to write about her because of having my own businesses, such as KP Equestrian. My latest novel, *He's The One,* has a heroine who is a single mother, a way of life I know very well. I like my novels to be about strong, passionate women, and the world of the novels is the world I know, the celebrity world, reflecting my experiences of being famous but still living what I think is a normal family life.

I'm hugely proud of the fact that I've sold over three and a half million copies of my autobiographies, novels and children's books. It all started with my first autobiography, *Being Jordan*, that came out in 2004. It sold over a million copies. Then I branched out into novels, working with a ghostwriter.

Even after nine of them I've got loads more ideas for plots up my sleeve. For instance, I'd love to write another novel about Angel. She's happily married now to her gorgeous ex-footballer husband, Cal, and has two children, but I'm sure there is plenty more that could happen to my beautiful heroine with the stunning green eyes. I know from all the tweets, Facebook messages and emails that it's something my fans would love to read. So, watch this space!

CHAPTER 10

STANDING UP FOR HARVEY

I want you to imagine something. I want you to imagine that someone made these comments, on television, about your son. What I am about to write will shock you, but imagine how I felt as Harvey's mum. Here it is:

'Apparently Jordan and Peter Andre are fighting over custody of Harvey. Eventually one of them will lose and have to keep him.' Pretty disgusting but there's worse to follow. 'I have a theory that Jordan married a cage fighter because she needed someone strong enough to stop Harvey from fucking her.'

I was horrified that the so-called comedian, Frankie Boyle, could say such a disgusting thing about my son, an innocent child. Whatever anyone thinks of me, there was no way that a little boy like Harvey deserved to be the subject of a sick joke like that. People think that because

Riding in Cordoba, Argentina, with Leo.
Riding was one of the few things we had in common…

Keeping dry with my mates.

You know me, I strike a pose any time, any place, anywhere!

Party animal! Not bad for a
mother of 3! Out with Ben
Algar, a member of the camera
crew on my beauty show.

Don't know whether
I'm about to do a pole
dance, or stopping myself
from falling over. Either
way, the woman in
white doesn't look very
impressed…

Above: About to hit the slopes with Derek, Jane, Leo, Junior and George.

Above: What happens in Vegas, stays in Vegas.

Top left: Getting glammed up for a night out!

Top right: A bit of après-ski with Jane.

Right: Up close with Leo, early days when I couldn't get enough of him…it didn't last…

Cuddles with Harvey.

Harvey loves
sneaking into my
bed for hugs.

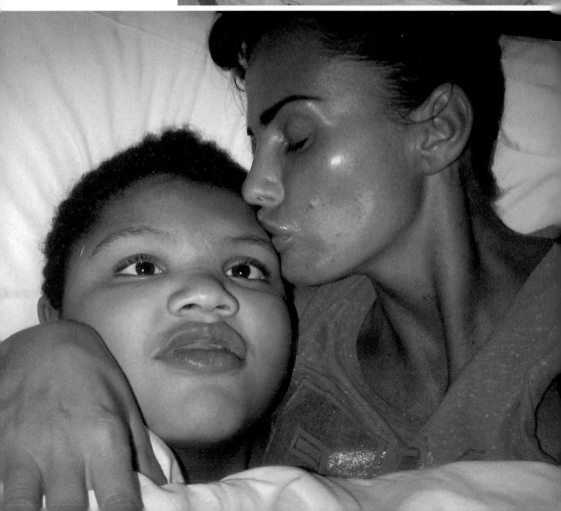

Messing about on the river with my cubs!

Sports Day! Go Junior! So proud of you!

I do love my motors…and my airbags!

I'm in the public eye I should just take everything on the chin, but I won't when it involves my children. And I didn't this time. I immediately contacted my lawyers. I had to defend my son.

I wasn't the only one who was outraged; Boyle's Channel 4 programme provoked around five hundred complaints from people who were shocked that a mainstream broadcaster had allowed a discriminatory attack on a disabled child, who has more courage in his little finger than Boyle will ever muster in his life. In response to my lawyer's letter, Ofcom the TV regulator launched an investigation and ruled that Channel 4 had broken the rules by broadcasting material which appeared to 'target and mock the physical and mental disabilities' of Harvey. But that was as far as it went; neither Boyle nor Channel 4 was asked to apologise, which I found disgraceful. Channel 4 went on to broadcast the Paralympics so how could they justify airing Frankie Boyle's comment about a child, insinuating that because he's got disabilities he's more likely to rape his own mother? If Boyle's wife or children had an accident and were paralysed that would absolutely change his life, and then I'm sure he'd think twice about making jokes about people with disabilities.

When Boyle made a series of sick jokes about the Queen and the Duchess of Cambridge, his entire sketch was cut from *Give it up for Comic Relief* on BBC3. And I thought, So it's okay to make jokes about people with disabilities but not the Royals? I fought back by making my documentary, *Standing Up For Harvey.* If Boyle had taken up my invitation to meet him he would have seen that Harvey overcomes more problems before he has his breakfast every day than Boyle would have to in a month of Sundays.

*   *   *

I believe many people look at Harvey and think he is just a big kid who is blind. They don't appreciate the full extent of his disabilities. I've had a set of cards printed so that, when I see people staring at him, I can simply hand them one. The card says: 'You're obviously looking because you're interested. This is his condition, Septo-Optic Dysplasia, and if you want to donate to a charity that supports children like this then do.' The details of Vision charity (which works with blind, visually impaired and dyslexic children) are also printed on the card. I have noticed that the stares are worse in posh places like Harrods and Selfridges…and whenever we eat out at a restaurant we get stared at because Harvey is very sensitive to noise and hates the sound of cutlery being clattered, or doors banging, and can easily get upset – and this is especially difficult because he's obsessed with food. That's because of one of his other conditions.

Septo-Optic Dysplasia caused his blindness. Besides that, put simply, his brain didn't develop properly and that is the reason for all his other medical and behavioural problems. He was born with a limited pituitary gland, which is like the body's chemical regulator, so is deficient in all the hormones the body needs to help it function. He also has cortisol deficiency, which affects his stress responses and makes it harder for him to fight off illness and cope with shock.

When he suffered horrific burns to his legs in 2006, I was terrified that he would go into shock, that his windpipe would close up so that he wouldn't be able to breathe, and he would die. An emergency cortisone injection has to be administered to him in such situations. The accident happened on New Year's Eve when he got into a bath full of scalding hot water. The house was completely baby-proofed, with stair gates and the upstairs doors locked, but that day we were having a party and I can only imagine that one of our guests left the gates open and the doors unlocked, and Harvey, who was obsessed with water, slipped upstairs without anyone seeing. I wasn't at the house when he had his accident but returned to discover him screaming and thrashing around on my bed in agony. The sight of my son in so much pain is something I will never forget. Thank God he has fully recovered from the accident now.

Harvey also has Prader-Willi syndrome, a genetic disorder that means he is likely to eat to excess and is prone to obesity, and Diabetes Insipidus where he can't regulate how much he needs to drink and without medication would have a continual thirst. As if that isn't enough he is also autistic. Recently he was diagnosed with ADHD (Attention Deficit Disorder) and ODD (Oppositional Defiance Disorder). His autism means he has to follow a strict routine, ADHD means that he finds it hard to concentrate and focus, and ODD makes him aggressive, so all three of those conditions really affect his behaviour.

While Harvey is the most fantastic little boy and I love him very much, it is a constant challenge looking after him. He has to have medication every day, at 7 a.m., 8 a.m., 12.30 p.m., 2 p.m., 4.30 p.m., plus hormone injections at 8 p.m. I am not exaggerating when I say that, without regular medication, Harvey would die. He needs to be supervised all the time, and his condition constantly monitored by us at home and in regular hospital appointments. He has to have regular hospital blood tests to check that all his medication is balanced, and to do this has to have a general anaesthetic where a line is put into his arterial vein so they can take blood every two hours. He is so brave about this, especially since he hates needles, though he is fine with me giving him his hormone injections at night. I find it really upsetting going into theatre with him. I stay by his side while he is given the anaesthetic, I have to be brave for his sake. I hope people understand that when I say Harvey needs specialist nanny care while not at home, this is no dramatic overstatement. It is a simple fact that there has to be someone always on hand who is trained to deal with his many issues.

When Harvey was born he seemed like a perfectly

healthy baby boy. But at his six-week check up the midwife shone a torch into his eyes and commented that he didn't seem to be following the light. It was a complete bombshell. The doctors told me that my son was blind, that he would never be able to see and would hardly be able to do anything either. Just as I was coming to terms with this, twelve months later he was diagnosed with Septo-Optic Dysplasia. Thank God for my family and their constant support, especially my mum who gave up her job to help me look after him. I must say a few words about my family here.

My mum is my rock. She gets all my emotions and helps me deal with them. I would be lost without her. She is so good with Harvey, and I have always employed fantastic, highly trained nannies to help us.

When it comes to looking after my son, I've never looked for sympathy. My attitude has always been that I have to deal with it, get on with it, be strong and give Harvey the best possible life. Of course there are times when I've cried, but I know I would be no good at all to Harvey if I wasn't fighting for him, especially as he only has me to parent him. His dad is Dwight Yorke, the footballer, but he doesn't play any part in Harvey's life at all. When I fell pregnant with Harvey, Dwight wouldn't even admit that he was the father until we both took a DNA test that proved he was.

What has always upset me greatly is when the press or others suggest that Harvey's disabilities may be my fault in some way. When he was a baby there were suggestions in the press that I had caused his problems, that I was a bad mother. One newspaper blamed me because I went clubbing when I was pregnant. But for God's sake! People can still socialise when they are pregnant, and I was only twenty-two! They printed pictures of me coming out of a club, but they never printed the pictures of me driving home afterwards perfectly sober. I'm pregnant with my fourth child as I write this and that all seems like a very long time ago. Now I'm such a homebody I hardly like going out at all. My idea of a good night is watching *The Voice* and *Britain's Got Talent*. How times have changed for the Pricey...

I've often asked the doctors what might have caused Harvey's condition and they always say that it's nothing that anyone has done; it is genetic. No one is to blame. But some people still can't seem to understand that and can be so cruel. Only recently in 2013 Katie Green, some model or other, suggested on a live TV show that Harvey was disabled because she had heard that I had taken drugs when I was pregnant. She has not apologised properly for this so I am taking legal action. And some MP's son tweeted a vile comment about Harvey being a vegetable. His father is the patron of a brain injury charity, so you would really think that he should know better... It just shows what kind of attitude parents of disabled children, and people with disabilities, are up against. I wish all those people who show such ignorance could spend a day with Harvey and see the reality of looking after a disabled child.

Although we were told at first that Harvey would be blind, in fact he has limited vision. He can see at six metres what a normal child can see at sixty. He can read text in a size **48** font. He has glasses, which he is supposed to wear, and if he wore them all the time then he would be able to read a smaller font. However, he hates wearing them so he'll put them on and say, 'Wow,' and then take them off a few minutes later. He can use a touch-screen computer, write and draw pictures, and if he needs to see fine detail he has a special glass to help him. His right eye is better than his left, where he has a nystagmus. This means his eye turns in towards the centre, so when he looks at something he has to turn his head and his eye is constantly moving. Imagine how hard it would be to look at something when your eye was constantly making involuntary movements in another direction. It must be so frustrating for him.

At one of his check ups at Moorfields Eye Hospital, we showed his consultant some of Harvey's drawings and he was really impressed by one of a frog and a rainbow. 'That's amazing,' the consultant said, 'I would never have expected him to see colours.'

Harvey's sight is actually the least of his problems. The same consultant told us that if my son didn't have any of his other disabilities, including the behavioural ones, then he would have been able to lead a full life, have a job and live completely independently. But that is not going to be possible for Harvey; he will always live with me.

Harvey and I have a very close bond. My mum and his teachers say that everything he does is for Mummy and that he always wants them to tell me how well he has done at school, and to show me his pictures. I think it's unusual for a child with autism to feel this strong bond with a parent but it's unbelievably strong in his case, to the point where if ever Harvey is having a tantrum and lashing out, he might hit someone else but he would never hurt me. In the mornings I can't be the one to get him ready for school because the moment he sees me he would want to spend the day with me and refuse point blank to go to school. So my mum and the nanny are the ones to help get him ready and take him there.

Recently Harvey has started drawing pictures of me. I think he's captured me pretty well; the big boobs are there, along with the long eye-lashes, pink lips, and the long black hair! He's captured me pretty well, but he always makes my skin the same colour as his. Is he trying to say that I've overdone it on the sunbeds? Cheeky! He also draws a love heart on me and writes 'Day 22', which was the name of my fashion range. I have no idea how he knows about that, I guess he must have heard it in conversation.

When we were looking into new schools for him, we went to see one in Exeter that looked amazing and had the most incredible facilities. We wanted to see what was on offer and to get Harvey assessed there. I think it would have been a brilliant place for him. But it was a boarding school and there was no way I could imagine him living there. It would break my heart, and his. The moment I come home he says, 'Mummy, shoes off!' because he knows I'm going somewhere if I'm wearing them. And if I am going out he gets really upset.

His dad has nothing to do with him. There was a time when Dwight would occasionally see him, but that was years ago. He actually spoke to Harvey on his tenth birthday because my mum had phoned his manager to say that he should. I think Dwight was gob-smacked when Harvey said to him, 'So when am I seeing you?'

I texted Dwight to ask him if he wanted to see Harvey, although he seemed to be in no particular hurry. I thought that, while there was no urgency as such, the sooner he started seeing his son the better.

We ended up arranging to meet at a restaurant in Manchester in November 2012, to discuss the matter. We sat at the bar and didn't eat. It wasn't a friendly meeting. Dwight didn't smile the whole time I was there. He accused me of stopping him from seeing his son, which I absolutely never have. I always wanted him to see Harvey regularly. It's important for a boy to have a relationship with his father.

Dwight's attitude made me really angry. 'I'm not sitting here to be bollocked by you!' I shot back at him. 'I'm sitting here because you have a son...a son you could get on with and who you could see at weekends. Are you interested?'

'I'll have to think about it,' was the reply. 'And if I do decide to see him it will be on my terms, not yours or your mum's. And I only want to deal with you.'

Dwight gave me such a hard time that I felt like standing up and saying, 'Fuck you!' Why was he being like this? It was his son we were talking about! I suppose I should have been used to it, as he had hardly been involved in Harvey's life to date, but I still felt hurt for my son. I'm the only family Harvey has got, along with my mum, dad, sister and brother, there's no one else.

I didn't hear from Dwight afterwards. It's such a shame. All I can say is that he is missing out on a very special little boy. Personally I think he is scared of seeing Harvey because he doesn't know how to deal with him. And while I can understand that, I still don't get why he doesn't want to see his own child. I could help him connect with Harvey and there would always be a specially trained nanny there anyway. The door is always open to Dwight and his family, so long as they realise that it would have to be a regular commitment, not simply random visits when it suited them. It wouldn't be fair on Harvey to settle for anything less. Dwight should try. He would get so much love in return.

*   *   *

One of the hardest things about looking after Harvey is dealing with his autism. Everything has to follow a strict routine or it can send him into a total tailspin. And by that I mean he can kick off with a massive temper tantrum, where he will lash out, head butt the wall and floor, and throw things. Recently he smashed the glass door of my oven because I didn't do the usual thing of clicking my nails on the kitchen door before I walked in. He pulled open the oven door and slammed it shut, and the glass shattered and fell out.

I have lost count of how many TVs Harvey has destroyed when he's had a temper tantrum and thrown something at them, even when they have been protected with a Perspex screen. Now I've had to put even thicker screens up. The worry is that he will hurt himself or whoever is near him, which is why he is always supervised and never left alone with Junior and Princess.

We try and anticipate when he's going to have a tantrum and deal with it before it happens, but we can't always do that because sometimes it happens too quickly. At other times there are warning signs. Harvey's expression will change and his eyes roll more than usual and he begins making a moaning noise. If we can catch him at that point we can say, 'No, Harvey, stop making that funny noise. If you don't there will be no cake and you won't get your treat on Friday.' We are trying to show him that there will be consequences to his behaviour.

Usually that will do the trick, he'll say 'Sorry', and there won't be an outburst.

'Good boy!' we'll reply. He is motivated by food and praise, which almost always win him over. But we have to intervene quickly. Harvey gets really upset after he's had a tantrum because I think it wears him out emotionally and he doesn't like being told off.

Because he needs one-to-one attention and can dominate family life it is sometimes hard on Junior and Princess. I am sure that is the experience of many families with a disabled child. But it has definitely got easier now. They are still wary of him at times, although they do interact far more with him as they have grown older and Harvey has got better at communicating.

They can have fun together, playing on the trampoline outside for instance, or drawing, or we all watch films together in the cinema room. Junior, who is a born performer, has discovered a useful accompanist as Harvey will play the keyboard while Junior sings a Bruno Mars song.

On school days Princess and Harvey get up at the same time and have breakfast together, which is such a great development – sleepy head Junior is usually still zizzing away in bed. I used to lock Harvey's bedroom door at night to make sure he was safe, and didn't wander downstairs in the middle of the night, but I don't have to do that any more. Princess and Junior used to worry that if Harvey's door was open he might come into their rooms, but they're not concerned now they know how to talk to him. The other morning I could hear Princess telling him to go back to his room because he was eating toast before Lizzie the nanny arrived and he is supposed to wait for her. Off Harvey went.

Both Princess and Junior copy the way I tell Harvey to do something or not do something, as if they are adopting my role. For instance, Princess will say, 'Come on, Harvey, eat your tea.' Sometimes that works and he'll reply, 'Okay, Princess.' At other times he'll put his foot down and say, 'No, Princess' or 'No, Junior, only Mummy [can tell me this].' It works both ways because if I ever have to tell Princess and Junior off and shout out, 'Kids! Will you stop it!' you'll hear Harvey repeating it a few minutes later, imitating my voice exactly, so it saves me having to say it again!

We all have to be incredibly patient with Harvey. You can never rush him. For example, if we are running late at any time, we have to go at his pace and accept that there will be a delay. In the past we had a board with pictures on it so we could show Harvey exactly what was happening that day, but he's progressed beyond that and we don't have to rely on pictures any more. Instead, in the evening, we always run through what he is doing the following day. If we want him to finish an activity we have to say, 'Right, Harvey, we are going to count down from ten and when we get to one we are going to move on to something else. Is that okay?' Everything has to be negotiated and explained. We have all discovered reserves of patience that we didn't know we had! Harvey also knows Makaton, which uses signs and symbols and helps people communicate straightaway when they can't get the words out. So he can sign things like, I feel angry. And we can quickly respond.

135

His autism also means that he gets obsessed with things. At the moment it 's frogs and has been for a few years now; he also loves drawing Christmas trees. He'll spend hours drawing colourful pictures of frogs and saying, 'Ribbit, Ribbit,' as he does so. His entire bedroom is decorated with pictures of frogs, and I've lost count of the number of toy frogs he has. Kieran bought him some frogs for his eleventh birthday and Harvey was over the moon when he saw them.

Recently I had my London flat redecorated and had all the walls painted white. Without me knowing, Harvey drew the biggest frog ever on his bedroom wall in crayons. It was quite a sight, I can tell you. He told me that he wanted his room in London to be exactly the same as the one in Sussex, where there are frogs painted all over the walls. Can you imagine if someone in the family had a phobia about frogs! Fortunately none of us do, and so we embrace Harvey's frog obsession. Then again, you never know when he might become obsessed with something else, and that's just part of his autism.

In 2013 we discovered that he had two more conditions – Attention Deficit Disorder (ADHD) and Oppositional Defiance Disorder (ODD). ADHD affects his ability to concentrate and focus, and ODD means he can become very aggressive. If he doesn't want to do something, or something upsets him, he will immediately bang his head against the wall or the floor or throw the nearest object to hand. It is this behaviour that has always held back his progress. It has affected his ability to learn, but if his aggression can be controlled and his concentration span can be increased, then it will open up new possibilities for him.

It took over a year and a half for the doctors to do their research into Harvey and come up with the latest diagnosis. They want to target the ADHD first. Of course this means yet more medication when he is already on so much. This time they started him off on a low dose of Ritalin. It is always a delicate balancing act giving Harvey a new drug, as the doctors have to ensure that it doesn't affect the medication he's already on. At home we have to keep a daily record of his dosages, along with what he's had to eat and drink and what his weight is, so we have all the information at our fingertips for every hospital visit and also if he were suddenly to become ill.

Ritalin can also be an appetite suppressant, which could be beneficial as one of Harvey's other conditions is Prader-Willi. This means he can't control his appetite; has no idea at all when he is full. If, for example, we left a chocolate cake in front of him, and didn't stop him, he could easily eat it all. We have had to move all food out of his reach or move the fridge to a room where we can lock the door, otherwise Harvey would raid it constantly. In the past he has taken frozen pizzas and cakes out of the freezer and hidden them in the cinema room, so that in the night he could sneak down and eat them. Well, not any more! The only thing he can reach now are the vegetables and salad, and so far we haven't found any stashes of broccoli...

I wasn't sure if I could see a change in him at first from the Ritalin, but my mum was convinced that it was having an effect: that he was concentrating more as well as talking and becoming better at expressing his feelings. Hopefully it will mean fewer tantrums in the future as he will be able to tell us how he feels. Lately we have noticed that he has been able to say why he got upset and kicked off; usually it will have been because of noise.

At the same time Harvey is definitely becoming more independent. He is able to dress himself in the mornings for school, go downstairs and make his own breakfast, brush his teeth, tidy his bedroom, strip his bedclothes if he has wet the bed at night – that's to do with the Diabetes insipidus which means his body can't regulate fluids. Above all he enjoys doing things for himself, which is a huge step forward.

He is such a character and is turning out to be a really good mimic. He can take me off perfectly. 'He-e-ey, hello!' he'll say to visitors. 'Oh my God! So sorry I'm late! The traffic... what a nightmare!' He also did a very good impersonation of Leo and kept saying, '*Fantastico*!' Recently he has become obsessed with filming and recording all the conversations that he hears around him in the house or in the car. I keep having to say, 'Harvey! Delete that!' Can you imagine having a recording of everything that is said in your house! All kids go through stages where they know what swear words are and they like saying them to shock, and Harvey is just the same. We can be sitting at the table eating and he will exclaim, 'This is shit, isn't it!' And I'll reply, 'What did Harvey say?'

And he'll say, 'Oh, goodness, gracious me!'

And I'll say, 'Hmm, I thought that's what you said!'

The latest thing he likes saying when we're out in public, in a loud voice, is: 'Mummy is Katie Price!' And I swear he does it to be cheeky and to get a reaction from me. I am so embarrassed when he comes out with that!

I'm constantly amazed by how much progress Harvey has made. I used to worry that he would never be able to tell us how he feels or what he wants, that he would be lost in his own world, but he can communicate so much better than he used to. If he doesn't want to do something he can tell you, if he doesn't feel well he can tell you – though you have to watch that he isn't faking it! He talks all the time now and he wants conversations, which is something he wouldn't have wanted a year or so ago. He will ask, 'When am I going to school? What's happening on Monday?' And although it is still all about his routines, his conversational range seems to be broadening. He can also come out with completely random things and one of his favourite sayings is, 'When can I go in the racing car all the way to Tesco's on a windy day and go to Andrew's?' I've no idea where he's got that from! And he will often ask, 'When are we going on the white boat?' Again, I've no idea why.

In the car, when my mum is taking him to school and she is looking out of the window, he will grab her hand and say, 'No, Nan! Look at me, talk to me!' He has a strong character and always wants his own way...I wonder who he gets that from? He'll say, 'Oh, look at the traffic! I must ring the school to say that we're going to be late.' And my mum will call up the school and Harvey will speak to the secretary. He can definitely get his own way – though not with me, I have to say – with other people. Every morning my mum has to record him playing the keyboard and he won't go to school until he is happy that she has the right recording. His latest favourite is Lady Gaga.

In April 2013 he started at a new school in Wimbledon. His old school, Dorton House, where he had been since he was a baby, was being closed down. Dorton had been brilliant for Harvey and the teachers had brought him on so well, I've nothing but praise for them. It was an extremely stressful time when we found out that the school was closing as we didn't yet have a place somewhere else for him. We got together with the other parents at Dorton and even tried to start up our own Free School for children with special needs, but the Government turned down the proposal on the grounds that there weren't enough pupils. I think they were wrong because there is definitely a need out there.

One of the big things about having a disabled child is that you feel you have to fight for everything for them, every step of the way. We had to fight for the correct support for Harvey, for his statement of educational needs. We had to go to a tribunal because I didn't want him put in a rubbish school. With any child you want to give them the best start you can in life, and just because a child has disabilities that's no excuse for anyone to think that their education doesn't matter; that they won't be able to achieve anything anyway. That's so wrong! We have proved with Harvey that the more stimulation we give him, and the more we push him, the further he progresses.

The new school looks as if it is going to be fantastic for him. It's bigger than his old one, with 145 children with special needs. Harvey is one of nine in his class and he might not always have one-to-one support as the teachers don't think he will need it – I never thought that would happen. There is always a great atmosphere in the school, and it feels really lively and friendly. I think the new environment will bring Harvey on even more. He has made such great progress there and continues to learn new things. He seems to have a real hunger for learning.

Like any little boy he is very active. He loves swimming and trampolining; plays football using a ball with a bell in it. He can ride a three-wheeler bike, but you have to go with him as he has absolutely no sense of danger because he can't see what's coming. 'Turn now, Harvey!' you have to shout, to stop him from riding into a fence, ditch, or whatever! He also absolutely loves going on the quad bike, he's a complete speed freak. Just like me, I guess. You can have so much fun with him. And now I feel that I can take him anywhere I go. We can stay at friends' houses for weekends, which I never used to do. I would worry that the change in routine would be too much for him and that it wouldn't be relaxing for anyone else. In the morning, if he wakes up too early and starts making all his frog noises, I will say, 'Harvey, come to bed and have a cuddle before we have breakfast.' And he understands that he can't get up yet, and will cuddle up with me.

There was a time when we had to take the wheelchair, or black chair as Harvey called it, out with us everywhere because he would hardly walk any distance, but not any more. So, for instance, he comes shopping with me, we go to the cinema and we go bowling. If we go shopping at Churchill Square in Brighton, we have to finish up by going to Costa where he always has to have a sandwich and a cake. He will eat the sandwich and then ask the waitress to put the cake in a bag so he can bring it home. He puts it on the bedside table, and won't eat it until the morning. Such self-control! I don't know if I could do that. A lot of his treats are about food. It's part of his condition. He always wants to know when he is getting his next meal or snack.

During the week he has a strict routine because of school so at the weekend I like us to be more relaxed and let him do what he wants. I don't have a nanny then, though I do have to watch him carefully and it's usually because of food. I can suddenly discover that he's hidden a bag of sweets somewhere. I'll find him licking his lips and ask him what he's doing and he'll pretend to be all innocent. And I love that because it shows he's just like any other little boy. He has a cheeky side to him as well, especially when it's to do with not going to school. On Sunday night he'll say, 'Mummy, Harvey's got a poorly belly. You must call the doctor and call the school.' Monday mornings are especially difficult.

He loves music and has taught himself how to play the keyboard. It used to be that he was obsessed with Usher and had to listen to him whenever we drove anywhere. Thankfully that phase is over and he will now listen to pretty much anything, not that I've got anything against Usher! Harvey loves Jay-Z and Drake.

At night he is really good at going to bed. He takes his iPod and listens to music, plays with the frogs on his bed, and when he's had enough he'll turn off the iPod and switch off his light. Sometimes he'll come into my room and chat away and I'll have to say, 'Harvey, it's time for bed! Go back into your room.' And off he'll go. I think he knows he's being cheeky and likes it.

He loves going on holiday and is the easiest one of my children to fly with. He is used to travelling first-class where there are flat beds and screens and dinner is served. Harvey is in heaven with a screen he can control, and food coming round regularly every few hours. It's a bit of a shock to his system if we ever fly with budget airlines! I was so embarrassed when we were boarding an easyJet plane recently and he said in a very loud, clear voice, 'Mummy, where are the beds and duvets?' I bet all the other passengers must have thought: What a spoiled brat!

When he was much younger Harvey didn't seem able to show affection unless you asked him for a cuddle. It was as if he had to learn how to show it, which is part of being autistic. But he's very affectionate now. He has definitely become close to our family and knows exactly who everyone is. He likes going on the quad bike with Granddad Price and being thrown by him into the swimming pool. He likes Uncle Dan Dan (as he calls my brother) bouncing him up and down like a frog. He'll give my sister orders and say, 'Aunty Sophie, can you get me…?' He knows how to work us, put it that way!

Having Harvey has taught me so much. I have definitely learned patience and have a lot more empathy with other people now. I know I've changed because of my son. I would love to adopt a child with disabilities, but the trouble is adoption can take years and years and I hate that because there are children out there who are desperately in need of a home now.

Because of Harvey I've got involved in things I perhaps wouldn't otherwise have done. I'm patron of Vision charity and take part in fund-raising events for them, and I've raised money for Autism Independent UK. I've met people, such as parents of disabled children, and young people with learning difficulties I might never otherwise have met.

Thanks to Harvey my family were guests at a charity event at the Olympic stadium in 2012. Harvey was asked by Vision to start the charity mascot race. It was such an honour to be there. I was also asked to appear on Channel 4 during their coverage of the Paralympics, and I invited the para-equestrian Natasha Baker to my house to ride one of my dressage horses. She rode him brilliantly and I told her she was always welcome to come and ride whenever she wanted. In fact, I thought she looked better on my horse than on hers! However, she won two gold medals in the 2012 Paralympics, and you can't do better than that.

Having Harvey in the family has had an impact on us all. My brother has got very involved in fund-raising for charity. In 2013, for example, he ran the London Marathon to raise money for the Jeans for Genes charity, which raises money for children born with genetic disorders, like Harvey. In 2012 my mum went to India and spent three months working with children in the slums of Goa. She already has other plans to work with the charity Chain of Hope that arranges open-heart surgery for children from undeveloped countries. She will look after the children, as a kind of surrogate mum, when they come to London for their operations. As she said, being with Harvey, 'Puts life in perspective and makes you appreciate it more. Seeing what a disabled child has to go through makes you want to give something back.'

I don't know what the future holds for Harvey. My

mum is convinced that if all his medication is balanced and his ADHD and ODD are controlled, then he will be able to hold down some kind of job when he finishes school, so long as it is repetitive and not too challenging. There is a charity called Remploy, which specialises in finding and providing work for disabled people. She thinks he could become more independent and live in the log cabin in the grounds of my house with a carer. Maybe she is right. Harvey has already surprised us with his progress and he continues to do so.

You have to take every day as it comes with Harvey. We have good days and we have bad days, we have funny days and challenging days. But I love him to bits and he's perfect to me. Harvey might not have his biological dad or Pete in his life any more, but he still has my family and we will fight all the way to give him the best possible life.

CHAPTER 11

LEO MOVES IN...
AND OUT

'What is it with you, that all your relationships happen so quickly and become serious so soon?' my friend Jane asked me when I told her that Leo was moving in with me.

'I don't know. I think it's because I'm so open and I wear my heart on my sleeve. And when I fall for someone, I really fall for them. I can't help it. It's just the way I am, all or nothing,' I replied. 'I always have been and I think I always will be.'

Jane raised her eyebrows and gave me a look that said, What are you like!

It's a nightmare when I fall for someone. Other people are able to play it cool, play games, but I have never been able to do that. When I fall for someone I pretty well let my guard down. I still keep some barriers up, though, because of what happened with my first marriage, and from the way one of my former boyfriends, Dane Bowers, left me broken-hearted all those years ago, in such a terrible state that I took an overdose. Should I have been more cautious with Leo? At the time I believed I was doing the right thing, one hundred per cent.

*   *   *

Those first months Leo and I were together were wonderful. I had the feeling that this really was a fairy-tale romance, that our meeting had been intended all along and here we were together. Everyone who met Leo really liked him, including my family – and they can be a tough crowd to please! My step-dad Paul thought Leo was a man's man, and joked that he was all right even though he was an Argie. Typical Paul! My brother said that he would always distrust men's motives for getting involved with me, but because Leo didn't know who I was when we met, that was a positive sign.

The language difference was still an issue, but Leo enrolled in a language school and I was hopeful that he would make rapid progress and then we would be able to communicate more easily. I felt really optimistic about our relationship. He was into country life, just like me, but he also liked socialising. I could take him anywhere and he would fit right in and be charming and friendly to everyone. And at least I didn't have to worry that he'd change into a dress halfway through the evening.

At the end of May we went out to Marbella for a short holiday with my friends Jane and Derek. Overall we had a good time: sunbathing, swimming, eating out, then hanging by the pool at the exclusive Ocean Club, drinking cocktails and messing around in the water. Leo and I re-enacted the iconic scene from *Dirty Dancing* when Patrick Swayze lifts Jennifer Grey above his head. Yeah, nobody puts Katie Price in the corner ... We got the first part right and then Leo dropped me and I tumbled head first into the water, very inelegantly.

But it was here that I started to see a flaw in the man I had thought was so perfect. Leo had a jealous side to him. We went out clubbing one night, and he made it clear that he didn't like me wearing a short dress. Well, screw that! I wear what I want. No man is going to tell me how to dress! I hit the dance floor and, because he didn't think I was paying him enough attention, he got the hump and ruined the night with his attitude. Back at the hotel he said, 'We finish, we finish!'

Well, we made up that time, but I wasn't impressed.

Other problems started to surface, the biggest of which was Leo not having a job. While his English was so appalling, he wasn't likely to get one either. At first it didn't seem to matter so much because I was taken up with filming my new series, *Signed by Katie Price,* and Leo would come with me while we filmed, and we went here, there and everywhere together, and it was busy, and it was fun. But it got to a stage where his lack of a job really started to grate on me. It wasn't long before he dropped out of English classes. I never understood why, his English had hardly improved at all. As a result he would be at the house, in my face, all the time, from the minute I stepped through the door after work. And then, when I would be getting up early to go to work, he would be lying in bed because he had nothing to do that day, other than go to the gym, which I paid for, in my car, using petrol I had paid for. He'd make out he did things round the house and in the garden but he kept breaking things! Like the garden tractor, for example. I'd tell him that I didn't need him doing jobs for me, that I paid other people to do those things and wanted him to concentrate on language school. I didn't think it was good for him always to be hanging round the house. I couldn't understand why he wasn't trying harder to make a career for himself in the UK.

I wanted a man with a job, someone who was engaged and interested in their work, so that we could have good conversations in the evening. There are only so many times that you can ask how the gym was... Again, at first it wasn't such a big problem; after all, I had wanted him to move in. But the man I had wanted to move in with me was very different from the Leo who would spend hours on the phone or his laptop, claiming that he was working when I had no idea what he was really doing. He often seemed miserable and subdued and yet when we went out with friends he would be completely different, the life and soul of any event. It crossed my mind that he was feeling homesick and depressed because he wasn't working, but it wasn't up to me to find a job for him and I didn't see how I would be able to anyway.

He kept asking if I could get him work with magazines. Here we go again, I thought...no way was I doing that. In the early weeks of our romance we had done a shoot together, and later we had done one shoot and interview with *OK!,* but it was all very low-key and I was determined that I wasn't going to go down that road again of doing shoots and interviews with my partner, just so they could get famous on the back of my name. I told him that I didn't want to work with him; that I'd done that in my previous relationships and wanted to keep ours more private.

I used to say to people, 'What do you know about Leo?' And they'd reply that he was a polo player, or that he was a model, but that was pretty much the extent of their knowledge. And I'd reply, 'Good, that's exactly how I want it to stay.'

'But I moved over here and gave up everything for you,' he said, during one of our conversations about his lack of work.

My heart sank when he said that. It sounded as if he was expecting me to transform his life. It wasn't fair.

'Don't say that,' I told him, feeling upset. 'It was your choice. I never made you give up your TV work and move over here.'

He was an intelligent guy; he should have been able to get a job for himself. My step-dad, Paul, even offered him work with his fencing company. Okay, it wasn't glamorous, like modelling or TV work, but it would have given him some money and some independence. But Leo turned it down; I got the impression that he thought it was beneath him. Well, he didn't think it was beneath him to live off me.

Why couldn't he get a modelling job? I know at twenty-five he was getting on a bit in model years, but he was still a gorgeous guy and I'm sure he could have got work if he'd put his mind to it. I tried to tell him that he wasn't going to get a TV presenting job in the UK because, for a start, he couldn't speak English, and nor was he well known enough. By now I had seen his Argentinian TV game show. I had thought he must be the presenter, but no, he was the sidekick who got to hold up the scores, a bit like the girls on something like *The Price is Right*. Leo was the eye candy.

He was appearing in my reality series, but that was purely so we could see each other. He got paid ten grand to be in my show, and to be honest I hated that because it felt as if he was making money out of me. And I didn't like the way he seemed to put on an act for the cameras and come across as this fun-loving guy, when the reality once filming stopped had become so different.

And I couldn't help feeling that he was lazy, enjoying the life-style I could give him while not really putting in any effort himself. An example of this was in July during one of the signings for my novel *The Come-back Girl*, where I was trying to beat the Guinness World

Record for the longest book-signing by a single author. It was a very big deal for me. Leo had come with me to Leeds but instead of supporting me he lay in bed, moaning while I was getting ready in the hotel room, as if I was interrupting his beauty sleep! I lost it with him and shouted, 'If you're going to come to work with me, don't think you can stay in a hotel room and sleep! You've got to get up!'

In the end it took my manager going in and giving him a talking to before he finally shifted his arse. And while I was in the O2 Arena signing away for all my fans, Leo strolled around with my brother looking at the crowds and apparently lapped up all the attention when they noticed he was my boyfriend and wanted to take his picture.

*   *   *

In July I finally managed to complete the purchase of my new house: a farmhouse outside Horsham in West Sussex. It was set in over fifty-two acres of land, and I planned to build stables and an indoor school, and keep my horses there. I was convinced that I would be able to ride more often if my horses were just outside my back door, and I loved the fact that the children were going to have so much space to roam around and play in. The house needed a massive amount of work, though, including an extension, new kitchen, bathrooms and a cinema room. I had employed an interior designer to work on the plans for it. I like a minimalist, stylish look, with muted colours, lots of cream, taupe and silver. The only bedroom that I planned to be pink was Princess's. There we were pinking it up to the max, with a pink fairy-tale castle bed and hot pink walls, with fairy-tale figures painted on them. I knew Princess would absolutely love it. Junior was going to have a football-themed room as he was getting into sport, and Harvey's room was going to be painted green with frogs all over it, his obsession.

While the work was being done we stayed with my friends Jane and Derek and I also had a log cabin built next to the house so that we could stay there temporarily. The tabloids made out it was a shack. I promise you, it was far from being that! It had three bedrooms, two bathrooms, an open-plan kitchen and living room…not exactly what I would call a shack.

It was such a relief to leave the old house in Surrey, the background to my two failed marriages. I couldn't help feeling that the place was cursed in some way, a misery mansion. I'd often heard strange noises when I was living there (no, not from Roxanne) and weird things would happen, like water suddenly pouring out of taps without anyone turning them on. Strangely enough the same thing happened when I moved into the new house so perhaps it's me, perhaps I give off a weird energy…who knows?

In August we went off on holiday for a month to Marbella with the children and some of my friends, while the house was being done up. I rented a luxury villa with a pool. It was brilliant spending that relaxed time with the kids. But things still weren't going at all well with Leo. In fact, by now everything he did annoyed me. The lack of a job, the lack of money, the way he always wanted to have sex...even his personal habits when he was asleep in bed. Everything! He probably only had to breathe for me to feel irritated. I was totally off him. I didn't look at him and think he was good-looking any more. I thought, You absolute ponce!

It felt like I had another child to look after, not an equal. He had made out that he was a successful model and TV presenter in Argentina, and the way he had treated me and paid for nearly everything during my visit there had led me to believe that he had plenty of money. But it was becoming clear that he had very little. At first he claimed that his credit cards weren't working as he was abroad and he was having problems transferring his money, which was plausible the first few times but surely by now the problem would have been resolved? He didn't treat me to anything and nor did he contribute anything towards living in the house. And yet, whenever we went out shopping, he would always head for the most expensive designer stores; he was a man with a taste for luxury. He would spend ages trying on clothes and all the assistants would be telling him how good he looked. Yes, he definitely looked the part, I'll give him that. But he rarely bought anything. When we were in Marbella I remember going into Dolce & Gabbana with him. He tried on all these designer tops and looked the nuts in them. He acted as if he could afford to buy anything he wanted, and it was only because he didn't know which one to choose that he walked out without buying anything.

And that reminded me of the time in Brighton when we were in a designer boutique. He went to pay for the designer tops and boxers he had chosen, but his card kept getting declined. In the end I'd paid. And yet whenever we went out to eat with friends he would always make a grand gesture and pay for everybody. But believe me, that was it.

His sister and her husband and two of their friends came to visit us in Marbella. Of course I wanted them to have a good time because of the hospitality that she had shown me in Argentina. I did really like her. But Leo made a big fuss about how everything had to be right for their stay and insisted we have a special barbecue. That meant a big food shop. (Guess who paid?) And when they arrived he gave them a tour of the villa and grounds, and I got the feeling that he was boasting about where we were staying. It was as if he was putting on a show, saying, 'Look what I've got with her.' And in a way I was part of that show because I pretended to be happy when they arrived since I didn't want to upset his sister, even though I really wasn't getting on with Leo.

Suddenly he wanted to go out in Marbella so that, I reckoned, he could be seen with me, showing off to his sister and friends how we were followed everywhere by the paps. One night something happened to make me mistrust her friends. We were in a restaurant and one of them was taking pictures of our group with their phone. I said, 'Oh, let's see them,' as you do. And as my friend Jane and I looked through them we found pictures of me sunbathing topless. I was furious and instantly deleted them.

In September Leo flew back to Argentina as he had an ongoing court case with the mother of his daughter. I think being around my children had maybe made him realise what he was missing out on and he wanted to become more involved. I think he was also motivated by the way the child's mother had done a series of stories on him over there, and didn't like having his name dragged through the mud.

I breathed a huge sigh of relief that I was going to have a break from him. After thinking that we had a perfect romance at the beginning, I now felt that the relationship didn't have a future. It couldn't unless Leo got a job and learned the language, and there was no sign that he was planning on doing either of those things. I didn't miss him at all while he was away. I loved having space to myself, and not having to worry what he was doing and how he was feeling and if he was okay.

We limped on for a few weeks more when he returned, but my heart wasn't in it, not one bit. His sister and her husband, their friends and his brother, came over for a visit and Leo insisted that they should stay in my pink horse lorry so that they could see my new house. The log cabin wasn't even finished and the whole house was like a building site. We were still staying with friends.

'Why can't they book into a hotel?' I asked, baffled as to why anyone would choose to stay in my horse lorry, even though it's a really flash one with a double bed and pull-out double bed, a small kitchen and bathroom.

'No, no, they must come here,' Leo went on. When they arrived he switched on all the lights along the driveway and in the indoor sand school. And again to me it felt as if he was saying, 'Look at everything she has.' I didn't like that at all…But as it was Leo's birthday, I put on my act that we were okay and arranged a whole night out for him and his family and friends, with a luxury limo picking us all up to take us to London to a restaurant and then on to a club. But Leo didn't seem to appreciate any of it. At the club I was talking to ex-*TOWIE* star Lauren Goodger and I just wasn't interested in being with him at all. In fact, I ignored him, thinking that he was with his family, and no doubt enjoying himself catching up with them. I had paid for the whole night and felt that I should be free to enjoy myself. Leo came over to where we were standing and was really aggressive. He was apparently jealous that Lauren and I were taking pictures together. I thought, OMG, you have got to go! I just didn't want anything to do with him.

As soon as his family and friends had left I told him we needed to talk and we sat down, together with the translator – I wanted him to understand everything. I said, 'It's over, you have to leave.'

Leo got very emotional and cried. 'Please, I want to stay. Please, I love you!' he kept saying, over and over.

I could hardly bring myself to look at him; I couldn't believe that this was the man I had fallen for. 'Get him on the plane tonight,' I told the translator.

I thought, Fuck you with your tears. You've had ages to change and get a job and get off your fucking arse. You're suffocating me and annoying me. You don't contribute anything to this family.

Just as I had paid for everything else, I paid for his ticket back to Argentina. Then he was driven off to Heathrow and out of my life, I hoped. But even when he was on the plane he sent me a picture of himself sitting in his seat and crying. Let me tell you, that was *not* going to win me back. We were finished and I wanted to enjoy myself. No more having to have sex with someone I didn't want to have sex with. I was free at last!

CHAPTER 12

SIGNED BY KATIE PRICE

In 2011 I began filming a series that I had wanted to do for years and which had been my idea: *Signed by Katie Price.* The idea was to find someone with the looks and personality to develop their own brand. I wanted to give someone a stepping-stone so that they could have a similar career to mine, with their own products, modelling shoots, calendars, perfume and TV show. I wasn't looking for a new me – face it, there can only be one Pricey! I wanted to find someone who could achieve the same sort of success. To me, it was like bringing out another product, but this time I was expanding into people!

I wasn't simply looking for a model. I wanted someone with more than good looks. They needed to have an aura, charm, presence, that all-important charisma, be confident and articulate, plus have a good head for business. I knew it was a big ask but I wanted the works! The winner would be signed to Black Sheep Management, which manages me. I would support and mentor them, along with input from the management company.

The series kicked off with the auditions. I was one of the judges, along with Bayo Fulong, a renowned street-caster who casts major advertising campaigns, so he knows what's hot and current and what's about to be hot and is very commercially minded. Glen Middleman was the other judge. He is a TV executive with years of experience in the industry and knows exactly what makes good television and what audiences want. I was the judge who had strengths in both areas as well as my own unique take on the industry. I hit it off straight away with both judges; there was none of that behind-the-scenes bitching and backstabbing you sometimes get in other talent shows. They often played bad cop and were brutally truthful with contestants; I was more good cop, sugar-coating the bad news.

The auditions were held in four large shopping centres around the country (Bristol, Birmingham, London and Leeds). They lasted all day, often until really late, but I never got bored or complained...and I admit that I can be the first to moan if I think something is dragging on too long! I can honestly say that I loved every minute, especially as I saw the show as my baby. It was the first formatted show I had fronted on my own and I felt I was really broadening my TV experience.

The production team would meet the contestants first and vet them to see who was good enough, quirky enough and individual enough to put through, as all talent shows do. They all had to have the character to make good TV. Over 10,000 people auditioned.

The three judges sat on-stage in front of a live audience. The first time I went out there and saw the crowd, I thought, Bloody hell! I can't do this! It was nerve-wracking initially, but I quickly got used to it and then enjoyed the adrenalin rush I got from performing in front of a crowd.

'Next!' I'd call out, and a set of pink (naturally) sliding doors would open to reveal the contestant. They had to strut their stuff along a catwalk while they were being photographed and end up standing in front of us, where they had to tell us something about themselves and then wait anxiously to hear our verdict. First up we saw them in their regular clothes and then they had to make a quick change back-stage into their bikinis or swimming shorts. I'd dreamed up this part, knowing that if I was at home watching the show, that's exactly how I would like the contestants to appear.

I hated upsetting people and giving them bad news. People think I'm bolshie and outspoken but I don't want to hurt anyone's feelings. I didn't want to be the baddie who destroyed their hopes, especially when some contestants begged for a place, saying, *'Please!* Just give me a chance.' It really tugged at my heartstrings. But there were only a certain number of places so we had to be strict.

It was so hard knowing what to say when you had someone standing in front of you who thought that they had what it takes, when it was completely obvious to everyone else that they hadn't. And I had to be the one to break their hearts and shatter their dreams, by saying, 'Sorry, you're not what we're looking for.' Most people accepted it, but there were some who were so deluded about themselves that they argued back. Then I had to say, 'Look at your attitude! You won't get anywhere being like that. In this industry you're going to get criticised. If you can't even take that at your first audition, what hope have you got?'

Some moments were pure cringe, especially with the contestants who thought that they had what it took to be famous, but so hadn't. I felt sorry for them. They didn't have the attitude or the body. Or there were those who had great personalities but who looked minging! Then I would have to tell them how awful they looked. Often they simply wouldn't believe me, and would exclaim, 'What do you mean? I spent ages getting ready, how can you say that!' Or we'd get contestants who really didn't have the looks and told us that they already were a model. And I would think, Well, what the f*** have you been modelling! I think someone must have been leading you up the garden path. You do get some unscrupulous model agencies who take money for a six-week course and tell people that they're going to be the next big thing, when they haven't got a chance in hell.

Rylan Clark stood out a mile at the auditions. I just loved his personality, his humour and warmth. True, he didn't have a muscular, pumped-up body like some of the other boys, but he had so much natural charisma. Amongst the girls Amy Willerton stood out for her incredible body.

Out of the auditions we had to choose fifty contestants for Bootcamp. Here they were going to be set different tasks and challenges, either working with a group or on their own, to find out what kind of business mind they had and how good they were at coming up with ideas for products and marketing them.

Day one of Bootcamp was brutal. All fifty contestants arrived by coach expecting to take part, and within an hour we had split them up and told about half of them that they were going home. They'd had no idea that this might be on the cards. I really felt for them because they would have taken a day off work and spent all morning getting ready, thinking that they were in with a chance, only to be told that they were out. That was one of my worst moments from the series, having to stand in front of those contestants and tell them that they weren't through. I absolutely hated doing it. I thought it was too cruel. The aim was to produce a dramatic scene, and I'm afraid that's TV for you. If you don't like the heat...

The contestants were told to come dressed to impress but their first challenge, also dreamed up by me, was to strip down to their underwear. And there was more... The girls had to take off all their make up and take out their hair extensions; the boys had to strip down to a pair of pink swimming trunks and wash out any hair product. I told them that I wanted to see the blank canvas I was going to be working with. I needed to see if they had the confidence to make it as a successful model – where you could be asked to adopt any number of looks that are out of your comfort zone. It might have seemed cruel but I honestly wasn't trying to humiliate them or make them feel bad about themselves.

I was amazed by how different the girls looked in their natural state. They had all looked stunning in make up but some of them were absolute piglets without their slap on, completely unrecognisable. Anyone can look good with the right make up, but to succeed as a model you have to look good without it. I'm not saying that my looks are perfect, not by a long way, I'm just saying I know what you need to look for. The other thing that shocked me was how many women don't match their underwear! Take the shame, ladies! I *always* match mine.

From Bootcamp we selected twelve contestants and they moved into a luxury house and were faced with more tasks, from photo-shoots, to marketing, to coming up with a viral video campaign to promote themselves. As I said, right from the start Amy and Rylan stood out. But I always felt that there was a problem with Amy's attitude. The other contestants didn't warm to her and there was often conflict in group tasks. I sometimes felt that she was a game player. When a focus group we'd set up were shown a video that each of the five had made about themselves, she didn't score well with it at all. In contrast they absolutely loved Rylan, who has the gift of the gab and such a warm personality. He's a great role model for anyone who wants to be different. I was convinced that Rylan should win the series.

And then it was the final, with just Rylan and Amy fighting it out. Their last task was to hold their own press launch for the perfume brand that they had designed. They had to come up with their look and choreograph their entrance, along with a group of models, in front of the waiting press pack. It was a really tough challenge. Then they had to get up on-stage, give a presentation about their perfume and take questions from the press about themselves. A final chance for them to shine. They were both impressive in different ways, but for me Rylan had the edge.

Back-stage I insisted that I thought he should win, and everyone else, the production team and the other judges, told me, 'But, Kate, the press won't write about him. Girls sell. The press will want to write about Amy…she's sexy and she's different. Amy has to win.' I know that people will say, yeah, yeah, but it is true.

'I admit that she's incredible-looking, but I still think it should be Rylan,' I argued. But the others had their way. Even when I went on-stage to announce that Amy was the winner I so wanted to say that it was Rylan, but whoever won would have to work with my team and, though everyone in it loved Rylan and thought he would have a great future, they felt that Amy fitted the criteria of what we had set out to find.

* * *

Winning the show meant Amy would be managed by Black Sheep, which is run by my brother and my manager, Andrew. The whole point of the show was to find someone in whom my team would invest considerable effort over a period of time to build into a 'brand'. It was not about quick wins, and for that type of investment the contract needed to be exclusive (as everyone knew in advance). Amy also won a luxury holiday and the use of a designer Range Rover for a year. But very quickly it all unravelled. She was too young to insure the car herself and my team had to look for alternatives for her. It wasn't anyone being difficult, it's standard practice in these situations. My friend Michelle Heaton said it was exactly the same for her and her group Liberty X when they were given cars.

But for me, it was Amy's attitude that was really the problem. It seemed that she expected to have overnight success and did not want to put in long-term effort to make the project a success. There was a delay with the show being broadcast and that meant we could not start working with her or it would compromise the surprise element. Amy would continually call the office, asking, 'Why aren't I doing this or that?' but our hands were tied. There were other issues too that my team had to deal with that I won't go into here, but the main problem was that Amy would not sign an exclusive contract with Black Sheep. That was her choice and I have no problem with it, but obviously none of my team wanted to put in the hours that would be required to build her profile in those circumstances. To be honest, by this time I think everyone was a little relieved that it would not be a long-lasting association.

I tried to explain that you don't get overnight success unless it's from something like *The X Factor*. But that kind of fame can be hard to cope with; have it all too soon and it can go to your head, and then it's over for you very quickly. In my experience it's better to build up to success gradually, so you become used to it and can deal with it and have a long-term career. But that didn't seem to sink in with Amy. Her boyfriend would even go and see Andrew and tell him that she should be as famous as Cheryl Cole by now, and why wasn't she? Talk about deluded.

Personally, I think she got too big for her boots, too soon. She is an attractive girl but the world is full of them. Apparently she did a radio interview and a story on me. I didn't hear it or read it. It did not surprise me though.

And now look at Rylan and how successful he is. I felt like saying 'Up yours!' to everyone who told me to choose Amy over him because I knew I was right at the time. I'm still good friends with Rylan and he came to my wedding to Kieran. I told him that I was very pleased it had all worked out for him, and that if he had signed up with us he might not have got the chance to go on *The X Factor*. He brushed himself down after being on my show and came up fighting again. That is what it really takes to be successful: guts, self-belief, determination, and plain old hard work. You cannot manage without those qualities.

I was thrilled he did so well on *X Factor* and that he went on to win *Celebrity Big Brother*. He is such a genuinely warm, gentle person and deserves all the fame he's won. He's worked hard for it and it's what he really wants. I think he'll do very well in the industry; personality gets you a long way in this business.

Overall I was really pleased with the way the show went, but disappointed that Sky Living didn't seem to want to give it as much promotion as it deserved.

I'd love to do another series of *Signed by Katie Price,* either here or abroad, as well as some other formatted shows. I've got so many ideas!

CHAPTER 13

I GET LEGAL

Throughout my career I've noticed that the press likes to have a pop at me, and sometimes it has felt as if I get more than my fair share of adverse coverage – more so than other celebrities anyway. Some of it probably stems from me always being myself, and not putting on a polished act. I accept that when you are in the public eye, the press are going to write about you and it's a two-way thing; if they hadn't, I wouldn't have become famous. But while I can take criticism for things I've actually done, it's when lies are printed that it really eats away at me. People read those stories and believe they are true, and end up forming a bad opinion of me. After the break-up of my first marriage, for instance, the stories were horrendous. I was portrayed as a bad mother, as out of control, it was said that my businesses and books were failing, and that I was desperate to get back with Pete. It felt as if sections of the press were out to destroy me. It was tough for me to be taken seriously for a while because everyone thought I'd gone off the rails when Pete left, and I was portrayed as someone whose career was over.

The constant battering really got to me and there were times when I felt very low and depressed. I took the decision at the end of 2009 to withdraw from doing magazine interviews and to step out of the public eye for a while. It was a risk but I had to do it. I needed to get on with my life without the constant criticism of every single thing I did. I would still do my press calls and interviews when I had a new book, TV show or product to launch, but that was it. I was sick of the press twisting what I said, sick of the lies that were printed about me. It didn't seem to matter how many times I pointed out that something wasn't true, no one seemed to want to believe me. I felt that some of the tabloids and magazines had treated me like shit; they showed no respect for my feelings. I lost all faith in them. In fact, it felt as if they didn't even think I was a human being with feelings at all. It felt as if no one was giving me any room to breathe, no one would give me a chance. It was a horrible, horrible time.

One of the worst experiences I had was when I tried to stick up for Alex early on in our relationship. He was in a film that the press claimed glorified rape. In defending him, I said that he would not make such a film because he knew that, early in my glamour career, I had been raped by a celebrity and what a devastating experience this had been for me. Of course I was naïve to think that the press would not want to know more and I was put under intense pressure to name my attacker, but I will never do that. For some that means they feel they can pour scorn on my story and basically accuse me of making it up. I was vilified by sections of the press, and it was a real low point in my life to be accused of making use of a terrible thing like that in order to drum up publicity for myself – that simply was not true.

Victims of sexual abuse deal with it in different ways. My way of dealing with what happened to me was to lock it away and speak to very few people about the details. I believe it has driven me on to make a success of myself. I made a personal decision that I was not going to report the attack to the police – partly because I did not think I would be believed, and partly because I did not want to have to relive the experience over and over throughout a police investigation and trial. My way of dealing with events would not be right for everyone and I understand the counter-arguments, but it was my choice. Having made that decision years ago, I feel it would be wrong for me to name my attacker now. I believe that is the victim's choice.

However, in a way my fears were coming true. I was being publicly doubted and accused of fabricating the incident. In defending myself against these accusations I said that Pete knew this had happened to me. He then denied this, saying we had never discussed it. This was not true. I will never understand why he did that when it led to me being castigated and belittled all over again. Made me a victim again. Given what I now know, this is a huge issue between us...but that is for later!

*   *   *

Things were going from bad to worse with the press. In 2011 my then management team had the idea of inviting a group of journalists over to my house for dinner, saying to me, 'Come on, let's get them on side.' But I felt I didn't need to get them 'on side' because there was nothing bad about me for them to write about! It was the press who kept choosing to make things up. But I went ahead and invited the journalists round, and gave them the full Pricey hospitality: more food than they could possibly eat, plus wine and chocolates. I was completely myself, didn't dress up. In fact, if I remember correctly, I wore my trackies and had my hair in rollers. We all got on well and had a laugh. But it didn't make a blind bit of difference to the coverage I continued to receive in the press.

I had tried so hard to stay strong and put on a brave face, no matter what was written or said about me. I had this terrible anxiety that if I showed any weakness, and had a breakdown, my children might be taken away from me. But enough was enough. I had to take a stand against those parts of the press that had written such lies about me. I instructed my legal team to start building up a case against those publications that had blatantly done so. This was not something I did lightly because I knew that some in the press would simply redouble their efforts to harm me, but I had taken as much as I could. I wanted to scream out loud that I could take criticism for the things I actually did, but making things up and then criticising me for those things was just wrong.

If I listed all of them there would probably be enough to fill another book. But here are a few examples...

First that *Daily Star* story that Princess had been covered in a 'bizarre' set of bruises. They later admitted they were wrong.

There had been a front-page story in *Star* magazine saying that I wanted Pete to dump his then girlfriend Elen Rivas, that I was obsessed with looking at pictures of her on the internet and upset by seeing photographs of her with Pete. As it was front-page, of course my picture was splashed all over and the coverage made me look like a mad and embittered woman. And it was entirely made up! When we took legal action the magazine accepted the story was false and printed an apology.

In another example, the *Daily Star* published an article which claimed that I was involving my son Junior in a violent sport and that this was of deep concern to my ex-husband. This time I was being made to look like a bad mother. Again, completely untrue. The paper had to admit their story was made up and that I had simply taken Junior to a non-contact fun fitness class.

There were plenty more ridiculous made-up stories as well. Take this one, again from *Star* magazine which printed a story that I had a bizarre obsession with the Kardashians and had been bombarding them with messages. And that I had begged Living TV to consider a reality show based on the same premise as *Keeping Up with the Kardashians*. And that I wanted two more daughters who could star in a Kardashian-style reality show with my daughter Princess! Okay, you might think that's funny, but again it makes me look like a mad, obsessed woman and a bad mother. To make matters worse, this magazine published a reader's letter (in its 'star' letter spot) the following week saying how funny the article was – only that letter was not written by a reader at all but by a member of the magazine staff! And yet again, after we took legal action, they had to apologise and admit the claims were untrue.

I also had to sue a couple of magazines for falsely claiming that they had interviewed me. One magazine did this and lifted an interview that I had given to another journalist some time before – but added in their own questions, which made it look as if I thought Pete and I would get back together. The next week they published an interview by Pete hitting back at me! Stuff that, I thought, and they had to pay damages for making this up.

I know I upset Richard Desmond who owns Northern & Shell when I sued *OK!* magazine for claiming to have an exclusive interview with me and publishing a front-page picture of me, Pete and the kids under the headline 'Katie and Peter: Spending time together at Christmas'. The problem was Pete had done a Christmas shoot with the kids and I had been superimposed on to it! Pete and I were *not* spending time together at Christmas as I then had to explain to a very upset Junior, who had seen the magazine. Richard probably felt I was disloyal as he had paid me good money to appear in the magazine before, but I felt I had no choice given the trouble this coverage had caused.

There was one particular journalist from the *Daily Star,* Gemma Wheatley, who had written a number of upsetting articles about me. Between 2010 and 2011 I had complained to the Press Complaints Commission about seventeen *Daily Star* articles, which contained appalling and false allegations about me. At about that time the publishers of the *Daily Star* pulled out of the PCC! (Maybe they could not face any more of my complaints.) My legal team changed tack and eventually a settlement was reached, with the *Daily Star* admitting the most serious allegations were false. Of the seventeen articles I originally took to the PCC, eleven were written by Gemma Wheatley.

Ironically, when I had been on holiday in Egypt with Alex in 2010, I had rescued her from a difficult situation. We had visited a water park and been pursued by journalists and paps. We told security at the park, who rounded them up and held them in a room and were threatening to lock them away in a police cell. When

Gemma saw me she begged me to help her get out, and so, being a big softie, I said to the security guards, 'It's okay, let them all go.' Well, I regret that act of kindness now.

As if her string of untrue stories about me were not shocking enough, I then found out that Wheatley left the *Daily Star* and was taken on by Claire Powell and Can Associates to work closely with Pete as his PA. What I can't understand is why, if someone was writing all these horrible stories about the mother of your children, you would even want to associate with them, never mind have them as your PA! This was the journalist who had written the 'bizarre' bruises story. She had also claimed that I wanted a child to save my flagging career; that my book *Paradise* had been put straight into the bargain bins on the day it hit the shops; that during a web-chat with fans I had refused to answer any questions that were not about my products; that I had a 'drunken night' with Amir Khan...Believe me, if it had been the other way round and someone had said bad things about Pete that I knew weren't true, I would have stuck up for him. I wouldn't have worked with them, that's for sure.

*   *   *

So I was prepared to get legal with the press. But that wasn't all...since the end of my first marriage, I had suspected that my former management company had been agitating the press against me. I felt that they had decided that the best way to build up Pete was to knock me down. Can Associates was run by Claire Powell and her then partner, Neville Hendricks.

For five years Claire, Neville and their assistant Nicola Partridge had been a huge part of my life. I'd thought that they were my friends, I had trusted them and confided in them. And overnight they cut off all contact with me. Not once did any of them check that I was okay after Pete walked out. I felt completely lost. My husband had left me, I had no management, the press were printing all kinds of lies about me. I was portrayed as the bad person while Pete was painted as the perfect dad. It really affected my reputation, and my career. I started to feel such anger towards Claire Powell, and it was hard not to be disappointed in Pete as well for the way he never once stood up for me. People might say, why should he? But for me it's simple. I am the mother of his children. I admit I have my faults but being a bad mother is not one of them. And I hated the way he seemed to be building up his career by playing himself against me.

I have since had a reconciliation with Neville and Nicola. We got some stuff off our chests and it was quite emotional for me. Neville is currently fighting ITV2 because they terminated his company's contract to film Pete's reality show after Neville's personal relationship with Claire ended. I know Neville has been deeply shocked by what he has discovered since commencing that litigation, and he has had to dig deep and fight hard.

In late 2011 I was shown information by my lawyers

that devastated me but also made me realise that my feelings about what Claire had been doing were not simply me being paranoid. I don't want to say too much about this as I am currently involved in litigation against Claire, Pete, Jamelah Asmar and Can Associates – or, to put it another way, my ex-manager, my ex-husband, my ex-best friend and my ex-management company. Oh, and the cherry on top is that my ex-husband is being represented by my ex-lawyers! This litigation is a deeply unpleasant experience for me. Naturally sections of the press have sought to suggest that I have taken these proceedings out of spite or from some sort of desire to attack Pete. Nothing could be further from the truth – I simply felt I had no choice given what I had discovered. The defendants all deny my claims.

In a nutshell, my ex-best friend Jamelah swore an affidavit that contained personal information about me. I will not go into details other than to say that one piece of information in that affidavit is the name of the man who raped me and who, in September 2009, I made it clear to the world I was not going to name. This affidavit was sworn on 18 September 2009.

On 14 September 2009 Pete had denied knowing any-thing about this rape or having discussed it with me, in his *new!* magazine column. He repeated this claim in an *OK!* magazine interview the same week. In his defence to my claim, his position is that we had discussed it but that I'd told him I had been too drunk at the time of the attack to remember what happened. Pete's denials of any knowledge of the matter in 2009 had led to me being attacked by the press over and over again.

This affidavit was prepared for legal proceedings, according to the defendants. I won't express a view on that but it is admitted that Jamelah then met with the *News of the World* and that this meeting was arranged by Claire Powell. She also arranged for Michelle Clack to do an interview, "setting the record straight", with the same paper. There is so much more to this case but I will leave it there.

What is for certain is that I am not the first client Claire has fallen out with after they have left her. She had to apologise to the actress Martine McCutcheon, another of her former clients, for comments made about her.

I had always hoped that Pete and I could meet and talk about why our marriage ended, get some closure, but that's never happened and I don't think it ever will. The way he behaved after we split proved to me that I could never trust him again. Ever. It's sad because I think he chose to believe the lies other people around him were telling about me. Over the years there have been some crazy stories in the press saying that I wanted to get back with him. Trust me, I never did. Even before my legal case against him and Can Associates I felt that we could never be friends, which is just horrible for the kids.

CHAPTER 14

MY MOMENT OF MADNESS

October 2011. A date I look back on and think: What the hell was I doing? I had a brief, intense relationship with a certain rugby player that completely screwed me up. I behaved in a way that just wasn't like me at all. I think it stemmed from the events of the last couple of years catching up with me. I was still recovering from what had happened in my marriage to Alex and how shocked and disturbed I had been by his behaviour. The emotional scars from that time still ran deep. And I had just found out what my ex-management, husband and friends had been up to. I felt besieged from every side. I was vulnerable. I wanted reassurance. I wanted, needed, to be loved. It was just a pity then that the next man I got involved with shattered my already fragile self-esteem. Danny Cipriani. How I wish I had never met him.

I'm friends with the boxer David Haye, and one night early in October he texted me to say that Danny wanted to get in touch with me and could I give him the PIN for my BlackBerry so we could message each other? I had met Danny before at The Worx, when I was on a shoot, and he'd invited me to some charity event. I'd thought he was fit, but he was with Kelly Brook at the time so nothing was going to happen. I remember he had a cute pug puppy with him, little realising that next time I saw that puppy it would be in Danny's bedroom...

I suppose I was curious to find out more about him, so I gave David my PIN to pass on to him. To my surprise Danny got in touch straight away. Instantly we seemed to hit it off and BBM-ed each other non-stop. It was good not having to use Google Translate to have a conversation, I can tell you! Danny was very full on and seemed to really like me, paying me lots of compliments. This makes a change, I thought, as I'd just broken up with Leo and was bitterly disappointed by the way our relationship had turned out. Here was a man who sounded like fun, who I could actually have a laugh with. We got on so well that I arranged to meet Danny the following evening. Usually I never meet men I don't know well while on my own, but I thought, What have I got to lose? A lot more than I'd bargained for, as it turned out...

We arranged that I would pick him up but Danny had seemed paranoid about being spotted out with me when we fixed the meeting and I had said, 'Don't worry,

I don't want to be seen either as I've just split with Leo.'
At first we were both shy with each other when he got
into the car, but we soon started talking. It was a low-
key date. My friends Gary and Phil had said I could
spend the evening at their flat as we didn't want to be
seen eating out together at a restaurant. We decided to
get a takeaway curry and strolled down the road to get
one. Plus point to Danny, he actually paid. We were
both casually dressed, I was in my jeans, and a little
blue top and sandals. OMG, I thought, he is gorgeous!
That night we went no further than kissing...but I have
to say that there was chemistry between us and I was
strongly attracted to him.

I knew I should be wary, though. He was only twenty-
two and had a terrible reputation as a womaniser. In
contrast to Leo's handsome features, Danny had bad-boy
rugged looks. He had amazing thighs – and I love a good
pair of thighs! I should have been able to resist him, but
I just couldn't. From the moment we met...in fact even
before we met, in his texts...Danny said everything
he could to make me feel that he was really into me. It
seemed like the moment I was reading one message, he
was already sending me the next. He completely turned
my head, giving me all the talk, making me feel really
special. I thought, Wow, he's so fit, he's English and he's
got his own profession. He won't be a ponce, *and* he
knows the media industry so no problems there. This
could work! I had been so used to lack of communication
with Leo that it was refreshing and exciting to have a bit

of banter with someone who actually spoke the same language. And having a man pay me so much attention made me feel much better about myself. It was like medicine to me after everything I had been through. I craved his adoration. Looking back, I wasn't thinking clearly at all.

We would meet at his friend Rory's house where Danny was staying while he was in London. I did think it was strange that he didn't have his own place, but he was playing for an Australian team at the time and said that he'd got rid of his flat and sold his car. At the beginning I would see him in the evenings and stay over. In the mornings he would have training and I would drop him off there and sometimes stay and watch, then we'd go for lunch. He would tell me that he wanted to see me all the time, that he didn't know what it was about me but he couldn't get me out of his head. Because of the way he made me feel I let my barriers down straight away. He was the first guy I had done that with since Dane Bowers. I wish I'd known then that he would end up breaking me, just as Dane had. If I'd had any suspicion of that, I'd have run a mile.

Really early on Danny told me that he loved me and I ended up saying it back. I knew it wasn't love; it was lust. I just said it because it seemed romantic to go along with him. He definitely led me to believe that we were a couple. I absolutely fell for Danny and he seemed to have fallen for me too. I know it sounds mad as I write this down, it was so soon after me splitting with Leo and I had wanted my freedom then, but that's what happened.

However, Danny didn't want to be seen anywhere out with me in public. He made the excuse that we should wait at least six months before we came out as a couple, so that we really knew each other and would be strong enough to deal with whatever the press said about us. And he claimed it was important for his rugby career that we kept our relationship under wraps. I did think it was odd, but he made a convincing case. He also told me that he had spoken to his mum about me, and she had said that she was looking forward to meeting me, so that all sounded as if he took our relationship seriously.

When a picture of us together appeared in the press – I think it was after I'd spent the night at his place in London – Danny told me that his manager had accused me of setting it up, which of course I didn't! I immediately rang her up and put her straight. Danny blamed the story getting out on my distinctive Range Rover. 'It's your fucking pink car! Don't come up and see me in that,' he told me, sounding pissed off. And rather than thinking, Hang on, what's the big deal? Why won't you be seen with me? I ended up borrowing my friend Jane's car, so I wouldn't be spotted.

Looking back, Danny's concern about being seen out with me must have been because he was still seeing other girls... And it wasn't that the warning signs weren't there at the beginning. After the picture of the two of us appeared in the press, the former *Big Brother* contestant Imogen Thomas tweeted that Danny was a liar and a bullshitter after everything he had told her in Vegas. When I asked him about her, he replied that it wasn't serious and she had wanted a relationship when he didn't. That won't happen to me, I remember thinking.

At the beginning of our relationship it felt as if he was pursuing me. We saw each other all the time and he couldn't get enough of me. It had been very romantic. But once I'd started sleeping with him, things seemed to change. Everything had to be on Danny's terms.

'I've got a meeting tonight,' he'd say. Or, 'I've got to see the boys, I need to catch up with them as I'm going back to Australia soon.' And then he wanted to see me late at night, after his meetings or after he'd seen his friends. And I'd think, How many meetings has he got? So it would be eleven or twelve at night that I'd be going round to his house. It felt like a booty call. It *was* a booty call. I was such an idiot, where was my self-respect! God! I wish I'd turned round then and there and said, 'Forget it! I am worth so much more than this!' But because I was so into him, I didn't. I would turn up at the house, and he'd be sitting in the living room with his mates watching some crap on TV, and I'd sit next to him on the sofa, feeling awkward and out of place, exactly like a teenage girl.

What the hell am I doing here? I'd think to myself. I'm a mother of three, an adult! I have an amazing career! This feels like kid stuff. But I didn't say anything because I wanted to be with Danny. And then we'd go upstairs to his top-floor room and go to bed. The house was a proper bachelor pad, it was chaos...Seriously, what was I doing?

One night we went to see a film together – or rather he bought the tickets and I had to walk into the cinema without him and meet him once we were inside, so no one would see us together. Afterwards, in the car, he told me that we couldn't go back to his friend's place.

'Well, we can't go back to mine.' My house renovations still weren't finished and I was staying in the log cabin with the kids. There was no way I was taking Danny back there with me. He suggested we stay at his mum's, which wasn't at all what I had in mind, but I ended up driving us there.

It was late when we arrived and we had to tiptoe around as his mum was asleep in bed. Again I felt like a complete teenager as we crept upstairs to his bedroom. And his room was such a tip! I couldn't even see the carpet as it was covered in all his possessions, which were scattered everywhere. The sheets were half on, half off the bed. He said it was a mess because he was in the middle of packing to leave for Australia. I wondered how he could live like this. I would never bring anyone back to a room like that. But I gave him the benefit of the doubt and ended up staying.

He was due to go back to Australia for the rugby season and I asked him what was happening with us. Again he told me that he didn't want the press to find out: 'I'd rather we see each other, and get to know each other for at least six months. And then, when it comes out and people try to give us shit, we'll be so strong together that it won't matter what they say.'

To which I should have said, 'No, we're either a couple or we're not. And I'm not going to be treated like this.' But I didn't. It was as if I had lost all common sense. But as I said before, he did sound very convincing. I wish I'd turned round and said, 'What can you actually offer me? You haven't even got your own place to live.'

I ended up lending him my white Range Rover and insuring it for him because he didn't have a car. I hoped that he would drive down and see me so I wouldn't keep having to drive up to London, but it made no difference, I was still the one travelling up to see him. When he went back to Australia and the car was returned to me, it was a complete mess inside. There were about ten parking tickets in it, loads of empty beer bottles and champagne glasses covered in lipstick. And then I discovered that he may not even have had a driving licence! I had to pay £200 worth of parking fines and it felt like another example of Danny taking the piss. He had no respect for me at all.

He completely conned me. When I look back, his friends must have been laughing up their sleeves because he clearly had other girls on the go at the same time. I don't think my friends were impressed by Danny and the way he treated me when they met him, but I didn't listen to their concerns. I wanted to be with him and he made out that he wanted to be with me. Admittedly, as I have spoken about in my column in the *Sun*, I found him lean in the most obvious department, which is why I nicknamed him Danny Chipolata.

Late one night he asked me if I would drive him to a certain address outside London because he needed to collect something. Of course I agreed, though I wondered what on earth he wanted to pick up in the middle of the night! It took ages getting there as I kept getting lost on the M25, but there were love songs on the radio and I was happy to be with him on this little road trip. When we got to the address Danny said he'd just be five minutes. He got out of the car while I waited outside and then returned carrying a bag. Afterwards we stayed in a hotel in Kingston – he knew the manager there, who let him in the back way. I wondered if he'd taken other girls to the same place. Once we were in our room Danny asked me to do something that wasn't right at all. It wasn't of a sexual nature but I was totally shocked.

*   *   *

I kept thinking that he would drop his idea that we couldn't be seen out in public, but he didn't. David Haye, who had introduced us in the first place, had a birthday party at the Paramount Club in London and Danny and I were both invited, but yet again he said we couldn't be seen together. What's going on? We're supposed to be a couple, I thought. But I was sure that when he saw me at the club he would change his mind...I wore a very cheeky, attention-grabbing see-through black lace all in one, which flashed my underwear and quite a bit of my bum, along with some killer heels.

My good friend Melodie came with me, and when we arrived I saw Danny. I was stunned when he completely ignored me. One minute he said that he loved me . . . and now this? I felt hurt and confused. I couldn't believe that we had spent all week together and here he was, treating me as if I was nothing to him.

We went to the bar and David came up and introduced me to his mum and dad and we got talking, but all I could think of was Danny. Finally he came over and stood next to me at the bar, but he was still acting as if we weren't a couple.

'All right?' he said, really casually, as if we were acquaintances and that was it. He got himself a drink and then moved away; he was offhand to the point of rudeness.

I tried to hide how hurt I was by hitting the dance floor with Melodie. I saw Danny across the club, talking and laughing with a group of girls, and I thought, You absolute bastard. I was furious that he was treating me like this – like shit basically. After I'd left he texted me saying that he couldn't believe I'd worn that outfit. I replied that I couldn't believe he'd ignored me!

But I didn't want to get into an argument. I thought everything would be okay as I was seeing him the following night, having organised a box for him and some of our friends at a Katy Perry concert. I had also hired a limo to pick us all up from my house and take us to the concert and then back to the house for a party. However, when I saw him again Danny was still offhand with me. He wouldn't walk into the O2 Arena with me and he didn't stand next to me while watching the concert. But yet again I thought, It's okay, he's coming back to my house later, we can sort this out. Really I should have turned round and said, 'Fuck you! You can't even talk to me in a group of people! Do you really think I'm going to organise a party for you and your friends?' But I was in a fragile state of mind at the time.

I was completely different with Danny from the way I have behaved with my other boyfriends in the past. I was nothing like that with Kieran, where I followed the age-old rule of treating them mean to keep them keen – and it must have worked as we got married! With Danny it was as if I was a teenager again, putting up with all a man's shit, and going along with everything he said.

After the concert, as we were walking out, Catherine my PA said something to Danny, and he shot back angrily with, 'No, it's your job. *You* look after her.' It was clear he was drunk and he sounded aggressive. It got worse on the drive back. He said something to me, I can't remember exactly what, but he was trying to be a smartarse and because I'd had a few drinks I was gobby back to him. What happened next completely shocked me and everyone I was with. He got hold of me by the neck and pushed me against the window, saying, 'Don't ever speak to me like that again!'

'Hey! Get off her!' everyone exclaimed. 'That's out of order.'

'I don't fucking care!' he shouted. I just didn't understand why he was being like this. Looking back, I should have told him to go, there and then, but I was still under his spell. He was vile throughout the house party after the concert, downing drinks, walking around with a bottle of vodka in each hand, swigging it neat. My friends and I were amazed by what he was getting up to.

A few days later I went to the premiere of the film *Paranormal Activity 3,* which was held at the Big Brother house at Elstree Studios, along with two contestants from my own reality show, *Signed by Katie Price,* Melissa and Gemma. In the morning as we'd lain in bed together, Danny had told me that he couldn't meet up with me that night as he was staying at his mum's house. 'Well, can't I come over like last time?' I'd suggested, but he'd said no as he was going to be with one of his friends.

I had a feeling that something wasn't quite right and after the film I texted him again to ask if we could meet up. If it sounds like I was obsessed, that's because I was... Again he said he couldn't, and that he was having dinner with a friend. Then he actually sent me a picture of the pie they were supposed to be eating, as if to prove that he was where he said he was... Now I really *was* suspicious.

I texted Danny, *Are you sure you're at your mum's house?*

Yeah, why do you keep asking? he replied.

I was feeling more and more wound up.

I knew people and did my research to try and find out the truth and was able to get hold of a picture of Danny at the time sitting on the sofa, next to a girl.

I was so upset that he had lied to me. Right, I thought, I'm going over.

Then I found out that Danny and the girl had gone to bed together. I felt sick; I was shaking with hurt and anger. I couldn't believe how he had lied to me. Somehow I kept it together to drive from Elstree to where Danny was staying, but all the time I couldn't get what he had done, and what he was doing right this moment, with another girl, out of my head. In my mind I was planning exactly what I was going to say when I caught him, rehearsing my speech.

I deliberately parked at the end of his street so he wouldn't see my car, and then Melissa, Gemma and I tiptoed along the pavement so he wouldn't hear our heels clicking against the concrete. When we reached the front door I covered the little spy hole so that whoever answered the door wouldn't be able to see us. Then I knocked. One of Danny's housemates answered the door, and the 'Oh, fuck!' look on his face said it all when he realised that it was me, and that his mate Danny was about to be found out big time.

'Hiya,' I said, sounding calm even though I felt anything but. 'I realised I'd forgotten something...I'll only be a minute.' And before he could prevent it, all three of us walked in and headed straight for the stairs. My heart was pounding and the adrenalin was pumping through me as we went quietly up to Danny's bedroom. The door stood slightly ajar and we all walked in.

Then we froze as we looked down at the bed. My gut instinct had been spot on. Danny, who was supposed to be my boyfriend, was having sex with another woman. I was strangely calm, I guess because I'd had an hour to prepare what I wanted to say and because I knew what I was going to be confronted with. Deep down, I also think I realised by then just what he was like.

I gestured for my friends to go out while I waited, hand on my hip, getting ready to launch into my pre-prepared speech.

'Hiya,' I said.

The effect on the couple in the bed was instantaneous. They stopped what they were doing and grabbed the duvet to cover themselves. Both of them looked up at me, completely horrified. It would have been funny if I hadn't felt so completely cut up by his betrayal.

'Danny,' I said, sounding more together than I was feeling, 'I want you to know that I forgive you, but I never forget.'

At this Danny got out of bed and grabbed his clothes. I marched up to him and flicked his dick with my hand. 'All right, are you? You fucking dick!' I shot at him, struggling to contain my anger. He rushed out of the room.

Then it was just the girl and me, and I was still trying

to control the hurt and anger that was boiling up inside me.

'So how long has this been going on? Did he tell you that he was with me and that I'm his girlfriend?'

She shook her head, 'No way. He told me he was single.'

I couldn't believe what I was hearing. All those things he had said about us being together properly...all lies.

'So did he tell you that he was going back to Australia soon and that you could go out and see him there?' I carried on. I had to know everything, even though it was killing me.

'Yes, he did,' came her reply. Exactly what he had told me... I found out then that Danny had met her at David Haye's party, the night he had insisted we couldn't be seen together, the night he had treated me like shit. And now I knew why. He had been pulling this girl.

I couldn't really be angry with her as she'd been conned by Danny, just like me. I asked her if she needed a cab but she said she'd get one herself. I went downstairs and found Danny sitting on his friend's bed, looking upset. *He* looked upset...that was nothing to how he'd made me feel.

'I can't believe you did that. I'm going now,' I told him.

He pleaded with me not to go. I couldn't believe what I was hearing.

'Danny, is this for real? Do you seriously think I'm

going to stay with you after I caught you in bed with someone else? You fucking liar!'

He held on to my jacket to stop me leaving. This was a totally different side to him. He was like a lost puppy.

His display of emotion didn't work, though, because all I could think was, Fuck you for cheating on me.

'Don't worry about it,' I said, really sarcastically. 'I forgive you but you're never going to see me again.' I was quite proud of myself for holding it together.

Then I walked out of the room.

As I was leaving I saw his housemate and said, 'The look on your face when you opened the door! It's all right, I'm fine about it. These things happen, I'll move on. I can't believe he did that, but there you go.' I was still being really calm, eerily so.

I thought, Kate, don't you dare give in to him and stay. But it was like a battle being waged inside me. I knew I should go, but part of me wanted to stay and argue it out, make up and cuddle Danny. And I know this is going to sound weird, but in spite of everything I wanted to fuck him. I left.

He texted me later and told me he had put it on his BBM status that I was his girlfriend. 'That's funny,' I replied, 'it's not coming up on my phone.' But somehow he talked me round to seeing him, and the following day he came to my house and did the big 'I'm sorry' number again. He sounded desperate. He was about to go back to Australia, as he was playing for Melbourne, which gave it all added urgency.

He convinced me that he was sorry, that it would never happen again, that we were going to be together, properly this time, that he wanted me to be his official girlfriend, that he would tell his PR to release a statement saying we were together, that he would tweet it...Anything I wanted him to do, he would do it.

He actually texted his manager in front of me and showed me the text, which said: *Just to let you know Kate is my girlfriend and we're going to be together whatever anyone thinks.* He did such a good job of persuading me that it had been a mistake and that he loved me that I was eventually won over. I guess I wanted to be because I still had such strong feelings for him. I wanted to believe him so basically I let myself down by getting back with him.

He had to go training and asked me if I wanted to go with him. As we drove there he said, 'So how does it feel now that you're officially my girlfriend?'

'It feels good,' I replied, but somehow I just didn't believe him. And what happened next showed that my gut instinct was right. He was due to fly back to Australia in the next week and I told him that I would really miss him when he was gone. 'Come out and see me soon,' he said. I said that I would, but I had work commitments to sort out first. He certainly seemed keen for me to visit him though.

But within a couple of days he had changed again and I was back to not knowing where I stood with him. I had been so strong when I caught him cheating, but now all the hurt and insecurity were creeping back. On a night out together he was really nasty to me. I ended up drinking way too much because I was so upset. Did he want to be with me or didn't he? I just didn't get why he was behaving like this when he had told me he loved me. Later, Gary and Phil found me at one of their friend's houses and took me back to their place where I just broke down. Danny had completely fucked with my head. He had played with my emotions, convincing me that he was into me then turning on me again. The strong impression I got was that he needs to feed his own ego in any relationship, whereas I don't.

I was in such a mess that I had to cancel the launch of my seventh novel, *Santa Baby*, because I was in no fit state to do anything. That had never happened before. They had even flown reindeer in, specially for the shoot and press call. But I couldn't do it, I couldn't face seeing anyone, let alone the press. My manager actually phoned Danny, the day before he flew to Australia, and said, 'What are you doing to this girl? Just be honest with her. If you don't want to be with her, tell her. She doesn't deserve this treatment. She's a decent girl.' But it made no difference.

I was a broken woman. I went to a country hotel and stayed in one of the private cottages in the grounds, so no one would see me. Danny was all I could think about, all the time. I wanted him so badly and I didn't understand why. It was probably the shock of his rejection on top of everything else that had happened to me. I was on my phone non-stop, texting him, or seeing if he had texted me. I didn't care about anything else; it was all Danny, Danny, Danny. If he texted me, I'd say, 'See, he does want to be with me!' Driving myself mad. It's shocking, reading back over this, to see what a hold he had over me, and I think I can only explain it as being the result of what I had been through and how he had played me.

The rescheduled launch for *Santa Baby* was on 4 November, after I returned from my trip to the country. When I look back at the pictures of the occasion I can tell that there's something wrong with me. I don't have my usual sparkle; I look subdued. And it should have been brilliant as I was wearing a fabulous outfit, a kind of sexy Mrs Christmas, a fur-trimmed basque, suspenders and a long red cloak. Plus there were the reindeer and the elves. But I still felt crushed. I knew I should cut all contact with Danny as it was so destructive, but I just couldn't.

He hardly texted me once he was in Australia, but I didn't want things to end on a bad note, I never do. So I decided to send him an iPod with the tracks of some of my favourite love songs on it. This wasn't a gesture meant to win him back, and he isn't the first guy I've done this for, me being such an old romantic...But I thought to myself, This will be the last time he hears from me. Michelle Heaton and her husband helped me set up the iPod.

'Why are you doing this?' Michelle asked me, looking concerned. 'He doesn't deserve it.'

She was right, of course. Along with the iPod, I sent

Danny a new BlackBerry and a new iPhone. And he didn't even say thank you! He had the cheek to say that he needed to know a certain PIN to make the phones work as he was in a different country, but he didn't mention the songs. I thought, You rude fuck! He still said that I should fly out and see him in Oz, and I was planning to go, but there would always be some excuse why he couldn't make it then after all.

Eventually, I got over him. Time was probably the healer and I went out with my friends and realised that Danny wasn't right for me at all. I started to feel stronger and decided that it had been a moment of madness and I had other, more important things to worry about. Now I would advise any woman to stay well away from him. He's got issues. I'm a strong girl but he completely messed me up.

But that wasn't the last I heard from Danny...He emailed me in January 2013, asking if I wanted to meet up with him, even though he knew I was with Kieran by then. He asked me if the paps were still following me because he wanted to meet up in Manchester without being seen, adding that I had to keep my mouth shut if we got together. What a charmer! I showed Kieran the emails; I had absolutely no interest in seeing Danny again.

CHAPTER 15

A BLAST FROM
THE PAST

Since Leo had left, to be honest I hadn't given him much thought, though we continued to be in touch, sending each other texts, him more than me. Three weeks after we split he even sent me a picture of his dick. God, the sight of it. I didn't want it anywhere near me! I thought our relationship was well and truly over. He had mentioned several times that he was planning to come back to the UK, but I'd always say, yes, I could meet him, and then change my mind and say that I was busy. I just wasn't bothered about seeing him again.

But then, unexpectedly, a week or so before Christmas, he flew over and we met up. To my surprise Leo seemed to be a changed man, a million miles away from the blubbering wreck who had left in September. He was more confident and looked incredible, as if he had been working out big time at the gym. I mean, he was always fit but now he was super-ripped and buff. He had rented a studio flat in London, near Sloane Square, and while it was a tiny apartment, it was at least in a smart area. His English seemed to be better, and he had enrolled in a language school in London. He'd hired a car too. He seemed back to being the Leo I had first met, full of energy and charm, the Leo who had swept me off my feet. It felt as if he had come back intending to impress me, and it worked. He had also proved in his absence that he didn't sell stories to the press...well, he didn't then...and that was another major plus. So many times in the past that was the very first thing my exes did when we split. Leo and I went out for dinner a few times and seemed to get on really well. We spent the night together and it was good.

But I didn't know what to think or do. Could he and I give it another go? Did I want to? At the beginning of December I had met a guy – he's not in the public eye, so I'm not going to say who it was – and we had been seeing each other. We got on really well and enjoyed each other's company but it was a casual thing, not a serious relationship. At that time I didn't want a serious relationship. My confidence had been knocked by my experience with Danny and I wasn't ready to commit to anyone. When Leo unexpectedly returned, I was still seeing this other guy.

Before I knew it, it was Christmas and Leo asked if he could come over to my house. He gave the kids

Out with Princess and Harvey filming.

So proud of my brother Dan for running in the 2013 London Marathon to raise money for Genetic Disorders UK, which supports families affected by genetic disorders.

Riding - my life
long passion, and
modelling one of my KP
Equestrian t-shirts.

Check us out! With
good friend Jane, who
I've known for years.

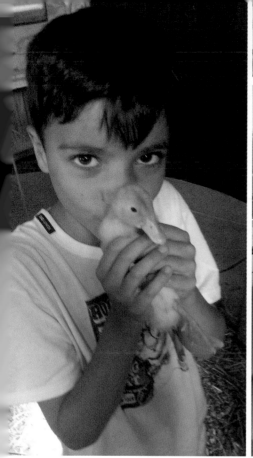

Above left: Cheep cheep! Junior and one of our Easter chicks.

Above right: I love Harvey to bits and wouldn't change him for the world!

Right: I know I'm biased but Princess is so cute! And Junior too of course and Harvey!

Romantic bathtime, rose petals check, champagne check, candles, check. Shower cap, err check!

Doing a signing for KP Equestrian but never too busy for a kiss from Princess!

Style rules pah! Who says you can't wear a bathrobe and sunglasses?

Lazing around, perfect time for a snap.

Planet Katie – Keiran and his friends on his stag do in Berlin – they may need to work on their cleavage…

Top left: About to have my say at the prestigious Cambridge Union on celebrity. Never underestimate the Pricey!

Centre left: Film night with my man.

Bottom left: Kisses with Kieran, my Prince. Well, I've kissed enough frogs in my time…

Kieran showing off one of his poses. I have no problem at all with him being a stripper. In fact I love it!

Opposite: My gorgeous husband Kieran! Phwoar! He is ripped!

A romantic dinner for two.

and me huge piles of presents each, all of which had been bought from Harrods and gift-wrapped. I don't think I've ever seen such a big pile of presents in my life. He must have spent an absolute fortune as he had bought me all these Dolce & Gabbana designer clothes and shoes. I thought, Where the fuck has he got all that money from? It was such a dramatic turnaround from what had gone on before. He insisted that I open all of them in front of my family and friends, as if he wanted to impress everyone with his generosity. There was one final present, which was in a large gift-wrapped box. But when I ripped off the paper, there was another box inside, then another and another and so on, like one of those Russian dolls. I had a feeling I knew exactly what the final box was going to contain. Shit! I *so* didn't want this! I glanced over at my mum, who rolled her eyes and I knew she was thinking exactly what I was.

'You'd better not have bought me a ring,' I said to him. But as I reached the tell-tale jewellery box, it was obvious that he had. When I finally split up with Leo the second time, he did a number of stories about how I had reacted when I first saw the ring: that I'd had tears in my eyes when I asked him if it was an engagement ring, and how he had said it was even though he didn't mean it to be. Absolute crap. This was no engagement. At that moment getting engaged to him was the last thing on my mind.

The ring was not my cup of tea at all. He had bought it from Boodles, an expensive jewellery store, but you know I like my bling and this pretty diamond ring in the shape of a flower was way too small for me. Tiny, in fact. It reminded me of a ring that my nan had bought me when I was little. Leo had had our names engraved on the band.

'Thank you so much!' I told him, and deliberately put the ring on my right hand, i.e. not on my engagement finger.

When Leo went out of the room for something I turned to my family and said, 'Fucking hell! Why's he bought me that?' A little later, I told him that I was never going to wear the ring because it wasn't my style and that he should return it and get his money back. If he really wanted to buy me a ring, he should get one made by my favourite jeweller, Bill Forman. I told Leo I would like a pink love heart, and he should talk to Bill about how much he could spend. But it was not an engagement ring at this point.

While Leo stayed with me over Christmas I told him that I wasn't going to have sex with him. I didn't want to make whatever we had between us all about that. 'You've only just come back,' I told him, 'I want to take things slowly.'

But Leo seemed so into me, so passionate and loving. He told me that he was following his heart and his dream to be with me; that I was the love of his life. Just the kind of words I want a man to say to me...but I wasn't sure I felt the same way. It sounds like a proper love story, that he comes back a changed man in order to win my heart again. It turned out to be nothing like that...And there was still this other guy I liked. I couldn't help thinking that Leo had come back at the wrong moment. I didn't want to commit to him because of this other guy, so I was happy keeping things casual. But I didn't want to commit to the other guy either...I guess I thought I would carry on dating both of them and see what happened.

In the weeks that followed I started to see more of Leo and began to feel more for him. I forgot about all the bad times, and only remembered the good. I started fancying him again. He seemed more independent, which I found very attractive. I felt that at heart he was a good guy, and he definitely seemed to have changed for the better. And everyone around me, all my friends and family, really liked him and said I should give him a second chance. And I thought, Okay, I'll try and make a go of it even though it's not really on my terms. It was more because everyone else was convinced that he had changed and that I'd be mad not to give him a second chance. I felt under pressure to do it and, looking back, that was never going to work.

So that's what I did. I was spending a lot of time travelling to see Leo in London at his apartment, and he was spending a lot of time travelling to see me – and a lot of money. I didn't see the point of that, and so I suggested he should move back in with me. At first it was great, we got on well, he made me feel safe and loved and all those things he had at the beginning of our relationship. But I think I was trying to convince myself all the time that this would work. And I sort of resented him for coming back when he did, when I was single and actually enjoying myself. I'd always gone from relationship to relationship in the past. The thing with the other guy fizzled out. Once again I was in a relationship, this time almost despite myself.

Leo didn't seem to have any such doubts, though. He took me to Prague for Valentine's weekend in 2012. I knew a proposal was on the cards as by now he had had the replacement ring made for me: the pink heart that I'd wanted, surrounded by diamonds. When we were at the airport, Bill's wife turned up to give it to him, as Bill had only just finished making it. It all felt very rushed, and of course now there was no element of surprise.

Leo proposed to me over dinner at a restaurant. I knew he was going to do it, and thought, This is so cheesy. There was no going down on one knee or anything, he just got the ring out of his pocket. To be honest, he didn't even get the words out properly, but said something like, 'Will you marryiout me?'

I said yes, but I didn't feel passionately in love with him. I didn't gaze into his dark brown eyes. Looking back, I think I agreed because I wanted security. I thought: Leo's gorgeous, he will get a job, he will learn to speak English. Everyone likes him…so commit to him. But it didn't feel romantic or special. I was only doing it because I thought I should, and put it this way – I wasn't excitedly planning my wedding with him. I had learned my lesson about rushing into marriage from the mistake I'd made with Alex. Getting engaged was one thing, but it would take a hell of a lot to get me down the aisle and saying those vows again, because the next time I did I wanted them to be for ever. I loved the idea of a big old fairy-tale wedding, but it would have to be for the right reasons. In fact, I never had any intention of marrying Leo.

I was busy filming the second series of my reality show *Katie* for Sky and again Leo ended up being in it, which I had mixed feelings about. But we did some great things together, and with my family and friends. We did all kinds of country pursuits, like clay pigeon shooting, we went riding and took part in a ten-kilometre extreme run. Leo was great at getting involved in those kinds of things.

In May we went off to South Africa on safari. The reality show made it look very romantic, and there were times when it really was. But we also argued a lot. Leo could be very arrogant and stubborn; he never thought he was in the wrong, and if you said no to him he would get the hump. It was his way or no way, and because we are both strong-willed and have strong personalities we clashed a lot. On our second day at the hotel, which was in an amazing national park, we both got very drunk... so drunk that we had to be escorted back to our lodge in the grounds. We had a massive row because Leo wanted to have sex and I didn't. I think I shouted that I didn't even want to be with him any more... then I pulled off my ring and threw it into the surrounding bush and ran out of the lodge. The rest is a blur. The following morning I woke up feeling horrendously hungover. The bed was covered in twigs and I wasn't wearing my ring.

'What the fuck happened?' I groaned to Leo, who was lying next to me.

Apparently I had run away from him and hidden underneath our lodge. Leo hadn't been able to find me and had had to call the manager. He turned up with some of his workers, carrying torches, desperate to find me quickly because we were surrounded by wild animals, including hyenas on the prowl which would gladly have eaten me. I know I say never underestimate the Pricey, but I think in that situation it would have been game over...Eventually they tracked me down underneath the lodge, stark naked and fast asleep with my head on a pillow. I didn't wake up and they had to drag me out and put me to bed.

Take the shame! Leo told me that the hotel manager was furious and said I could have been killed if they hadn't found me when they did. There was no sign of my ring. The film crew then arrived – we'd had two days on our own – expecting to get on with the filming.

'It's really not a good day to film,' I told Ben, the director. I explained about the massive row and about losing my ring and said that I would have to fly to the nearby town and find a metal detector so I could try and find my ring again. It sounded like the script to *Hangover 4*...Fortunately it turned out that the manager had a metal detector, which he used for checking his staff hadn't stolen anything when they clocked off work. Off he went, zapping away with the device where I thought I'd thrown the ring, and sure enough he found it. We never would have found it without the detector. Despite that rocky start, the rest of the trip was brilliant. We went on several amazing safaris, seeing all the animals close up: giraffes, elephants, hippos. I quite fancied adding a zebra to my collection of animals back home.

* * *

So there were good times...but there were starting to be too many bad ones. Leo had returned from Argentina and showered me with presents, but it quickly became clear that this had been the grand gesture meant to win me back when in fact he still had no money and, of course, no job. When we went to Prague in February, as we walked round the city, going in and out of the designer boutiques, I thought, I'm the Richard Gere character out of *Pretty Woman* in this relationship. It would be so nice if the roles could be reversed and Leo was the one whisking me into the stores and buying me things.

Another time we were lying in bed together and he told me about a plot of land he was planning to buy in Argentina. He meant to build on it as his big money-making scheme.

'Why don't you come in on it with me?' he suggested. 'If you give me fifty grand, I promise you will make a lot of money.'

Instantly my heart sank. It definitely wasn't something I wanted to get involved in.

'No,' I told him, 'I won't be allowed to give you any of my money.' My brother oversees all my finances and would never agree to me investing in such an uncertain project. 'And anyway, I like to keep my money in this country, so I know where it is.'

Straight away Leo got the hump with me and sulked. And I wondered: Has this all been about my money?

Then he would look at expensive cars to lease, like BMWs and Bentleys, and I would think, There's no way you can afford them! He rarely bought anything when he was living with me. I would still be the one paying for the petrol he needed for trips to the gym while he drove my car. I think at heart Leo was a bit of a fantasist, a dreamer.

In the weeks leading up to my thirty-fourth birthday in 2012 he said that he was going to buy me a Hublot watch. That is a really expensive brand that I've always loved. He involved all my friends, showing them various watches, asking them which one they thought I would like. He was talking about spending thirty grand. Then he showed various watches to me and asked me which one I wanted, so I picked one out, thinking, That is one hell of an expensive watch; I can't imagine where he thinks he's going to get the money from to buy that. But I just went along with it. And in the end he didn't buy me a watch. In fact, he didn't even get me a birthday present. All these things started tallying up in my head and I decided he was turning into a professional bullshitter.

On top of that he was once again showing signs of the jealous streak that I had seen in him before. In May, just before my birthday, I was planning to go to Vegas with the girls. It was supposed to be my friend Danielle Lloyd's hen weekend but she'd had to cancel. As I'd already booked the flights and hotel, I thought I would go anyway with a group of friends. I paid for Leo to fly first-class BA, along with my friend Derek. Once we were out there, I paid for everything. One night we went out to a club and I bumped into a guy I know called Bert, who invited us all to join his table. Obviously if someone does that I'm going to be polite and talk to them! But I could tell that Leo was getting jealous. When it was time to say goodbye, I kissed Bert on the cheek, a peck, nothing more. In front of everyone, Leo grabbed my neck and slapped me. I was stunned by his aggression, as were all my friends, who told him he shouldn't have done that.

Ironically there had been lots of speculation in the press that Leo and I had come to Vegas to get married, just as I had with Alex. Nothing could have been further from my mind. I was starting to hate Leo. You must be wondering why I didn't dump him after he behaved so badly. I think it's because I don't like being the one doing the dumping. I don't like hurting people, even when it's hurting me to be with them.

All too quickly Leo seemed to revert back to how he

had been when we'd split. He went to Brighton to look at language schools, but for some reason never signed up at one. (Even though his English had improved, he still had a very long way to go.) He got rid of the hire car and was back to driving my pink Beetle. I had lent him my white Range Rover one time when his sister and her husband and some friends were over, and he had taken them all out in London. He was twice caught speeding and didn't tell me. Because my house was still being done up and I wasn't living there I didn't receive the penalty notices, so couldn't inform them that I wasn't driving at the time the tickets were issued. I was taken to court over it and actually disqualified from driving for a year. It was a really stressful time. Fortunately I appealed against the decision and won.

Leo would go to the gym in the morning and then just hang around the house. Before I knew it we were back in the same rut as before. However, he had signed up with a modelling agency, which I'd helped him to do, so I hoped he would get a job. I was convinced that if he did our relationship would be much better. We would be more like equals, rather than me feeling that I was constantly subsidising him. But the agency began complaining to my manager that Leo failed to reply to their emails and never turned up for meetings when he was expected. When I asked him about it, he replied, 'No, me no email.' See what I mean about him needing English lessons...

After this happened a few times the agency didn't want to know any more and they dropped him.

'I have jobs abroad,' Leo told me.

'Okay, you can go and do those jobs, but let me get one thing straight,' I told him. 'If you want to work abroad, go off and do it but we won't be together. Afterwards, if you come back, we can see if we still have a relationship.' Really it was my way of saying, Go on then, fuck off. Because I knew I didn't want a long-distance relationship with anyone, it just wouldn't work out for me. I want that family unit.

He did take part in Argentina's version of *Strictly Come Dancing* in June, but didn't last long. He actually had the cheek to blame me for it! And told me that the reason he left was to come back to me, when in reality he had been voted off for being a terrible dancer. Then he claimed he wasn't paid all the money he was owed from the show and that they were only going to pay him half. He also made out he had businesses in Argentina, but if he did, then I never saw any of the proceeds. I really didn't believe anything he said.

Then Bill, the jeweller who had made my pink heart-shaped ring, got in touch with my manager to say that Leo hadn't paid him for it and the money had been owing for over six months. I couldn't even wear the ring because it was too big, and when I found out that Leo hadn't paid for it, I certainly didn't want to wear it. When we confronted Leo about this he got all defensive, saying that he wouldn't pay for it until Bill had altered it to fit me.

'Bill's not going to do that until you pay for the job first,' I told him, really annoyed by his attitude.

'Not my problem,' Leo insisted. 'Not paying.'

I should have told him to go then because that said it all really.

*   *   *

Everyone who knows me, knows that I longed to have another baby. I say 'a' baby, but actually two or three would be perfect. And I know that Leo would have liked nothing more than to marry me and get me pregnant. But I never fell pregnant with him, even though we weren't always careful. At one stage, when things were okay between us, I started a course of IVF, but stopped it after a week when I realised that I didn't want a baby with him. I wanted another baby, but it had to be with the right man. Looking back, the fact I didn't fall pregnant was like fate telling me this wasn't going to work out and that things would only fall into place with the right man. Leo was not that man. I wasn't planning a wedding even though I was with him, on and off, for two years. Yet I met Alex and married him after seven months, and Kieran I married within three because it felt right.

I had started to question Leo's motives for being back with me. Did he really love me, as he claimed to, or did he just see me as his passport to fame? Increasingly I thought it was the latter and that he had come back over to the UK with the sole purpose of using me to make himself famous.

When he was at home with me he seemed so miserable. If we had friends over he'd go into a different room and play about on his computer. He wouldn't even say hello to people when they came to the house. He was quite boring really. If I wanted to go out with my friends, I knew he would be at home on his own so I would feel guilty and have to ask him. But all our nights out together ended up in rows between us, and my friends Jane and Derek would have to calm Leo down. I hated the situation, and I hated being a burden to my friends.

And Leo's jealousy was something else I couldn't bear. One night we were out at a club in London. He thought I was not paying him any attention, and he was right because I just wanted to be with my friends. In a jealous rage he grabbed my neck, the way he had in Vegas. It was shocking that he thought he could behave like that.

By now I didn't want to do anything with him because I didn't find him interesting and would still be the one having to pay for our entertainment. I thought, Why should I always have to pay? I'd started really resenting him for that and went off sex with him big time. I felt angry and pissed off with him, so of course I didn't want to have sex! If a man interests me, and we have a laugh together, then I'll want sex. As soon as a relationship gets miserable, I don't want to, I shut down. Any woman would feel the same. I thought, Why would I want to have sex with you when you make me so unhappy? I knew I couldn't go on like this...

* * *

I had to go back on anti-depressants in September; I felt under so much pressure from my failing relationship with Leo, I could feel myself sinking as I had when I suffered from post-natal depression. I had actually come off the medication when I split up with Pete, but right now I felt I needed something to help me. And there was also the ongoing court case. It was all very stressful.

I knew my relationship with Leo had reached the end of the line. By September 2012 I'd had enough. I had been patient, given him time to get a job and earn some money, but he had done nothing. It started to get so bad between us that I called him a 'gigolo'. He hated that and denied that he was anything of the sort. Yes, he was good-looking, but looks aren't everything. He needed a job but I had the feeling that as long as he was with me, he would never get one. He just didn't *do* anything.

He nearly left one weekend. He packed his bags and went off somewhere. Then he texted me asking me if I still loved him. I didn't want to be with him but I guess there were still some feelings there, so I replied that I did, but I couldn't carry on like this, I needed him to get a job, I needed him to be independent. And on we limped for a few more weeks. But the atmosphere between us was awful, and I lost count of the number of times I said, 'If you're not happy, just go.'

'If you want me to go, I go, no problem,' Leo would reply, sounding not in the least bit bothered. Not like the first time I had told him to go when he had cried his eyes out.

That said it all really. I'd reply, 'And that's exactly my problem, Leo. If you really wanted me you would fight for me, you wouldn't have this blasé attitude.'

It was a very long way from the romance we had first experienced.

Finally, just as I was at my wits' end, I got a call from my manager telling me that Leo had sold a story to an Argentinian magazine where he said that he had walked out on me and God knows what else. I confronted him in front of my friends about it.

'No, me no interview,' he protested.

But then my manager emailed me the entire article and still Leo denied it. I saw red. 'I want you to fuck off out of my house. Now!'

'No. Me no go. Me stay,' he replied.

That made me even angrier. 'Well, I don't want you here! Go!'

Later I found out from my nanny that he had already packed three suitcases and sent them back to Argentina.

'Okay, me go,' he answered, not seeming upset or even bothered.

But he still made no move to leave.

'I meant now!' I told him. 'You could check into a hotel.'

'No.'

It was like a re-run of Alex, I couldn't get rid of him! So I said, 'I don't want you in my bed, you can fuck off out of there.'

For a day or two he moved into the guest room. I couldn't believe that he had so little self-respect that he would hang around when I'd told him it was over. On the morning Leo finally slung his hook, I didn't even say goodbye to him as I was at my friend Melodie's, having my hair done. I only know what happened from the nanny, who was there. Apparently a taxi arrived to collect him but Leo took his time about leaving, saying goodbye to everyone, trying to wring out the emotion. The kids were glad he was on his way. They couldn't bear him by the end. Junior even chanted 'Hip hip hooray!' when Leo had closed the door. Only Harvey mentioned him again because he is used to routine and he remembered Leo taking him out on the quad bike.

Apparently there were paps waiting by my front gate, and I wondered if Leo had tipped them off.

As soon as I knew he had left I breathed a huge sigh of relief. It was over. I could move on with my life. And even though things hadn't worked out with him, I felt I could trust him not to sell any stories. I never thought he had it in him to stab me in the back and come up with a load of rubbish just to make money and get his face in the mags. How wrong can you be?

*   *   *

I actually heard from Pete after I'd ended things with

Leo. It was Bonfire Night and I was at Melodie's when I got a phone call. I didn't recognise the number.

'Hi, it's me,' someone said.

'Who?' I asked.

'It's me, Pete,' he said, and then went on to say that I shouldn't worry and he hadn't called me to have a go at me. He never phones me so it was a complete surprise to hear from him. He told me that he'd heard that Leo was trying to sell stories on me and that he wanted to stick up for me as he didn't want to see me get hurt. As the mother of his kids he said he would do anything to help me out as Leo wasn't going to be nice about me.

This was completely fucked up! I thought, as Pete carried on about how he didn't want to argue with me any more, how he was in a happy place and wasn't going to be in this industry much longer. How he was really happy with his own life, how he wanted me to be happy, how he didn't want anyone to say a bad word about me...

I thought, You absolute hypocrite! What have you been doing to me for the past four years? Never once standing up for me in the press, allowing them to rip me to shreds, making out that you are the good father and I'm the bitch!

But I kept it all in, I didn't bite back. I wondered what his motive was for calling me, because I didn't believe that it was out of concern. It was way too late in the day for that, and too much had happened. Then it all became clear this was about the court case I had against him and Claire. He must really want me to drop it, I thought.

'Let's just get on,' Pete repeated, and said again how he wanted to protect me. He even suggested we should meet up.

Since he'd left me in 2009 I had frequently suggested that we meet up, to discuss the children, and to get closure finally on why he had walked out.

'I've always said that I would meet up with you, Pete,' I told him. We actually arranged a time and place. But when it came to it, he had to cancel and we rearranged and then I couldn't do it. I wondered if we both knew all along that it was never going to happen.

A couple of weeks later the story of Pete wanting to help me appeared in *Now* magazine. There I was on the cover looking all sad-eyed, and there was a picture of Pete looking all sincere and concerned, next to the headline 'Let Me Help You'. And inside an article where 'friends' said that Pete was trying to help me through this time. I felt that whole phone call was a set up so that he could then go and sell a story on me. I had no faith in him at all. It felt like everyone around me was ready to shit on me. I could never trust Pete again.

But he was right about one thing: Leo did a kiss and tell on me. Within a couple of weeks there he was on the cover of *Now* magazine, selling his story. Even though I say I'm desensitised to what the press writes about me, the fact that Leo went and sold a story did hurt. I did feel betrayed. This was someone I had been with for nearly two years, he had been part of my family, I had loved him and he'd said he loved me. It brought back a lot of bad memories.

According to Leo I was more interested in Googling myself than in having sex with him. Well, I didn't want to have sex with him because it was boring! And as for Googling – *he* was the one continually Googling *himself*... There were more lies about how I had begged him to marry me. More rubbish about how he'd spoken to Pete and wanted to be like him.

Lots of people have sold stories on me in the eighteen years I have been in the business: friends, people I thought were best friends even, but I can honestly say I was genuinely shocked that Leo had done the same. Although I'd had my doubts about him, I'd thought he had a strong character and that he came from a good family.

Incredibly, after he had sold the story he emailed me, saying he was sorry. Well, it was a bit late for that.

I replied and told him that I was very surprised that he had emailed after he'd said very bad, untrue things about me. I would never have sold stories about him and had never thought he would do that to me. 'I guess I was wrong about you,' I said. 'If it makes you happy to make money doing stories, then that is your choice. It's a shame you didn't have the same energy to work and learn English when you were with me.' I told him he had behaved exactly like the mother of his daughter, who had sold stories on him.

He replied that he was very angry with *Now* magazine, that he was very nice about me in the interview and they had changed everything. How he had said that I was a good parent, worked hard for my children and was the best mother to Harvey. Yeah, I can just imagine the journalists wanting to write positive things about me.

I replied, 'Leo, if you're angry with *Now* magazine, why did you tweet the article? If it really isn't true then why don't you tweet to say that they changed what you'd said?'

He replied, 'It was in my contract to tweet.' And told me the magazine had promised to fix the article next week, and he was going to talk to his solicitor and fix the problem. 'I apologise, Katie. Peter is not my friend, nor do I want to look like him. The journalist changed everything I said. I am very angry because I do not like lies, I only wanted to speak well of you and say how important you were. Sorry.'

It was pathetic! And yet again my name was being dragged through the mud and people were making money out of me by telling lies. And yet again I thought, Who the hell can I trust? In spite of all the things Leo had said about me he carried on sending me texts saying that he loved me, how I should go and meet him, and he texted all my friends, telling them that he loved me! But how could he possibly love me if he was selling stories to the press? One thing was for sure: I didn't love him. He had destroyed any feelings I'd ever had for him, any respect.

To cap it all I had to return the pink love-heart ring to Bill because Leo had never paid for it. A courier actually came to the house to collect it because Bill was going legal. Even then Leo had the audacity to say that the ring I wore was never the real one; that he had never been in possession of the real ring, so why should he pay for it? He totally lied. He even tweeted that I was a prostitute, though he claimed that someone else had written it. So I went legal and we got a copy of his signed apology.

I really hoped that was the very last I would ever hear of Leo. At some stage I'd have to get round to altering the tattoo of his name on my leg into something else, just as I'd had Pete's name on my wrist altered into a rose. I know my mum is rolling her eyes as she's reading this, she hates my tattoos and always has a go at me for getting them done. But at the time they always seem like such a good idea...and there's nothing you can't change into something else.

CHAPTER 16

UNDER THE KNIFE AGAIN

I'm well known for having had a number of boob jobs. It's something that I've always been upfront about. And up until recently I always thought it was fine that I'd first gone under the knife when I was eighteen. Now that I'm older and wiser, I think eighteen is way too young. You should wait until you are twenty-one at least. At eighteen you still have a teenager's body and I don't think you're mature enough then to make an informed decision about something as life-changing as cosmetic surgery. So I would definitely advise any girl to wait until she is twenty-one.

Also, she should be really clear about why she wants the surgery; she should only be doing it for herself, not because she thinks it will please a man. I've always had my boob jobs done for me and no one else. In fact, there have been times when the men I've been with haven't wanted me to have surgery. It is serious and always carries risks, I don't think anyone should be under any illusion about that. I should know, I've had enough…which is why I say you need to be mature enough to understand that. And, of course, you should do your research carefully and choose a surgeon with a good reputation, never go to one just because they're cheap.

I was shocked by the scandal involving the PIP implants, when it came to light that industrial-grade silicone, which is only supposed to be used in products such as mattresses, was instead used in the breast implants of over 40,000 women in the UK. I was fortunate enough not to have these implants myself, but my heart went out to those women who did, through absolutely no fault of their own. It was disgusting that this company had done it, thinking more about their profits than the women involved.

In February 2012 I actually went on the current affairs programme *Newsnight,* presented by Jeremy Paxman, to talk about the scandal and to give my perspective on surgery. I think my friends and family were more worried about me appearing on it than I was! As my brother said, who could have thought that Pricey and Paxman would have been in the same sentence and then the same studio! My late nan would have been so proud of me as she used to watch it.

Paxman has quite a reputation as an interviewer, but having never watched the programme, I was not worried.

But I thought it was good that I had been invited on to it. Ten years ago I could never have imagined being on something as serious as *Newsnight*. I thought it was a sign that people knew I had opinions and something worth saying. You can't survive in the media industry as long as I have just by looking pretty and smiling. I've got common sense so I thought I would stick to talking about only what I knew and my own experiences, otherwise the other guests would be able to wipe the floor with me. In the end I think it went well, I didn't try to be anyone else but *moi*. I had to let off steam afterwards, though, and changed into a cheeky black leather mini-skirt and heels to hit a club. There's only so much serious debate a girl can take in one night…

*   *   *

Ever since I'd had my fifth boob job done in LA in 2009 I had known that I wanted to get them done again. I had never liked them. My nipples were slightly lopsided because the surgeon had cut around them when he performed the surgery – apologies to anyone out there who is squeamish! – lifted them up, and then stitched them back on. It's called the 'anchor scar' technique, in case you were wondering. As time had passed, inevitably my boobs had dropped, and they needed tightening again. There was also too much loose skin; I needed a bigger implant to fill the breast. And I wasn't happy about the scarring either. All in all, they needed to change!

Even I couldn't quite believe that it was going to be

boob job number six. Then again, some of the ops have been more like repair jobs, which I have to laugh about because it sounds as if I'm taking my car to the garage to have an MOT! The thing about having boob jobs is that there always comes a time when they will need redoing. In September 2012 that time had come round again.

I'd had a terrible experience when I had surgery in 2008, and it had almost put me off for life. But I knew that it had been down to me having too many operations in just one week. I'd had an anaesthetic when I'd had some dental work done, a general anaesthetic a day later when I had my boob job, and then another a few days later because there was a problem with my arm feeling numb, and finally a fourth anaesthetic when I had surgery on my prolapsed womb. Result, I had overloaded on anaesthetic and made myself extremely unwell. The pain had been excruciating, worse than anything I had ever experienced. Worse, I hope, than anything I will ever experience again. But this time round I was only having one operation so I was confident everything would be fine.

The last couple of times I have had breast surgery in LA but this time I went to Belgium. That might sound a bit random, but I was recommended this particular surgeon by the cosmetic nurse who does my Botox. Apparently she'd had 'work' done by him, including a boob job, and I thought she looked really good, an excellent advertisement for his skills. So off I flew to Belgium for a consultation. It was good news as he thought it would be straightforward to give me the boobs I wanted. Yes! I was still after the pert, high, stuck on look. I had never stopped wanting that!

People will say that I'm getting more and more fake as I grow older, and that's probably true, but I'm turning fake only so far. I may *look* fake but my personality is one hundred per cent real. Some of my friends suggested I should have a brow lift, but I didn't think I had reached the age where I needed that. Overall I didn't think I was in bad shape for a woman of thirty-four who'd had three kids. People ask me if it's harder getting older when you're a model, and you've made a living out of your good looks, but I've always accepted that I'm getting older, and been relaxed about it. I always make sure my hair, eyebrows and nails are 'done', but otherwise I'm pretty casual and don't think I have to look a certain way.

I think if you have surgery you should have bits done over time, rather than reaching a certain age and thinking, Right! I've got to have everything done at once! Because that's when people end up looking so radically different that everyone who sees them thinks, WTF! My motto is: a bit here, a bit there. But I don't rule out surgery on my face eventually, such as a brow lift. I'm too young for it at the moment, but as I'm getting older I would never say never... And I'm in the lucky position where I've got the money and can afford the best surgeons. I'll probably end up looking like Joan Rivers! In all honesty, can you see me ending up as an old wrinkly? And now I've got a younger husband...

I'm still a big fan of Botox. I get it done every four to six months, in my forehead and around my eyes. I really don't see it as a big deal. One time I didn't have it for six months and I could see the difference in the lines around my eyes. That's down to me abusing my skin in the sun – take note, you young girls. If you don't wear sunscreen, and if you go on sunbeds, you might be the colour you want to be, but it will catch up with you eventually, as it has me.

As for facial fillers – years ago I had some in my cheeks, but not any more because I heard that if you have too much filler, it can drop and leave you with that puffy-cheeked chipmunk look. No, thank you!

I mentioned my pot belly to the surgeon. Yes, yes, I know. After three kids, I'm not going to have the taut stomach of a twenty year old, but still, if there was something I could do... I thought I could have some lipo, get it all tightened up. I've had lipo before and it made no difference – that was on my legs – but I thought it was worth asking. But when I mentioned it to the Belgian surgeon, he said he wouldn't do it. That I would end up with a huge scar, and if I wore low-cut bikini briefs the scar would be visible and I wouldn't be happy. Then he showed me some pictures of people who'd had it done... and bloody hell! That put me right off! I'd never be able to wear any of my teeny-tiny bikinis again! Well, not unless I wanted to frighten small children.

The fact that the surgeon refused to perform the op reassured me that he was a good and reputable doctor.

Definitely not the sort to take the money and not care about the consequences. His charges were reasonable as well. It was going to be half the price it had cost me to have my last surgery in LA. But I wasn't going abroad because it was cheaper than having it done in the UK; it was purely because this man had come so highly recommended.

I would never advise people to choose someone just on price; you have to do your research. I don't want women to look at me and think, Well, if she's had boob jobs and Botox then she must know about it and it'll be all right for me to do the same. You have to make sure the surgeon, or cosmetic nurse, you go to is a good one.

So in mid September I booked myself in for surgery. The night before I was to have the op I was due to attend my friend Dawn Ward's annual charity ball, which I always love. But I knew if I went to the ball I'd have to delay my surgery, which would be frustrating, and if I didn't go to the ball I knew I'd feel I'd missed out. Crisis! At that point my very good friend Tanya, who was also going to the ball and is the most incredibly generous person, said that she would hire a private jet to fly herself, me and a private doctor to look after me, to Belgium straight after the ball, and then fly us back after the surgery.

'No way!' I said at first, but Tanya absolutely insisted and so we all went to the ball and left on the stroke of midnight to get to Birmingham airport. Cinderella had her pumpkin coach to whisk her away after the ball; I had my private jet...I know which one I prefer!

I was on the operating table at 7 a.m. the following morning, not something Cinders ever had reason to say. I still love the feeling of going under and asked the doctor to give me the anaesthetic slowly, so I could enjoy every second of the sensation. I know – weird. The op went well, I recovered at the clinic for a couple of hours and then we flew back.

Ever-optimistic, I had thought that it wouldn't take me long to get over the operation, but I had to rest in bed. I was sore and in pain. However, I am more sensible now and I do look after myself, not like after my second boob job when I went straight out to Britney Spears's birthday party. No, this time it was cups of tea and watching TV in bed for me.

However, my recovery didn't quite go to plan. I had kept the dressings on my boobs for twelve days as the surgeon said it would be okay to leave them that long, and that when I went up to London to see him on one of his visits there he would remove them. I didn't realise that I had an infection in one of my breasts. As it was getting close to seeing the surgeon I thought I could get away with having a shower and washing my hair, instead of having a bath as I had been doing since I wasn't supposed to get the dressings wet. But the shower sprayed water on one of the dressings and I peeled if off. OMG! What a sight that was! It looked as if there were ulcers along the scars. Yuck! It got worse when I checked out the state of my other boob. There was disgusting green pus oozing out of the scar under my breast and there seemed to be a hole by the scar. The smell was vile; I thought I was going to throw up! I'd have to get them checked out that day, I realised. I put the dressings back on and got dressed.

But before I had a chance to do anything, Junior suffered an unfortunate accident when one of my horses head butted him and left him with a nasty cut on his forehead. I immediately rushed him to the nearest A&E department. He was very brave while they glued the wound together. Once I was satisfied that he was okay, I mentioned to the nurse that I'd just had a boob job and was concerned about the scars and could she take a look?

She checked them out and instantly thought there was a problem, but the doctor she called for a second opinion took a look and thought the wounds were healing okay. I was still uneasy myself, but trusted him to know what he was talking about.

Later that evening, I was with my friend Louise. She was recovering from surgery herself and all the pair of us were up to doing was chilling out on the sofa watching *Silent Witness*. Both of us suddenly became aware of this rank smell and commented on it. It was so bad that not even the scent of my Jo Malone candles could disguise it.

'It stinks!' Louise exclaimed, covering her nose.

'God! I think it's me!' I told her. I went over to the mirror, lifted up my top and peeled away the dressing. When I pressed the hole under my breast a stream of green pus shot out. Eeew! I thought I was going to faint!

Straightaway I phoned Tanya's private doctor who had come with me to Belgium. He said that I obviously had an infection and must go to A&E immediately. He arranged for an ambulance to pick me up and phoned ahead to the hospital to ensure that there was a surgeon there to see me. The doctor I saw immediately thought there was an infection. By now the hole seemed to have got bigger and you could see the stitches unravelling.

He cleaned the wounds and arranged for me to see the breast surgeon, who works with women who have breast cancer. I saw him the following day and had a mammogram to check that the infection hadn't spread. If it had the implants would have had to be removed. See what I mean about surgery carrying risks? But thankfully everything was okay. He was very reassuring and said that although the wounds looked so shocking, it was good that they were weeping as it meant they would heal. He gave me a course of antibiotics and I saw him weekly for the next month and had several more mammograms. The infection soon cleared up.

And once the wounds had healed I was left with the best boobs I have ever had. Perfect! I loved, loved, loved them! They were exactly what I have always wanted. High up, stuck on, ready to fire bullets! The scars were amazing as well; you could hardly see them at all. But little did I know when I had them done that I would soon be meeting husband number three...and having baby number four.

CHAPTER 17

I'D RATHER BE HORSE RIDING

I've always loved dreaming up ideas for press photo calls to launch my products and books. I know that I've got to grab the attention and imagination of the press and give them something good to write about if I'm going to get publicity. I like to think that I always deliver!

I've dressed as an angel and been driven in a horse-drawn carriage along Park Lane for the launch of my first novel – they actually closed the road, get me! I've been a princess carried in a glass carriage by four handsome hunks. I've been a very sexy Mrs Christmas accompanied by reindeers and elves. I've been a space alien princess in a silver bodysuit and tiara made of iPods. I've been dressed as a Spanish flamenco dancer and ridden a rearing black stallion. I could go on!

In fact, the horse I rode for the press call for my novel

In the Name of Love was my absolute dream horse. He was a black Arab stallion. I've always loved black horses, from when I was a child and watched *Black Beauty* and then later on from seeing the beautiful black stallion called Cancara on the Lloyds Bank adverts. I had the idea of riding a black horse for my press call and had already seen the horse I wanted in the film *War Horse*. I went along to the stud yard and the trainer rode the horse, who was called Dante, and demonstrated all the things he could do. It was incredible how Dante would respond to the slightest of commands.

At the press call I was supposed to walk him round the room in front of the waiting journalists and photographers and then give him the signal to rear up. But Dante was so finely trained and tuned to every movement his handler made that I must have given him the signal by mistake and up he reared straight away! I kept my cool and acted as if I had intended that to happen. Then, later, when I deliberately gave him the signal and he reared up again at my command, it felt amazing.

I thought the shots of me on Dante as he reared up were really striking. But my all-time strangest and most eye-catching press call has to be the one I did to celebrate the fifth anniversary of my company KP Equestrian, and to launch my new show jumps and show jackets, in March 2013. This was where I dressed up as a pink panto horse, a kind of crazy My Little Pony. I wore four dip-dyed shocking pink wigs, furry horse's ears, a t-shirt from my KP Equestrian range, a tutu, furry front legs, sky-high glittery heels, and the rest of the horse was attached to my waist. I think it's no exaggeration to say that I've never seen another celebrity in such a bizarre outfit. I thought it was brilliant, and as I was three months pregnant by then it was the perfect way of concealing my bump.

But my manager and brother thought the horse costume was the worst idea they had ever heard of and were convinced it would damage my image. *Please!* I'm renowned for my outrageous outfits. The more outrageous the better. We had such a row about it that I ended up saying, 'If you don't like it then let's not work together any more, because I know I'm right.' I understand exactly how to work a press call. The sillier you look and the more fun it is, the more attention you will get. I'm not just going to stand there in a show jacket, it's boring! The press want something funny to write about and take the piss out of, and that's exactly what I was going to give them. I knew they'd love it.

Sure enough I got masses of publicity from the stunt.

By the end of it everyone knew that KP Equestrian was five years old, a huge achievement for a company when so many fail in their first year of business. There were plenty of shots published of my new range of show jumps and show jackets, so as far as I was concerned it was a job well done.

I am so proud of KP Equestrian. As you know, riding is my passion and life-long hobby, and to be able to create a business related to that has been such a thrill for me. I had always thought that riding equipment, from clothes to tack to horse accessories, could do with an injection of glamour and glitz. Before KP Equestrian, you only seemed to be able to get clothes in dull greens, blues or browns. So boring! And the same went for horse equipment. I saw a gap in the market for items that were glamorous, feminine, and in bright colours. As the KP Equestrian website says: we are putting glamour into horse riding! We are the fastest-growing equestrian brand. Recently we brought out a pink fly rug and mask, and as one of my friends said, it looked like the horse was a pink Power Ranger. The pink is so bright it can probably be seen by Google Earth. My mission to turn the horse world pink is working!

I am one of the directors of the company, along with Cath Hart, a keen horsewoman with a solid background in retail. After thirty years' experience in the business, she certainly knows her stuff when it comes to sourcing our products and what will sell. We sell online and have stands at some of the biggest horse shows in the country, where we always do a roaring trade. I regularly go along to do signings there and to meet the fans, and it's brilliant to see everyone enjoying the products. I get great satisfaction from seeing all the KP Equestrian carrier bags as I walk round a show. There are always more KP bags than any other brand. At the Olympia Horse Show we are upstairs, which can be death for some stalls because it's thought to be quieter, but we drive business upstairs and are always packed, which is why the organisers don't want us to move downstairs.

The response I get when I go to the signings is very positive. And when I'm not there, the girls who run the store always comment on how much everyone loves the products. There will be people queuing throughout the day to buy something, even if it is only a pair of socks. Though there are some people who will walk by the stand and say to the girls on it, 'Oh my God! Katie Price. I feel sick! How can you work for her?' They might think that they are better than me, but I just think they're rude and bad-mannered and, like I said earlier, it's their loss!

I want to make my range accessible to everyone, and anyone can buy into it because our items start at £5.99 for two pairs of funky socks with slogans, such as *Dressage Queen* and *Queen of Everything*. At the top end are the divine made-to-measure Italian leather riding boots at £500, in pink, gold, red and silver. We do black, but even those are blinged up with patent heels and diamante straps. They are made by the highly renowned Italian manufacturer De Niro and are stunning. These are the boots that I wear. In fact, I wear all the KP Equestrian products.

Along with wanting to inject sparkle into riding gear, I also wanted to bring out products that were affordable and good quality. Equestrian equipment and clothes can be very expensive. Take my show jackets, for example, which are blinged up with pink trim, lining and diamante buttons, and retail for £59.99. Show jackets by other companies can cost up to £200, often more, which I think anyone would agree is a lot of money. Plus our products perform really well, they last a long time and wash well. Whenever we send them to be tested in features for various horsey magazines they always come out with top marks, and we get so many people coming to the stand or commenting on the website that they were surprised and pleased by the quality of our products. Something else that I'm extremely proud of is that Cath has made sure all our products come from ethically tested sources, and we only deal with manufacturers who own their own factories.

We have two seasons, spring and autumn, when we bring out new ranges. I have ardent fans who will buy one of everything as soon as it comes out! And once a range has gone, it's gone, so we can keep everything fresh. We get plenty of orders from customers in Germany, New Zealand and Australia, and I'd love to expand further abroad. The great thing about KP Equestrian is that there are so many products we can bring out. We started with t-shirts and sweatshirts and have branched out from there. And, honestly, not everything is pink. We bring out ranges in blue, white, purple and black. But if an item is black there will be bling on it...and probably a bit of pink somewhere.

Our largest volume of sales still comes from our t-shirts and sweatshirts. I love the cheeky slogans on our t-shirts, such as *Horses are like chocolates, one's just not enough*. And the one that says, *Warning! Horses can seriously damage your wealth*. Yep, both of those slogans ring true with me... Apparently other equestrian companies are starting to take note and there are now riding hats with crystal-encrusted bows on them. I'd like to think that KP Equestrian led the way for glamour in riding. Because who says you have to look boring and dowdy to be taken seriously when you're riding? (Though I would love to know what the horses think of their bright pink rugs...)

My fans have always been so important to me. I know that without their support I wouldn't be where I am today, and on our KP Equestrian website we have a whole page devoted to the pictures they have sent in of themselves wearing KP Equestrian clothes, posing on their own or with their horses sporting KP Equestrian rugs. I love it!

* * *

I enjoy riding now as much as I did when I first started as a little girl aged seven. Riding has always been my escape and it's the best stress-reliever I know. When you're riding, you can't worry about anything else, you are there in the moment and that is such a good feeling. Relationship worries, anxiety about what the press had written about me, all disappear once I'm in the saddle.

Five years ago I decided I wanted to learn dressage. I bought my first horse and had lessons from one of the country's leading dressage riders, Andrew Gould.

I loved learning a new skill; it gave me such a buzz. I was really proud of my achievements, and the highlight was when I performed a dressage set at the Horse of the Year Show in 2008. The show is a big event in the horse world and so it was a huge deal that I performed there. It really was like a dream come true.

Unfortunately my taking up dressage and spending more time riding coincided with the breakdown of my first marriage. Pete never understood why I wanted to spend so much time riding, and why I always returned from the stables and my lessons looking so happy and full of energy. But as anyone who loves riding would immediately understand, it takes up a lot of time, is all-consuming... and makes you feel brilliant afterwards. Also, at that time I was feeling under such pressure from the constant filming we did that going riding was the one time I could switch off and have some space away from work. I can remember going off to the stables and feeling miserable and down because Pete and I weren't getting on, and by the time I'd had a dressage lesson I'd be feeling on top of the world because I had achieved something.

When I moved into my new house with all its surrounding land in 2011, I was able to keep my horses there. I still can't quite believe how lucky I am to be able to look out of my kitchen window and see them in the field. All I have to do is pull on my KP Equestrian riding boots and get out there!

I was also keen to take up a new riding challenge

and recently decided to learn show jumping. I haven't done it for years, but I love it! Show jumping is scary but exhilarating. A real test of courage for rider and horse. You have to remain completely calm as you're approaching a jump and not transmit your nerves to the horse. They are sensitive to a rider's mood, and if the rider is afraid then the horse is going to be as well and will more than likely refuse to make the jump. I have cleared some big jumps, but it's all about the proper technique. You have to be able to control your horse around every part of the course. I took part in a show and got a clear round, which I was proud of. I've been teaching myself mainly, and working with one of my grooms, and I've also had some training from Guy Williams, the international show jumper.

I was really getting into show jumping and making good progress when I became pregnant. My doctor told me it was perfectly safe to continue riding for as long as it felt comfortable to do so, but I suffer from sciatica when I'm pregnant and my back kills me! So I can't do as much as I would like now.

The great thing is that Kieran completely understands my love of riding and fully supports me. He has started riding himself and is surprisingly good – none of us can believe how quickly he has progressed. Princess and Junior have got their own ponies and they both love riding, though Junior is more confident than Princess and able to do more. He goes off riding across the fields with Kieran or else canters round my sand school.

Harvey has also ridden at school. A while ago he had his own mount, but back then he never wanted to ride and so I sold the pony. Now he keeps asking when he can go riding! So I'll let him ride one of the more docile ponies, though of course I will be leading him. It's wonderful that my family share my passion for riding.

CHAPTER 18

BRAND KATIE

PART I: BEAUTY QUEEN

I've never been one of those celebrities who puts their name to a product without knowing anything about it and then walks away with a nice fat fee and never gives it another thought. That's not the way I work. I'll only put my name behind a product or a new business project if I'm one hundred per cent involved at every stage. It has to be something I am passionate about and I have to know something about it. If I don't, I do my research and find out exactly how it works.

The beauty business has long been one of my passions. Even before I was a model I was interested in beauty products and techniques. As a businesswoman, I have brought out a wide range of products, from eyelashes, to hair products, to perfume. I think I must be a frustrated beautician because I have converted an entire room in my house into a salon where I can practise various beauty techniques on my friends and family. They are the Pricey guinea pigs! I've got drawers full of fake lashes, nail products and varnishes, fake tan and waxes. It's a girlie paradise. Maybe one day I'll open my own salon, but for now I want to learn as much as I can about the beauty business. And with that in mind, I've taken a number of courses in various beauty treatments and processes. I've got qualifications and everything! I'm not just a TV personality, author, model (not so much now admittedly, but never say never. I'm still itching to get my kit off for some smoking glamour shots), oh, no. I am also qualified in HD brows. If you thought high-definition only referred to your TV, think again!

HD brows are all about getting the most perfect eyebrow shape possible. So many people spend a fortune on make up and skin care products and yet they ignore their eyebrows, not realising that the brow frames the eyes and face, and that without that frame, well, frankly you're wasting your money!

I've always had a thing about having well-defined eyebrows. From the age of fifteen I started tinting my eyebrows and eyelashes jet black. It drove my mum mad, especially when I combined the black brows with red lipstick and black lip liner and my obsession with wearing catsuits...but there you go, I've always had my own unique style.

I've been on two HD-brow training courses at Milton

Keynes. Nilan Patel is the brains behind the HD brow and is the 'Eyebrow Queen'. She's worked in the States as personal brow-shaper to a number of Hollywood A-listers so I went to the very best place.

I love learning new things and had a great time in Nilan's class. It was like going back to school and I enjoyed mixing with the other students and bantering with them. No one made a big deal of me being there, which I liked. I paid far more attention to that class than I ever did at school, I promise you, and I needed to as it's not just about plucking. The full HD treatment is forty-five minutes, and involves an in-depth consultation, a patch test, tinting, plucking, trimming, waxing and threading. If you have thin eyebrows, with HD brows I can be your eyebrow fairy godmother and give you the gift of fuller, better-shaped brows! Though, as with everything, practice makes perfect and I haven't practised for a while now, so I would probably need a refresher course before I was let loose on anyone again.

Along with brows, I'm also qualified to do eyelash extensions – or, to give it its proper title...drum roll, please...I am a qualified Eyelash Artiste! A while ago I brought out my own range of fake lashes, and I'd like to bring another range out as soon as I've got some new ideas.

I'm also a qualified nail technician. I admit, I am obsessed with having perfect nails. I can go out of the house without a scrap of make up but I *must* have perfect nails. Maybe I'm a bit OCD about them, because when I went on *I'm a Celebrity...Get Me Out of Here!* the second time I didn't use insect repellent because I'd heard that it stripped off your nail polish. I might have stunk to high heaven when I walked off the show, and my six and a half grand hair extensions were ruined, but my nails had survived everything the jungle had thrown at me. I'd like to say that now I'm qualified I do my own nails, but I don't. Sure, I can paint them but, again, I haven't had time or enough friends and family to practise my acrylic nail skills on. One of the episodes of my reality series showed me trying them out on Leo – so he was good for something then...only joking!

I want to bring out my own range of nail products and the equipment you need to use with Gelish or acrylic nails, and make them affordable for younger women to buy. Plus I want to bring out my own range of nail varnishes.

I've also completed and passed a spray-tan course with Crazy Angel. I am Katie Price, licensed to spray and the proud owner of one massive spray gun, one smaller one, and a range of different tans. I've given spray tans to all my friends and family and I'm pretty nifty at it. But in the process I've managed to wreck my white carpet...even while using the special spray-tan tent. Grrrr. Now I've done the course I want to bring out my own line of fake-tan products. And you can trust me: along with my new tanning expertise, I've been using fake tan long enough to know what works.

But that's not all. My next plan is to do a couple more

courses in facials and then in massage – though I know the massage course will be challenging as you need to learn about all the different muscle groups – as I want to bring out a skin-care range. That's the beautiful thing about the beauty industry: there are so many products you can create!

So, as you can see, beauty is definitely my thing. My other passion is fragrance. I've already brought out three perfumes, Besotted, Stunning and Precious Love, and in July 2013 there's a new one out. It's called Kissable and appropriately I'm launching it on National Kissing Day. I absolutely love the scent! Love it! I ran out of all the testers the manufacturers sent me and had to keep asking them for more. To find the one I wanted I had to test out over forty scents. After each sample I had to take a quick sniff of coffee beans to refresh my olfactory sense – clear my nose – otherwise I'd overload on perfume. I took ages narrowing down my choice, and in the end Kissable was a mix of the two scents I loved the most.

PART II: FASHION QUEEN

Lingerie is another of my passions. I'm obsessed with it – and can't get enough of it! A few years ago I had a lingerie range with the label Panache, which was really successful, but when Pete left they dropped me. So I left it for a couple of years and then I brought out my own lingerie range – in bright, fun, flirty colours, of course. I actually did a photo call with Leo, thinking that I would give him a chance to prove what he could do work-wise. He might have looked good lounging in bed but he still managed to irritate me! I had given him instructions not to do anything other than lie in bed because if he did anything provocative or silly, that would be the photograph the press ended up using. So what does he do? As I'm posing by the bed, he leans towards me looking as if he's going to grab my arse! Like something out of a *Carry on* film! And that of course is the one the press used. I've had more professionalism from the many horses I've posed with.

If it glitters you know I'm going to love it, and in 2012 I launched my own line of costume jewellery with Love Lemonade. I chose glitzy crystal pieces that would be affordable for my fans, including necklaces and bracelets and crystal-encrusted lip-shaped clutch bags. To die for! I did a press call in London and it was all about white and glitz and glamour, so I was in a white leotard robe, thigh-high boots trimmed with marabou, a tiara, and a whole load of my crystal bangles on my arm. The *Daily Mail* said that I looked like a cross between a Vegas Showgirl and a bride. I take that as a compliment! Vegas Showgirls have amazing bodies!

Then in December I showcased KP Rocks at the Clothes Show in Birmingham, posing for press pictures and doing a signing. It went really well. Afterwards, as I walked round the show, I passed by Amy Childs' stand. She happens to be represented by my ex-manager. And who should be sitting at the till but Claire Powell? It had been three months since we filed high court papers against her and Pete for breach of confidence. She looked straight at me and I felt a moment of pure satisfaction when I saw how haggard she looked. I hoped that the impending court case was giving her some sleepless nights, as it had me. And I loved it when I saw that there were no queues at the stand, in contrast to mine which was buzzing. I didn't say anything. There is no point in speaking to someone who clearly doesn't care what they do to me.

It was only the second time I had seen Claire since Pete left. The first time had been in 2011, when I had taken Harvey to visit Pete for an hour. I had told the lawyers that I wouldn't take him if Claire Powell was going to be present, but there she was in Pete's kitchen, folding up his clean clothes. That was before I even knew about the situation with Jamelah, and it still stopped me in my tracks to see Claire standing in front of me, the woman I had blamed, and still blame, for the break-up of my marriage. It would have been easy then to tell her exactly what I thought of her and, God, it was tempting...but instead I killed her with kindness and made smalltalk.

Amy Childs also had a jewellery range at that time, which she was doing through a company I've always liked. They had asked me to do a range with them and I had gone to their London store and picked out all the pieces that I liked and even tweeted that we were going to collaborate. And then when Andrew, my manager, discussed the deal with them, it became obvious that it wasn't what it seemed. And I said, 'Oh my God! Do they think we're stupid! I would never do that deal with them, never, ever, ever!' And when Amy signed up with them, I thought, I bet she's getting paid practically nothing. It's all very well bringing out products or endorsing them, but you have to earn money from them or what's the point? It was the same with the sports label Lonsdale. I was going to do a deal with them, but the money and terms just weren't good enough. Then Amy Childs signs up with them, and I know the money she got for it.

But on to happier thoughts – I'm also bringing out my own range of wedding dresses. I feel I've done my research on this as well! I've been married three times, and have had five weddings, if you count the wedding blessings I had first with Alex, then Kieran, so I have worn five dresses … probably four more wedding dresses than most people.

When I married Pete, my dress was made by the haute-couture designer Isabell Kristensen, the creator of many glamorous and dazzling red-carpet creations for celebrities. I had told her that I wanted to look like a princess for my wedding day, and it had to be a fairy-tale dress: big, sparkling and pink! And, boy, I got it! Every time I had a fitting for the dress, I can remember saying that I wanted it bigger, with even more sparkle. It turned out to be a show-stopper, encrusted with thousands of Swarovski crystals – apparently it took twelve people over three weeks to hand stitch them all on. It was three metres wide with a seven-metre-long train. Because the bodice was entirely made of rose-pink crystals it was very heavy to wear. I can remember feeling exhausted by the end of the night. It was also staggeringly expensive; I reckon I could probably have bought a house for what it cost me. Now I look back and think that was an insane amount of money to spend on a dress I only wore once.

When I married Alex in Vegas, I bought my wedding dress off the peg from a wedding boutique, a couple of hours before tying the knot. Talk about last-minute – I didn't even have time to try it on first! I loved it on sight, and buying it in such a rush seemed to fit in with the spontaneous, romantic feeling of that Vegas wedding. I wouldn't recommend it, though; taking your time choosing your perfect dress is one of the lovely things about planning a wedding.

I'm bringing out three dresses to start with and I'm calling it the Royale Collection. I came up with the concept and the names and styles of the dresses. There will be the Queen Dress, which is modelled on the one I wore when I married Kieran, with a striking feather-trimmed bodice; the Princess, a gorgeous full-skirted style; and the Duchess, a fitted dress with a skirt trimmed with feathers.

I'm having the launch later this year. I mentioned my plans to bring out the wedding dresses on Twitter, just after I married Kieran, and had a great response. Of course I've been busy dreaming up ideas for the launch, to make the photo-shoot as eye-catching as possible.

The dresses will be sold initially through the wedding boutique at Rookery Manor, Somerset, and then we'll go out to the bridal exhibitions.

But that's not all! Before my bridal range launches, I'm bringing out a range of crystal-encrusted shoes, corsets and handbags. And no doubt by the time this book is published in October 2013, I'll have dreamed up even more ideas for Katie Price products.

CHAPTER 19

LOVE AGAIN

Even after my two failed marriages and the break-up with Leo, I still believed in love, still believed that there was a perfect man out there for me. I wanted a soulmate, someone who loved me as much as I loved them. I wanted a man to get down on one knee and propose before sweeping me off my feet. I'm the all or nothing sort.

By this stage I knew myself well enough to realise that the single life was not for me. I hated not having someone in my life to love and to love me. I wanted to meet someone I could commit to, heart, body and mind. I wanted that loving family unit. And I wanted to have more children. But I had learned some harsh lessons through my relationships with Alex and Leo, when they had moved in with me and I had started out wanting to be with them all the time. That doesn't work if the relationship is one-sided. To be my ideal match the man has to have his own career, his own interests. Also, my friends have told me that whenever I meet a guy, I want to buy them things, and treat them, and set up this chain of expectation that I will always do that – and that's when they end up taking advantage. So the next one had to be different...*Please God*, he had to be different!

My friend Phil texted me in October 2012: *Kate, there's a guy I know who really wants your number. Is it okay for me to give it to him? He's called Kieran and he's a really nice guy, I've known him three years. He's been asking me for the last year, he's driving me mad! What d'you reckon?* He went on to tell me that Kieran had worked as a topless waiter, and was a plasterer and part-time stripper, so at least he worked!

I reckoned, why not? I wasn't seeing anyone, though I was having a bit of flirtatious banter with a couple of guys. To be honest, I don't know how anyone can be a major player. It's such hard work keeping on top of it all when you have these guys constantly texting you and have to remember what you said and to whom! I asked Phil if Kieran had BBM, because the good thing about that is that you can give someone your BBM PIN and they won't have your phone number so if you decide you've had enough of them, you can just delete them. It turned out he did. But before I was willing to hand over my PIN, I had to check what Kieran looked like so I asked Phil to send me a picture. Good-looking as he was, I just thought, Oh, yet another muscular, fit guy. Gary and Phil know loads of guys with that look. I thought, I don't want another one; I've just got rid of one like that! As I knew only too well from my experience with Leo, looks weren't everything…But because Phil said that Kieran was such a nice guy, I thought, Well, I'm not with anyone, it's just BBM, it will only be a bit of banter, I may as well give him my PIN.

So Kieran started messaging me and I thought, Yeah, he seems nice. And he was so full on! Constantly sending me messages. The thing about BBM is that you know when the message has been delivered and you know when it's been read, so sometimes I would read his message and not reply and he would instantly message me again, saying, *I know you've read my message, so why aren't you replying?*

Bloody hell! He doesn't stop! I thought, but I liked the attention. He kept asking when he could meet me, saying that he really wanted to see me, and how much he had always liked me. And I suppose I was playing a bit hard to get so I'd reply that I was busy at the moment. But that didn't deter him, he would reply with, *Well, when* can *I see you then?*

Jesus Christ! You don't stop, do you! I'm busy, I'm not sure when I'm free, I'd reply. But he was so persistent and every day he would be on my case.

I'd call Kieran The Stripper to my friends, and say, 'That stripper guy doesn't stop!' And it got to the point where I thought, OMG, I'm going to delete him from my BBM contacts. This is too much. I'm enjoying the flirtation, but this is too full on – and that's saying something coming from me…Also, he hasn't even met me! He might not like me if he did.

And so I deleted him. Straight away he rang me up (I guess he must have got my number from Phil) and said, 'Have you just deleted me?'

Shit! He'd caught me red-handed. I pretended that I hadn't, being a big softie at heart and not wanting to upset him. And as we spoke on the phone I thought, Actually, you're all right. You've got a sense of humour like me, which I'd never expected. I really liked the way he sounded.

So when he asked again if we could meet, I thought, Why not? I've got nothing to lose by it. We spoke on the phone and I questioned him about what he did, where he lived and what he liked doing, just to see if there was any connection there. And I felt there was definitely something. We could banter; I liked his dry humour. It reminded me of the TV programme Snog, Marry, Avoid, where if I had only seen a photograph of him I would have thought he was so into himself and vain. And people probably look at me and think, She's so fake, she's got no personality, she's thick and easy. But when we talked it was different, there was a connection.

It's funny looking back and seeing how blasé I was about meeting Kieran, when he was going to be the man who was finally going to sweep me off my feet…the man I had always dreamed of. I decided to ask him over that night as I had friends staying and they could vet him for me. I didn't have Princess and Junior with me, so that wasn't an issue, and Harvey would be in bed. I decided I wasn't even going to make much of an effort. I never really do at home so I decided to wear trackies and hardly had any make up. If he was expecting to get the glammed up, boobs out Katie Price he could dream on. He was going to get the natural-looking Katie Price. I was just going to see how it went, no pressure.

But as I was getting ready, and the time was getting closer to him arriving, I realised that I was looking forward to meeting him. We had got on well when we spoke on the phone and I was half excited, half nervous.

When he arrived, I made sure that I was upstairs and my friends Mikey and Ross let him in. I texted Mikey to ask him what Kieran was like. I already knew that he was twenty-five and over six foot tall.

Does he smell good? I asked. *And what's he wearing?*

They completely wound me up by saying that he was in a pink onesie. Cheeky bastards! Surely they weren't serious? For a moment I actually believed them, and thought, oh, no! He must be a knob! But then Mikey came up to my room and admitted that they were taking the piss, that Kieran was really nice, that he looked good and smelled great. *And* that the poor guy was really nervous. I thought, I'm so cruel, making him wait!

So I went downstairs and met him. I was really surprised when I saw him as I thought, OMG! You really are good-looking – and you're really fit! He was muscular and thick-set. I absolutely love that look. Leo had been muscular but wiry...not so good. Kieran was chunky and ripped. He had a perfect body, from what I could tell. And I loved the fact that he was so tall. Pete had been a bit lacking in that department. Whenever we went out and I was in heels, Pete would put tissues in his shoes to make himself look taller than me, otherwise we would have been the same height. (Sorry, I couldn't resist putting that in!)

Kieran dressed exactly how I like men to dress, really bang on trend with that boy-band look. And he smelled delicious, I've always been into fragrance. Actually he was way better looking than I'd imagined he'd be. Head to toe fit in every way.

We all chatted for a while and then I got everyone into my cinema room for a thriller marathon that included *Eden Lake* and *Orphan*. Because of my dry humour, I'm not really into comedy, and the only romantic films I really like are *The Notebook* and *My Best Friend's Wedding*. Thrillers are what I really prefer. As I sat next to Kieran it was exactly like the scene in the film *Grease,* where Danny doesn't know whether to put his arm round Sandy but he really wants to. And I thought, What the hell! I'm single, why don't I just cuddle up to him? And as I did so, I thought, Wow! He is absolutely fit.

He had the most ripped body ever! I could feel ridges of muscle in his biceps and abs. Impressive! He must really work out to have achieved that. I loved how strong and solid he felt. You know how when you cuddle someone you either match or you don't? Well, this felt as if we were completely compatible. We didn't kiss, but we stayed cuddling up until four in the morning. And then he had to go because he had to get ready for work at six. I didn't let him stay, not that he asked.

When Kieran left I was thinking about him for a long time. He had made quite an impression. His looks were perfect and I really liked his personality. But he seemed quite shy and quiet, and I wondered if he might be too quiet for me. Overall, though, I thought he was gorgeous. Really gorgeous. And I wanted to see him again. I had started out thinking that this was going to be no big deal, a bit of fun, a bit of male attention. But it was already more than that.

But there was a problem. Later that day my sister came round and she said, 'Oh, yeah, so you had that stripper guy up here last night, didn't you?'

'How did you know?' I asked, taken by surprise by her question as I hadn't told anyone except the friends who were with me that Kieran was coming round.

'Well, obviously he's been talking,' she replied.

Instantly I felt disappointed. It turned out that Kieran had told his mum that he was meeting me, she had then told her boyfriend, who had told someone else, and so on. This had happened to me so many times before...Next thing I knew it would be in the press, which was the last thing I wanted.

So I texted Kieran. *Have you been talking about us? I'm not into all that. Who have you told?*

Instantly he texted back asking me to call him. I didn't reply. Then he tried calling me but I cut off the calls. I thought, Fuck you, you've ruined it now, you've obviously opened your mouth; you've got no chance with me. I liked you and this has put me right off you. I was so relieved things had gone no further than a cuddle. I was really angry and disappointed.

I've only told my mum! he texted me. And then he said that he'd had a real go at her for telling someone else. I still didn't know whether to see him again, but he sent me a huge bouquet of flowers with a card saying, *I'm never going to disappoint you or let you down again.* It was a sweet gesture and as he sounded genuinely upset by what had happened, I thought, Maybe I'll give him a second chance...

He came round to my house again. Because he seemed quiet I thought it would be easier to have a film on rather than sit on the sofa together, in case there were any awkward silences, so once again we hung out in my cinema room. I couldn't tell you what the film was because my whole attention was on him. This time we kissed. And a very good kiss it was too. I've always thought you can tell a lot about a man from the way he kisses and get a very good idea about what he is going to be like in bed...and from the way Kieran kissed me, I thought I was going to be in for a treat.

All the time I was falling for him. I had the idea in my head that I would stick to the five-date rule, and not sleep with him until then. We lasted until the third date. I fancied him like crazy and I knew he felt the same about me. I won't go into details, because of course he is now my husband and I respect him. When I saw his body, I was not disappointed. It is perfect. And put it this way: no woman would ask for their money back if they went to see him stripping! He doesn't shave so he doesn't have red rashes all over him; he's got hair on his arms and legs like a normal man (other men I have been with have shaved theirs, which I hated). He uses clippers on his chest and in other areas, so it certainly doesn't look like plucked chicken down there ... I've had that experience as well in my time. So all I will say is that he was fit in every sense of the word!

Kieran's body is a temple. I found out he's a complete fitness freak; he works out all the time and has a really healthy life-style. He doesn't take steroids or anything else to get that perfect body, and hardly ever drinks. And he had met me when I was completely sober, which felt good. I wasn't out on a wild one; I was at home, being myself.

Does it bother me that he is a stripper? Not at all. If anything I was intrigued that someone as quiet as he is could do something so extrovert. Before I saw the show I would tease him in front of my friends and say, 'Go on, get your kit off!' And he refused, saying that he only ever did that on-stage, he didn't do it any other time. That impressed me. I know I'm a terrible wind-up merchant but he's always stood up to me. Even if I went to lift his top and said, 'Come on, show us your abs,' he wouldn't.

Of course I had to see his show for myself. He's not the kind of stripper you see coming into a pub and getting their kit off. The audience can't take photographs and nor can women touch the performers. It's a proper choreographed show, with three strippers and a drag queen. When I saw it for the first time I was so nervous for him, because I couldn't imagine him taking all his clothes off in public, he just didn't seem the type. I already knew women wouldn't be disappointed with what they saw, and I had learned about the stripper's tricks of the trade. They use a cock pump before the show (who knows if that's the right term!), which gets the blood pumped into the relevant part, and then they have to tie an elastic band at the top to keep it in. It f****** hurts, according to Kieran. But like all good performers he suffers for his art.

The show isn't sleazy at all. It's very tongue-in-cheek, light-hearted, with plenty of comedy. There's also great music, which you can sing along to, and the guys wear all these different outfits, like a gorilla suit, Scooby-Doo, a fireman's uniform, a sailor suit. But not for long... everything comes off. They get girls up on-stage and do silly things with them, like wrap themselves up in Clingfilm then get the girls to spray whipped cream on them and lick it off. But like I said, it isn't sleazy, it's funny.

The first time I saw the show, if someone had been

filming me and my friends you would have seen that our mouths were open in complete amazement and our jaws practically on the floor because the Kieran in front of us was so completely different from the one we knew. And as I watched him strut around the stage and strip off, inside I was thinking, Yes! Get in there, my son! You've got it in you. And I realised that I liked him even more because he could be this extrovert performer and he wasn't afraid. And because he wasn't like that off-stage, he wasn't cocky or vain, he was just a regular, lovely guy.

So we started seeing each other and we were getting on so well, *ridiculously* well, to the point that when I wasn't with him, I was thinking about him non-stop and getting butterflies and wanting to be with him! Was I worried about the age gap? To be honest I didn't think the nine years made any difference at all, because I think I'm quite a young thirty-five and he's quite a mature twenty-six. It wasn't as if I was in my late forties and he was in his early twenties. That really would be a big gap.

I was a bit worried that my mum would freak when she realised I was seeing someone, so at first we pretended that Kieran was gay. Funnily enough, no one questioned that, probably because he is so immaculate-looking! Even so, Kieran had only been in the house thirty seconds when she presented him with a confidentiality agreement to sign. That's typical of my mum, being so protective of me. And nor can you fool her for long. She quickly cottoned on that he wasn't gay.

However, even though we were getting on so well, I wondered if I should be committing myself to another relationship again. Maybe it was too soon after Leo. For once I thought: I shouldn't rush into things, I should see how it goes, not get caught up in a whirlwind romance, take it more slowly. But then I had a wake-up call. I nearly lost Kieran.

It was one night early in December and we were both up in London. Kieran had been performing and I'd had work commitments during the day, and was due to work the following day too, so I'd booked into a hotel. I planned to go and see a film and then meet up with Kieran in my suite. But then my friend Phil called and said there was some event or other at Mahiki, the club on Dover Street.

'Actually, I'm not really dressed for it,' I told him, 'I'm just wearing jeans.'

'Oh, pop in for a quick one,' he suggested.

I agreed but insisted it could only be a quick one as Kieran was back at the hotel and I didn't want to keep him waiting. I did call Kieran and told him I was going to be about half an hour and asked if he wanted to meet us there. But as it was only going to be for such a short time, he said he'd wait for me at the hotel.

I don't know what happened, but the one cocktail I had at Mahiki turned into a complete bender. I was out all night and half the next day. Possibly my drink was spiked, I don't know, but the whole night was a blur. Apparently, after Mahiki I ended up at Balans with

Charlotte Church's ex-husband, the rugby player Gavin Henson, and a group of other people. And I carried on drinking. I don't know how I did it as I'm such a lightweight. I can honestly say that nothing happened with Gavin. There was probably a bit of flirtatious banter, nothing more. But I was still at Balans at 11.30 a.m. the following morning, and after that we all went back to Gavin's friend's house.

It was a completely mad, lost night. My PR woman had to come and collect me and take me back to the hotel. Kieran had gone and I felt awful. I couldn't even call him as I seemed to have lost my phone. I collapsed into bed and slept for hours. When I woke up my sister was there with her boyfriend, along with my PA, but I still wasn't in a fit state to talk, and only managed to have a bath before going back to bed. That day I was supposed to be working on my *Sun* column and it was the first time in my career I think that I've ever missed work because I was hungover. I felt terrible for letting people down; it was so out of character. But worst of all was knowing that I'd stood Kieran up. What must he think of me?

I had dropped my phone in the hotel lobby and when it was returned to me by one of the staff the battery was flat. When I'd charged it, I saw that I had heaps of messages from my friends and from my manager, wondering what the hell I'd been doing. I discovered that Kieran had spent last night calling my friends and saying, 'Why has she left me like this? I can't believe

Gazing into each other's eyes…

Kieran and me. I'm so busy pouting I haven't spotted the wardrobe malfunction…

Top: Keeping cool! Junior, Kieran and Princess.
Above: Pulling faces with my little monsters, Princess, Junior and Kieran.

Left: Kieran loving the snow on his stag do in Berlin. . . in costume of course!

My very generous friend Tanya chartered a boat for us all the day after I married Kieran! (Left to right: Kieran, my mum Amy, Kieran's mum Wendy, me, Jane, Tanya and Derek.)

Top: My new husband and me making the most of the Jacuzzi!

Right: Posing on deck.

Top left: I do! I do! I do!

Top right: Mr and Mrs Hayler! My smile says it all, I am so happy!

Above: I've saved the best till last. A perfect moment on our wedding blessing.

You know me, I like everything big, which is why I had 12 bridesmaids! And two flower girls, my Princess and Jane's Ruby.

March Bride! It was a freezing cold day! But who cares about the weather when you are marrying the man of your dreams.

Inviting everyone to come on up to the dance floor. The entertainment was brilliant!

Clockwise from top left: Wedding fireworks!

My beautiful Princess.

His and hers rings…of course mine are bigger!

Harvey and me. He loved the wedding and stayed up all night dancing!

Ouch! True love! Kieran has our initials tattooed on his ring finger.

The party begins!

My man and me. I have found my happy ever after.

My dad, Ray, my brother, Daniel, my step dad, Paul, Kieran and Kieran's dad.

My mum and Princess sharing a hug.

My gorgeous little girl.

she's done this to me.' I felt awful hearing that. Really ashamed. I imagined how I would have felt in his place. I know that if he had done that to me, I would have told him it was over.

I left it a day before I got in touch with him, figuring he might need some time to cool down. When I texted him asking him if he was okay he didn't reply for a while and then he wrote back, *No.*

Shit! I thought. I've lost him now. And I admitted to myself that I really liked him and didn't want to lose him. Then we spoke on the phone and he was short and offhand with me. Part of me thought, Well, I'm not going to grovel! But the other part liked it that he wasn't running after me. I was in the wrong and he was letting me know that. We arranged to meet up at my house and I still felt very bad for the way I had treated him. He told me that he had been so angry with me that if I had called him any earlier than I did, he would have told me he didn't want to see me again. Wow, that really shocked me.

After I'd said sorry about ten times, I said, 'I hadn't committed to you as a boyfriend when I went out the other night, but even so the way I behaved is no way to treat anyone. I feel terrible for what I did and I swear I don't know how I got into such a state. But I promise I will make it up to you.' And as we spoke I realised that this was my wake-up call and that there was no way I was letting Kieran go. From that moment we made a commitment to each other. This was no casual fling, no rebound relationship. This felt like the real thing.

The press had a field day linking me with Gavin Henson, but absolutely nothing happened between us and if anyone says differently then my drink must have been spiked because I don't remember anything. They made out it was just the two of us, yet the truth is we were surrounded by a group of friends. One paper said that we had done a photo shoot together, which was completely untrue. Anyway, as I've said, I'm so used to them printing bullshit lies, it's like water off a duck's back.

*   *   *

I'd always said to myself, after my experiences with Alex and Leo, that the next man I was with had to have more than me, but yet again it hasn't happened, and it doesn't make any difference to the way I feel about him. The feelings I have for Kieran are very similar to the ones I had when I first met Pete: it's a complete whirlwind passionate romance, as if we were always meant to be together.

Kieran and I realised we wanted to be with each other all the time. It felt so right. I thought, Oh my God! He's actually perfect, he goes to work and pays his way. It is a physical and emotional attraction. Basically I struck gold! Kieran is a lovely guy, through and through. He's a clever little soul and did well at school. You can tell he's been well brought up as he's got good manners and is respectful.

The only worry I had about him was that he was too

quiet for me. I'm such a loud mouth myself and have always gone out with men who are equally as loud. But as we got to know each other better in the weeks that followed I realised that Kieran wasn't quiet or shy, it was more that he was thoughtful. He didn't just come out with the first thing that came into his head, for the sake of speaking and because he loved the sound of his own voice. Hmm, not like some of my exes then...And so when he spoke it made more of an impact. Typically we will be sitting having dinner with my friends and family and everyone will be chatting away, and when Kieran says something they all sit up and take notice because what he's said is worth hearing. I always say he's silent but deadly, he speaks only when he needs to.

Of course I wanted to know all about his exes. It's like I have to torture myself. Deep down I don't want to know the answer, but I still have to ask the question! I wanted to know all about his ex-girlfriend, and why they split, and who else he'd been out with, and what his type was. I wanted to know all about the competition I faced...And as I was asking all these questions and winding myself up, I thought, Bloody hell, you must really like him! I thought it might be strange for him because he'd know who I'd been married to, and who I'd been out with, but as we talked about our pasts it seemed he didn't know that much! He hadn't read any of my autobiographies or watched my TV programmes. But he admitted that he had always fancied me! See, the Pricey still has it. What was more I trusted Kieran and felt he trusted me. Leo had driven me mad by always wanting to know where I was going and who I was texting. I think he was obsessed with me because he had nothing else happening in his life, and that's why I felt so suffocated and trapped by him. My life was his life. But with Kieran our relationship is so trusting, I could leave my phone out and he could go through all my texts and it wouldn't bother me in the slightest. And it's the same for him.

And he actually had a job. OMG! A man I was with actually worked and earned money. So we weren't joined at the hip, he didn't rely on me for everything.

Kieran gets up at six every morning to go to work, then he goes to the gym, and then every Saturday night he has his stripping show. So he is the first guy I've been with who has kept two jobs. And from thinking that I wanted to be with a guy who had as much money as me, I realised that I liked Kieran having a normal job. Men with money think they can buy you. I've been on a few dates with rich men and, to be honest, I've always found them more tight-fisted than men who don't have much money – probably because the guys with less money have to make more of an effort.

I soon discovered that Kieran is also the most romantic guy I've ever been out with. He takes me out to dinner and pays, he takes me to the cinema and pays, and he always buys me flowers. Early on he treated me to a box at the musical of *The Bodyguard*. He is always thinking of me. He knows I love different fragrances.

Recently I happened to mention that I couldn't wait to go to America to get this particular perfume I love called Bijan, because you can only buy it there, and the next thing I knew a bottle of it arrived! He had ordered it for me. It's little gestures like that which mean so much to me. If I'm ill, when I wake up he's laid out all the medicines on the pillow next to me. He is so sweet!

So I feel really spoiled by Kieran and I buy nice things for him as well, but I don't feel that I have to in the way I did with others in the past. I told him that I've spoiled every man I've ever been with, especially Pete. I bought him watches, clothes, cars. It was the same with Alex and Leo, I bought them clothes, treated them to nights out and holidays, so they never had to put their hand in their pocket. When I met Kieran my friends told me not to buy him anything, but to let him treat me. I told him that I've been burned so badly by buying guys everything they want that I'm not going to do it again, but maybe that's a good thing... Ironically Kieran is the guy who deserves to be treated the most!

And, most important of all, when he met the kids he was brilliant with all of them. He was especially good with Harvey, really patient and calm with him. Kieran's mum used to do respite foster care for autistic children, so he was used to being around children with special needs. I always feel like he's backing me up with the children. It's not that he's trying to be a father figure, just to support me. For instance, if they don't do as they're told, he'll calmly say, 'Okay, well, if you don't go to bed now, I'll take your iPad away.' And it works with them. And whenever we're getting ready to go somewhere and I'm rushing around, trying to hurry everyone up and shouting, Kieran will stay laidback and quietly get everyone into the car. We complement each other very well.

He seems to have a good grasp of managing his money and is good at saving. When I met him he'd just bought his own place, which I think is impressive for a twenty-six year old. He was really looking forward to moving in, and then of course we got married and he moved in with me! Apparently he had been working non-stop to save up for the deposit and hadn't had a holiday for three years. All that grafting and saving is, I think, the sure sign of a good man. I cannot bear someone who is lazy. Nothing winds me up more than someone who expects to have something for nothing. And I've had first-hand experience of that for many years...I am used to paying for everything, and in a way I don't like to take anything from anyone because then I end up feeling that I owe them. But I'm getting better at letting Kieran pay. Although he's no millionaire, he dotes on me exactly the way a girl wants a man to. He's thoughtful, considerate and romantic. He told me that along with saving for the flat, he had savings to give him some security...and then he met me, bought me diamonds, and said his plan has completely gone to pot! I genuinely believe that he would give his last penny to me.

Plus, and this is a big one for me, we have lots of

banter together and a real laugh. But he can also put me in my place and won't put up with any of my shit at all, and I like that. For instance, if we're out together and I say I want to stay out longer, he'll say, 'No, you're coming home now.' And I respect him and listen to him, which I haven't done with anybody before — even if I said I did, I didn't.

And, very importantly, I'm a real family person and Kieran is as family-minded as me. I really got on with his family from the moment I met them. I felt I could be myself with them, and that his mum accepted me, and it was a comforting, reassuring feeling to know I didn't have to put on an act. I can go to their house and chill and feel as if I've known them for ages. And Kieran gets on equally well with my family. For the first time *ever* my mum and step-dad get on with my partner's mum and family, so they can socialise together. They have things in common, and that makes such a difference and is such a good feeling!

CHAPTER 20

THIRD TIME LUCKY

Within weeks we knew what we had was special, a once-in-a-lifetime relationship. I know people will be cynical and say, yeah, yeah, we've heard it all before from you, when you met Pete. And, yes, you did, but so what? You can fall in love more than once! And I know that everyone will think, But of course you were crazy about Kieran! Everyone feels like that when they fall for someone in the early weeks, it's the honeymoon period. I get that, but I also know when I've met The One. And with Kieran it was a proper, true-life whirlwind romance, a match made in heaven.

By early December 2012 we knew we wanted to get married and as soon as we possibly could. There was no big proposal. He didn't get down on one knee, whip out a ring and ask me; instead we both talked about it and agreed that's what we wanted. It seemed like the natural thing to do. I knew that I was in love with Kieran and that I was in a good place. My wedding with Pete had been ruined as I was suffering from post-natal depression; I had married Alex on the rebound. But now I was completely happy.

In late December Kieran and I were on our way to a meeting with Andrew, my manager, at his house in Weston-super-Mare. Funnily enough, though we didn't know it then, this would turn out to be near the venue where we had the blessing for our marriage. We were chatting about our wedding plans.

'Do you realise you haven't even proposed properly yet?' I commented, jokingly.

Instantly Kieran whipped a candy ring out of a packet of Haribos and said, 'Kate, will you marry me?' Resourceful guy, my man.

And when I said, 'Yes,' he slipped it on to my finger. A cute gesture, though as you can imagine I wanted a bling ring. I mean, I like Haribos – but I like diamonds a lot more.

I already knew how generous Kieran was, and how he was always spoiling me, but when it came to my engagement ring, he completely took me by surprise. We were out shopping and happened to wander into a jewellery store. My eye was instantly caught by a picture of an absolutely gorgeous diamond engagement ring. I think it's called a Princess setting, and it was a whopping square-cut diamond set in a glittering diamond band. I asked the assistant if they had the ring at that store, and they did. I tried it on and it was love at first sight. It was completely me. But I had absolutely no expectation that Kieran would buy it. Just as we were leaving, he said he had to ask the assistant something and the next thing I knew he had bought the ring for me! I was absolutely thrilled. Really blown away by his generosity, and by how romantic it was.

We kept our wedding plans to ourselves at first, knowing that everyone would say it was too soon, that we were rushing into it, that we didn't know each other, all the usual things. But I'm not nuts. I take risks. I've said it before and I'll say it again: I live life how I want to live it, there is no rulebook telling you how you should live. If you're in love, you're in love. And I was absolutely one hundred per cent head over heels in love with Kieran.

He is the loveliest guy you could ever meet: caring, kind, funny. It helps that he's gorgeous, but it's not just about his looks, it's his character too. I really do feel complete with him, protected and looked after. That feeling of insecurity I've always had with other men, I don't have with Kieran. I feel more content now than I've ever been. And a confession: I'm so relaxed with him that I even fart when he's in the room. I've never done that in front of a man before! Okay, that's not going to make it inside a Valentine's Day card, 'I love you so much I can fart in front of you,' but it shows how relaxed I am with him.

Around Christmas we started to break the news to everyone that we were tying the knot. Kieran did the old-fashioned thing of asking for my hand from my step-dad. He got a thumbs-up from Paul and a lecture about how, if he wanted to keep me, he would always have to work, and that he mustn't let me walk all over him and give in to me, or I would end up treating him like a little dog on a lead and he'd be gone…Hmm, sounds harsh! But probably true…and only my family could get away with saying something like that.

Kieran told his mum and she was really happy for him. They have a close relationship so she knew that if he wanted to marry me he really was in love with me. I broke the news to my mum, telling her, 'I'm doing it whatever you think, Mum. I don't have to explain myself to anyone. We're both adults and, even if no one thinks we should, we're doing it.' She's so used to me doing things my way that she just rolled her eyes and said, 'Well, if you don't mean it this time, don't do it! And you had better make this one last. And, by the way, this will be the last wedding of yours I come to.'

But we didn't fall out over it. She really likes Kieran and thinks he is the best man I have been with. She likes the way he's so normal and grounded and that he works. I don't even think she minds about him being a stripper, because it's work and means he's not relying on me.

And when I told Princess and Junior they were both excited as they really like Kieran. I think people worry because I have been married before, and have the impression that my children have been introduced to my partners too quickly. But the fact is, whenever Kieran first came to my house, either the children weren't with me, or there was always a group of my friends there, so they would think he was just another friend. They weren't introduced to him initially as my boyfriend so that they could gradually get to know him. And the only other men they've had in their life, apart from their dad, have been Alex, who I was married to, and Leo, who I was with for nearly two years. And that was over the course of four years... it's not like there was a different man every month!

We held a little party at my house, where I met all Kieran's friends, and announced our engagement then. Everyone congratulated us, and seemed genuinely happy for us. I think they could see how into each other we were. You can tell a lot about a person from their friends and all of Kieran's were lovely, and a lot of them were in couples and around my age. They were all educated, friendly people with good manners.

We wanted to get married in January, as soon as we possibly could, though we didn't tell anyone at this stage. We planned to have a tiny ceremony with only our mums present, along with three of my closest friends, Jane, Derek and Tanya. There was no point in waiting; the big question was, where? We both thought it would be great to get married on a beach. I imagined beautiful white sand, hot sunshine, the ocean, a private idyllic setting. What could be more romantic? I wanted to go to the Maldives because I absolutely love it out there, but we discovered that you can't legally get married, you can only have a blessing. And at other places we considered there seemed to be so many rules and regulations about how long you had to stay there before you got married and we didn't have much time, as both Kieran and I had work commitments.

Then I remembered that my friend Michelle Heaton had got married at a Sandals resort in the Bahamas. She had sold the pictures to *OK!* magazine and the place looked stunning. I asked her if it had been private and she said it was (although it may well have been that she bought a private package). From the pictures and Michelle's description it didn't seem that we could get anywhere better than that, so we went ahead and booked our wedding at the Royal Bahamian Resort and Spa, a different resort from Michelle's but it looked just as lovely. The brochure and website made the place out to be idyllic, with gorgeous white-sand private beaches. And the package was going to be all inclusive. Our whole wedding would be planned for us. The hotel arranges the ceremony, the flowers, the food and photographer. It would be completely stress-free. It seemed too good to be true. Unfortunately, as we found out when we arrived, it *was* too good to be true...

I knew we would also have a big wedding blessing back in the UK where we would invite all our family and friends so I thought I would save the big white dress for then. Meanwhile I wanted something I could wear on the beach, and I ended up asking Adrian, the dress designer who makes all the outfits for my launches, to come up with a dress. He had made me a little black number that I had worn to the premiere of *Skyfall* which I loved, so I asked him to make me exactly the same dress in white, but with crystals all over it. It was a halterneck style in white silk, short at the front and long at the back, and yes, it did flash some cleavage, but I wanted to show off my fantastic new boobs, little knowing then that they wouldn't be looking so good for long...Adrian also found me a little diamante tiara that went with the dress perfectly. He made it in a record two days. I didn't even bother to try it on before we flew out because I knew it would fit. I didn't have to worry about shoes because we were going to be barefoot in the sand.

Everything was going so smoothly and I was filled with this lovely feeling of excitement and anticipation. I had my outfit and Kieran had bought his. He was going to be in ivory – ivory-coloured trousers and a matching shirt with an unusual collar. We had bought his wedding ring in the Lanes in Brighton. It was a simple platinum band. Because of his work he didn't want anything too fancy. I, on the other hand, did! A day or so before we were due to fly out I was getting my hair done – of course – and looking at wedding rings online. I texted Kieran the ones that I especially liked, never dreaming that he would buy any of them, but he replied asking which one I liked best of all.

No way! I texted back. *I don't expect you to buy any of these, they're too expensive!*

But he insisted I tell him which one I liked, saying that I shouldn't worry about the cost. And OMG! He only went and bought me the ring I most liked. It's the most beautiful, elegant ring made up of five diamond-studded platinum bands.

At first the press didn't know we were seeing each other, but by the end of December the news was out there and all my exes had to trot out their opinions. Who gave a shit what they thought? One of Kieran's exes sold a story on him too. It was the same old, same old...

*   *   *

In January 2013 Kieran and I flew out to the Bahamas. It was so exciting flying over together, knowing that when we returned we would be husband and wife. I couldn't wait! The press thought we were going to the Caribbean to get married and for once I was hopeful that we wouldn't be plagued by paps. One of the reasons I had wanted to go away was because my last two weddings had been made stressful through too much press attention, especially the blessing with Alex where some of the paps had behaved like animals in their desperation to get shots of me. It had been horrendous. Sandals looked like the perfect choice. I was going to have a stress-free wedding day. I was going to enjoy every moment. There was going to be no drama (for once).

But from the moment we arrived at the resort I started

to have my doubts that this was the right place. As we were shown up to our suite we walked past a lively bar, where guests were singing round a piano, then we passed another area where they put on shows, and the music was pumping out. Next to that was a pub. Peaceful? Idyllic? Hardly. And the place seemed to be full of English people...

Shit, I thought. This isn't what I wanted! To me it looked like an adult version of a Club 18–30 holiday. It wasn't at all how I'd imagined the resort would be.

'Let's quickly get to our room,' I suggested to Kieran. I didn't want to be spotted by anyone.

There was a further disappointment when we saw our suite. We were supposed to have a beachfront one, which suggested to me that we would be able to see the ocean. But we couldn't. Instead we overlooked one of the pools. When I phoned Reception to point this out, I was told that, yes, we did have what they called a beachfront suite, and if we went out on the balcony and looked to the left we would be able to see the sea.

Okay, I thought, don't be ungrateful; just enjoy it. Make the best of it. We're here to get married, that's what matters. But the fact was the décor wasn't up to much, it certainly wasn't like a home from home, and to cap it all, it was freezing! I'd thought it was going to be hot. I couldn't help feeling that I had let Kieran down by coming here; I'd wanted everything to be perfect for us.

The following day it was cloudy, with no hint of sun. Bollocks! But then I said to Kieran, 'We've got so much to sort out, it doesn't matter if the sun's not shining, at least we won't feel that we're missing out.'

We could hear loud music playing outside and when we went out on to our balcony we saw that a load of couples were playing organised games in the pool, with someone on a mic telling them what to do. It *really* was like a Club 18–30 holiday. Again, my heart sank and Kieran and I looked at each other as if to say, WTF! We both wanted to stay as far away as possible from all that kind of thing, and be private.

It got worse when our butler arrived. I explained to her that Kieran and I wanted complete privacy; that we wanted to be able to sunbathe on a beach, on our own. Ideally I wanted to be able to sunbathe topless. I can't get tan lines because of my work. She seemed surprised by how insistent we were on that point, and said that Sandals was a place where everyone got involved in the various activities.

'No, that's not what we want,' I told her. 'That's the last bloody thing we want!'

She said that she would be able to set up sun loungers for us at the far end of the beach where there weren't so many people. Okay. Maybe that would work. Next on my list of questions was the all-important venue for our wedding. On the website I had seen the various locations the resort offered, and one had been a pretty white gazebo flanked by two statues of angels, with a beautiful view of the aquamarine sea in the background. It looked absolutely beautiful and I had thought that it would be the perfect place for Kieran and me to hold the ceremony. But since arriving at the resort, I had noticed that the gazebo was bang, slap in the middle of the pool area, and if you looked away from the sea, your view was not of some idyllic scene but the hotel buildings and pool...And, of course, there would be people milling about.

'Do you have anywhere more private than the gazebo?' I asked her.

'Oh, yes, you can get married on the beach, around the same place where I will be setting you up to sunbathe.'

'But do people come and watch?' I asked.

'Oh, yes,' she replied cheerfully, as if that wasn't a problem at all.

'But we don't want anyone watching our wedding. We just want it to be us, and our friends and family. From the pictures on the website we assumed the venues were completely private.' By now I was really pissed off, and feeling that the website had been misleading with its beautiful photographs which didn't tell the whole story.

Again she seemed surprised that we would want privacy and seemed to be implying that if we had wanted that then Sandals was not the resort for us...

'So are you famous or something?' she asked.

'No, I just want privacy,' I replied.

Kieran could sense that we weren't getting anywhere and he said, 'Yes, actually, she is well known and we don't want any English people coming to our wedding.'

Her reply left Kieran and me completely gobsmacked. 'So are you a porn star?'

I looked at her in astonishment, before saying dryly, 'Actually, no. That's one thing I haven't done.'

She didn't exactly seem apologetic about her faux-pas and continued to ask me what I did for a living. Was she ever going to give it a rest! Kieran took over and told her that I was a well-known model and TV personality.

'So what's your name then?' she asked.

I felt I had to tell her, even though I never usually tell people what I do when I'm away. Usually I say I'm a hairdresser if people ask. As soon as I told her that I was Katie Price aka Jordan, she exclaimed, 'Oh, but I have heard of you! I've followed your story! I'm so sorry I didn't recognise you!'

'Do I look rough then, in real life?' I asked her, wishing that we hadn't had any of this conversation. She seemed shocked that I'd chosen to come to Sandals, and I thought, I like to do normal things, but this is what happens when I do, I end up getting stung.

'Now I can see why you want privacy!' the woman exclaimed, and went on to say that there was a private island and we could hire that just for our wedding, but of course it would be an extra cost. All of a sudden, now she knew I had money, it seemed to be Kerching!

That really put my back up. 'Actually, we just want to get married somewhere private, exactly like it suggested we could on your website,' I told her. 'So are there many English people here?' I went on.

'More Americans,' she told us.

That, at least, was something…but she hadn't finished.

'So would English people recognise you then?'

'They might. And if I'm sunbathing, I don't want anyone taking pictures of me with their phones. The paps think that we're getting married in the Caribbean and I want it to stay that way.'

She assured me that no one would photograph us, that they had security everywhere. 'We protect all our clients,' she told us, 'and we will know if we get people checking in unexpectedly. That just doesn't happen here.'

But I knew how cunning the paps were and told her that they could easily pose as honeymoon couples. Frankly, I wouldn't put anything past some of them. But she assured us that no one new was due to check in. All in all, she made us feel secure and we noticed that there were plenty of guards patrolling the resort so we were a little more at ease. Okay, I thought, it is the cheapest holiday I've ever had but we wanted to get married quickly and this is the only place we could manage that. It'll be fine. And anyway, I had something else on my mind…

I had been feeling bloated and sick for the last couple of days, but had put that down to my period being due. Then again, it might not be that. So when Kieran and I went to explore the local town – the weather was too cloudy for sunbathing – I went into a chemist and bought a pregnancy test. Once I had it I was desperate to find out if I was pregnant or not. We went out for something to eat and I couldn't resist nipping to the loos to do a test. But it was negative. I couldn't help feeling disappointed and I know Kieran felt the same when I told him.

'Ah, well, I must just be a fat bastard at the moment!' I said, typically trying to downplay my disappointment.

We had a few days before the wedding and wanted to chill out but the weather continued to be cloudy. Where was the sun? So much for getting a tan before our big day. We went out for lunch and dinner a few times but often we'd have room service, because we didn't want to be spotted by anyone. We treated ourselves to some massages at the spa. We tried to sunbathe whenever the sun showed itself, like typical British holidaymakers, but often we'd be wrapped up in our towels because it was too chilly! And it was too cold to go in the sea.

Our butler set our sunbeds up towards the end of the beach, as she had promised. On the plus side there weren't too many people about, and those that were, were foreign, so I went ahead and sunbathed topless. But although the beach was private, it was still overlooked by the resort buildings. I really did miss my lovely Maldives beaches where you're not overlooked by anyone.

Once when we were sunbathing we noticed that they had put out stylish wooden sunbeds with cushions on them. We'd had plastic ones. A helicopter kept circling overhead with a camera on it and we realised that they must be taking photographs for the new brochure. So out came the quality sunbeds for the shots. But in spite of our disappointment about the resort we were happy and had a laugh together and felt really close.

We were still wondering where to have our ceremony. The wedding planner had been to see us and had mentioned the private island and the extra charge again, which didn't impress me. She knew who I was, as the butler had told her, and said that she had to let her manager know so that they could keep an eye on us and make sure we weren't bothered by anyone. Well, I don't know what happened there, but given that the paps *did* find out exactly where we were staying...someone at the hotel must have said something to someone.

'What are they up to?' I asked Kieran, as we were sunbathing one morning and noticed some of the hotel staff pushing a wheelbarrow along the beach. It all became clear as they began arranging scallop shells to form an aisle and we realised they were setting up for a wedding ceremony there. Curious to see what it would be like, we stayed put. They set up a small white gazebo and arranged some chairs nearby. Music was playing, and as we watched the ceremony we thought the location would work for us too. It seemed private, no one apart from us was watching. Even though there were hotel buildings behind, it seemed that we weren't going to get anywhere better than that. At last, problem solved, we would have our wedding ceremony there. Now we felt really excited!

I was still feeling bloated, though, and decided to do another pregnancy test. It was the day before our wedding. I realised that pregnancy tests are pretty accurate nowadays, but you never knew...maybe that first one didn't get it right. This time a lovely faint blue line popped up in the square! I left it a minute while I brushed my teeth and then checked again, and by now it was a strong line. I was pregnant! It was fantastic news! I wanted to rush out and tell Kieran. But my cheeky nature got the better of me. When I went back into the bedroom I lay on the bed next to him.

'Well?' he asked hopefully.

'No, I'm not,' I replied. And the poor guy was gutted and so I quickly said, 'I am really!' And of course he didn't believe me until I showed him the test. We hadn't been planning to have a baby, but nor had we been careful as we were getting married.

We were both so happy. It felt like the perfect seal to our relationship. I always said that it was fate that I hadn't become pregnant by Alex or Leo. It took the right man...it took Kieran.

The following evening my friends arrived. I've known Jane and Derek from way back. They're quite a bit older than me as Derek is fifty and Jane is in her late forties, but they're my best friends. Whenever we go out together I know people are thinking, They won't be able to stay up late, but trust me, they are total party animals! They stay out all night! Even better, they have two children exactly the same age as Princess and Junior and we all spend a lot of time together.

And then there was Tanya. She's an incredible businesswoman, the co-founder and co-owner of Bayliss & Harding toiletries. Again, people would never have us down as friends because she's older than me, but we have such a laugh together and she's a lovely woman. Our mums arrived much later when we had all gone to bed as we were so tired. I had to get my beauty sleep for my big day! We planned to tell everyone the baby news after the wedding.

CHAPTER 21

BAREFOOT WEDDING

On Wednesday, the morning of our wedding, Kieran had to go into town with Derek to get him an outfit. That's my friend Derek: lastminute.com all over. Kieran and I had broken with tradition and spent the night before together... Meanwhile the girls and I had some serious preparations to take care of and were getting our hair and make up done. It was completely relaxed and we were all having a laugh. My mum and Kieran's mum, Wendy, had immediately hit it off. They had only met the day before at Heathrow. Apparently my mum had suggested they should meet up outside W. H. Smith, a bit like a blind date! But from the moment they met they got on. In fact, they ended up being more or less joined at the hip throughout their stay. I was so relieved! This was the first time my mum has *ever* got on with a partner's mother. But Wendy is exactly like us, and she's young, trendy and normal.

'I've got something for you,' my mum told me, and handed me a pretty blue Swarovski crystal bracelet. Perfect for my something blue. Earlier, when Tanya walked into my suite, she had been wearing a pair of fantastic earrings, huge diamante numbers.

'I love them!' I'd exclaimed.

'Wear them,' she told me, taking them off and handing them to me. 'They can be your something borrowed.'

And so for the first time I felt as if I was doing everything right, with my something old (my diamond bracelet), something new (the dress), something borrowed (the earrings) and something blue (bracelet). And it was good to have both our mums here with us. I would have hated it if mine hadn't been able to come, and I know Kieran would have felt exactly the same if Wendy hadn't been able to.

My dress fitted perfectly as I knew it would – a big thanks to Adrian! I wore my hair down, with the pretty diamante tiara he'd found and a crystal-studded veil. I kept my make up quite simple, but of course I had my fake lashes on and went for my sultry-eyed look, which I love. I think I probably looked like a girl from *My Big Fat Gypsy Wedding*, but without the big dress, and of course I was barefoot.

'Come on, Kate, we have to go, we're late,' my friend Jane said, looking at her watch.

'It's only half-past two, isn't it?' I replied, having no idea what the time was.

'It's four o'clock!' Jane replied.

Shit! I was supposed to have been married an hour ago! And for once I had planned to be on time. Too late for that now. Poor Kieran had been waiting for me...

When we arrived at the beach, he was standing in the gazebo. Wow! He looked so handsome, wearing his ivory-coloured shirt and trousers, a single white rose pinned to his shirt to match my bouquet of white hydrangeas. He made my heart flip with happiness.

But as I got ready to walk up the aisle, with Derek holding my arm, I couldn't help noticing there seemed to be a lot of people watching. I didn't like that one bit. Had someone said something to tip them off? Would they take pictures? This was exactly what I didn't want to happen. I could feel stress building up inside me.

Just enjoy it, I tried to tell myself. It's your wedding day, ignore everything else.

The keyboard player struck up 'Here Comes the Bride' (we had wanted something traditional) and I began walking up the scallop-lined aisle and Kieran came to meet me so we could walk together. The registrar was about to start the ceremony when suddenly I noticed a woman on a nearby sunbed, holding up a phone.

'Sorry!' I exclaimed. 'We have to stop. That woman over there is filming.'

The wedding planner rushed over to the woman, who claimed that she hadn't been but left anyway. So we started again. But then we noticed there was a man with a camera, pointed right at us, on the balcony of the building that overlooked the beach. And so we had to halt the ceremony again as I asked the wedding planner to go up there and delete his pictures.

In total we had to stop the ceremony three times. The registrar had married over ten thousand couples and said he had never experienced anything like this before. It was so frustrating! We weren't saying, 'Oh, look at us, aren't we special?' We had just wanted to be treated like any other couple. But there were far more people watching our wedding than had watched any of the others, which made us wonder how exactly they had all known to come at that time. There were even people watching from their balconies. Part of me did want to shout out: 'Fuck off! What are you looking at!' But I kept calm and carried on, determined not to let anyone spoil our special day.

We had kept our vows very traditional. When the wedding planner asked us if we wanted to add our own personal words, we'd both said that we wanted the usual vows: to have and to hold, for richer for poorer, till death us do part. Getting married was all that mattered to us. We didn't need to say anything fancy, we loved each other, that was enough.

After the ceremony we had our photographs taken on the beach, by the photographer from the hotel. He had also been filming and photographing the run up to the wedding and the ceremony itself as part of the package. Our mums and Tanya snapped away at us as well.

Over dinner we told everyone the brilliant news about me being pregnant. Everyone was thrilled for us, though I noticed our mums exchanging looks, probably because it had happened so quickly. We went through the pictures and thought they were lovely. We both looked so happy and relaxed. All in all, in spite of the hiccups with other people photographing us, it had been a brilliant day. And now I was Mrs Hayler! This time I really was going to change my name outside work. I had always said I would with Pete and Alex, but I never had. This time it was going to be different.

*   *   *

The following morning my manager Andrew called me with some very unwelcome news.

'The *Sun* have got pictures of your wedding. And apparently all the photos are really clear.'

How the hell had that happened? I was livid. This was exactly what I didn't want. I discussed it with Kieran and we decided that we would send some of our own pictures, taken by the hotel photographer, to Andrew to see if he could do a deal with the *Sun*. That should really piss off the people who were trying to make money out of selling pictures of us. We selected fifteen shots and asked the wedding photographer to email them to Andrew. Then we tried to forget all about it and not get stressed, and that wasn't difficult as Tanya had chartered a massive yacht and treated us all to an amazing trip round the island. We went snorkelling, sunbathed, had lunch, relaxed in the onboard Jacuzzi. Just a perfect day.

Back at the hotel we checked the *Sun's* website. We couldn't believe it when we saw the pictures. They were definitely not our official wedding photographs. There were close-up shots of Kieran and me gazing straight at the camera, other shots of us posing by the sea, and him picking me up in his arms. Straightaway we knew these had to have been taken from inside the hotel grounds. There were also some pictures that had clearly been taken by a long-distance lens, which meant by a pap. We were absolutely furious. And because they showed us posing and looking at the camera, everyone was going to think that we had sold them! I know some celebs set up pictures when they go on holiday, but we genuinely didn't. We wanted our wedding to be private. We hadn't even told all our family and friends yet, so the pictures in the *Sun* caused real problems for us as we had many texts from friends sounding hurt as they wrote, 'Thanks a lot for inviting us!'

Even worse was to come when the following day the *Sun* had pictures of Kieran and me sunbathing, including ones of me topless, claiming that these were our honeymoon photos. We had been well and truly stitched up. Those pictures had been taken on our very first day sunbathing at the resort. There had to have been a tip off from someone at or in the hotel, as how else would a photographer have known to book into a room in just the right position to photograph us from? We had deliberately chosen the most private part of the beach, which wasn't the closest to the hotel building, and the photographer had to have been told that. It was too much of a coincidence for him to have found us by chance.

I felt I had to do something. I wasn't going to sit back and take this. So once our friends and mums had left, I asked to see the manager. I started off by showing her the pictures from Michelle Heaton's wedding and pointed out that Sandals had given her a free wedding because she had promoted the resort. And I said that her recommendation about how private the ceremony had been had inspired us to come here.

'We paid to come here and get married,' I said, 'and you've had publicity from that! If I'd wanted a free wedding, I would have sold the pictures myself. But I didn't. Someone here went and did exactly that behind our backs.' I had started out quite calmly but I was getting more and more angry as I spoke.

'We've been stitched up,' I burst out. 'This hotel did nothing to stop our wedding being ruined!'

'I'll look into it,' the manager promised. She was taking notes and I think she could see that we had valid reason to complain.

'Oh, and that's not all!' I continued. 'I've just got the bills for our hair and make up and I'm not paying all that! Just because you know I've got money, you're not taking the piss out of me!'

The morning of my wedding day I'd had my hair washed and blow-dried and they had charged me $150 just for that. Plus $50 for conditioning treatments that I didn't even ask for! I did most of my make up myself, and the make-up artist we had booked just applied my eye shadow and lashes...and then they had charged me $40 extra for sticking on the lashes. I've been in the modelling industry for years and no one has ever charged me separately for putting on lashes. It's part of make up, surely. I really felt as if we were being ripped off. I was paying for everyone else and they had all been charged exactly the same.

'We're leaving tomorrow and I want everything sorted before then!' I finished up by saying.

After the woman had left, Kieran looked at me and said, 'That told her then!' I don't think he had seen me go into attack mode before...but I hate feeling that people are trying to take advantage of me. Kieran is a very calm, laidback man – just as well really. We couldn't have both of us getting into a state.

I trusted the manager to deal with my complaints but the following day, which was the day we were leaving, when I went down to Reception to see her, I was told she wasn't in. What kind of place was this? I took a deep breath. 'Right, let's get some things straight,' I started. 'We came here to get married, thinking it was going to be perfect. Instead, someone at this hotel has stitched us up and sold our pictures to a national newspaper. Unless you get the management to come to my hotel suite before we leave and explain how they are going to sort this out...' There were other guests in Reception, and they were all staring at me, but I didn't care. I was absolutely furious that we had been treated like this.

'I'm going to the hairdressers now, so you've got an hour to get your act together.'

I was seething as I had my hair done, but I made myself write down notes about all I intended to say. I wanted to get my facts straight. When I returned to our suite I told Kieran what was happening.

'Oh, shit! Do I have to sit in?' he asked. 'I never know what you're going to come out with!'

'Don't worry, I've got it all under control.'

The bell rang and I opened the door to find five managers. In they walked, suited and booted, and sat down on the sofas. I had my notes ready in front of me as I got straight down to my description of our stay, from the moment the butler had asked me if I was a porn star. I showed them all the pictures of us that had appeared in the press, pointing out the ones where we had been papped as we sunbathed and the shots of our 'private' wedding ceremony which could only have been taken from somewhere in the hotel. Whoever had done this had been very sneaky as the pap shots only appeared after our official wedding photos, and the photographer had obviously been staking us out all week, knowing that if he sold his pictures any earlier, every other pap in the area would have known where we were and come and got a slice of the action.

'Sandals is a private resort, so surely you should be interested in the fact that a person is taking pictures of your guests, without your permission or theirs?' I said at one point. They had no answer to that.

Finally, I summed it up for them with the killer comment: 'I write a column for the *Sun* newspaper and the editor will definitely want me to talk about my wedding. You're not going to want me to tell the biggest-selling paper in the UK that my week here at Sandals was shit, are you? We have been set up and you need to get to the bottom of what happened because you've upset all of us. And I am not letting this matter drop.' Phew! I was on a roll. Katie Price, kickass!

They seemed genuinely shocked and were very apologetic. We also went through the receipts for the wedding make up and hair and they agreed to remove the charges for the hair conditioners and lashes. But they didn't discount the rest of the holiday. They gave me the name and number of their PR representative in Europe and told me to contact her when I returned to the UK and said she would be able to sort it out.

However, when my PA Catherine called her to arrange a time to meet up, she made it clear that she wasn't interested in such a meeting. And so, when it was time to write my column for the *Sun*, I didn't sugar-coat our wedding experience, I told it straight. 'The butler asked me if I was a porn star.' Our wedding tent 'looked like it came out of B&Q', and the atmosphere was 'more 18–30 than royal. Sandals, my a*** – it was more like a smelly old flip-flop.'

And in reply Sandals were quoted as saying that they were 'Disappointed Ms Price was not happy with her stay' and that the butler denied making any 'derogatory remarks', adding, 'As a gesture of goodwill we are willing to offer her a refund on condition she does not choose our resorts for any future weddings or stays.'

Unbelievable! I'd never go near there again, never in a million years. And as for the so-called refund, was that going to include our flights as well as the money that someone had made out of selling our pictures!

We didn't let it drop and I have instructed my lawyers. I wasn't going to let them get away with treating us so badly. They sent through the wedding photos a few weeks later and I have to say the pictures were lovely. However, the experience of being papped while we were being married was horrible. It was very creepy, knowing that someone had a camera trained on us all week. And even when we'd returned from our honeymoon more pictures came out, which this time had been sold to various magazines. Whoever had taken the pictures had been so cunning; they must have been rubbing their hands together, thinking that they could retire on the proceeds. Bastards.

CHAPTER 22

MR AND MRS HAYLER

But whatever had gone wrong on our wedding and honeymoon, it didn't take anything away from the love Kieran and I felt for each other, and how happy we were to be married. They do say third time lucky and I feel incredibly blessed to be married to him. And content and relaxed and excited about the baby!

Looking back over my first marriage, I can't remember a single moment when we made any decisions without the involvement of Claire Powell. When friends ask me what I can remember about my first wedding day, automatically I feel what I can only describe as a stress gremlin in my head, with images of Claire and Pete and magazine deals and being filmed for the TV series, and of Richard Desmond, the owner of *OK!* I don't feel that I have a single memory of that time which isn't about work.

Since then I've tried to keep my relationships more private. So Kieran and I haven't done any interviews or photo shoots together and we won't be doing any. We did a very short one with the *Sun,* but that's because I'm a columnist for them. I know I'm talking about him here, in my book, but it's in my own words. No journalist can twist or change them. Nor does Kieran want to do any shoots or interviews. He's not interested in fame. He wants to do his own thing, off his own back. He says he doesn't want to make money or get fame by talking about me, and I believe him.

Once in the UK it was back to work for both Kieran and me. Some of his friends asked him why he had bothered returning to his job, but why wouldn't he? I really respect him for that choice. He's not going to be a kept man; we are equals, both responsible for looking after our family. So he was back in the routine of getting up at six to go to work, then off to the gym when he had finished. And we both joined the same gym, so we could go together and play sports, like badminton and tennis, which was a first for me in a relationship. I was already feeling exhausted from the pregnancy, though.

And, of course, my exes had to have their say. Yawn. Pete had one of his rants at me, through 'a friend', of course, claiming that I hadn't told the kids that I was getting married again. But I had, two weeks before we flew to the Bahamas. He was probably annoyed because I hadn't told him – but why should I when we don't even talk any more? I think he was trying to get another heartbreaking story out of my wedding...And it cuts both ways. For ages there have been stories about him and his girlfriend Emily...will they, won't they get married? You don't get heartbreaking quotes from me about him.

Apparently Alex wrote a letter to Kieran, which was published in *Now* magazine. I say apparently because I'm not going to read rubbish like that. All about how I was supposed to have treated him, that I compared him to Pete, saying Alex was as bad as him, that I hated his clothes – well, the clothes part is true as I've already said! When someone told me about the letter, I thought, My God, that man really does have no shame. And Leo had to have his say in the same magazine, saying that he was shocked by how quickly I had married Kieran and how he didn't think we would last. Awww, like I'm bothered about what he thinks!

And then the press started sticking their oar in. They picked up on a throwaway comment I'd made, that a medium had said that I would marry a man called Kevin. *Please,* that is not the reason I married Kieran! It was just a funny near-coincidence as both names begin with K, and she said that I had already met the man I was going to fall in love with. In fact, when I saw the medium I had just met Kieran, though nothing had happened between us then. She also said that I was going to get married to someone very quickly.

Once I was with Kieran, we very soon had a Kevin in our lives when I bought him an adorable fox-red

Labrador puppy for his birthday and we named him Kevin!

But at least the story about the medium was light-hearted. What upset me were all the stories that came out that had a nasty, vindictive edge to them. Stories that said I wasn't happy with Kieran, that I had only married him because I couldn't bear to be on my own, that eleven days into our marriage I was bored. And they printed comments alleged to be from my 'friends', that I had told them I had made a mistake in marrying Kieran. All absolute crap. Those were no friends of mine, because all my friends knew that we were happy and that one hundred per cent I had made the right decision.

The magazines were only coming out with this kind of rubbish because Kieran and I hadn't given any interviews. Instead of them printing the truth, that we were happy and in love, it was easier to write headlines saying that we were having problems already. It felt as if they didn't want us to get on. That they were waiting and wishing for something bad to happen so it would give them something juicy to write about.

One example was a picture they printed of the pair of us at a petrol station, and how they wrote that because we both looked moody and weren't holding hands this was proof of how badly we were getting on together. The truth is that it was a freezing cold day, Kieran was suffering from tonsillitis, and after we had filled the car up with petrol we went into the kiosk to buy him some more Paracetamol and various drinks and snacks. As he and I rushed back to the car afterwards, he pointed out that someone had a camera directed at us, and hearing a click, I turned my head away. From that the press decided that our marriage was on the rocks. Pathetic! I mean, that really is the sound of the barrel being scraped.

Then there was the wife from hell story in *Now,* saying that I had come out with Ten Commandments that Kieran had to follow. Apparently I'd ordered him to take his shoes off before entering the bedroom. Well, *Now* magazine, you need to get your facts right because *everyone* has to take their shoes off at my front door! And here's another commandment: Kieran must never make eye contact with a woman aged between 18–40 unless he wants a telling off. Funnily enough, he has plenty of contact with that age group when he's stripping in front of them all! So I don't exactly think I'd be worried about him having eye contact.

Oh, here's another: apparently we can't sleep in a bedroom hotter than 10°C because I'm so worried about ageing. *Please!* Anyone who knows me, knows that it's like walking into the Caribbean when you come into my house because I always have the heating up full blast.

I can shrug off the articles because they're rubbish and all completely untrue, but all the same, yet again, I am being made out to be a bad person. As I've said before, after years and years of having such stories written about me, I am to a certain extent desensitised to them. Friends ask me how I can bear to read things like this about myself, but I don't usually read them and I'm used to it. It's a case of, here we go, yet another bullshit story. The stories upset Kieran more because he thinks that people will believe the lies, but I say as long as we both know the truth it doesn't matter. And, as I've said, I do sometimes resort to legal action now, and newspapers and magazines have been made to apologise and pay me compensation. But we can't do that for every single story, it would take over our lives and I want to live my life and be happy. And anyway, I was pregnant when we got back to England and didn't want the worry. The only major stress was the court case I had pending against my ex-manager and ex-husband and ex-friend (represented by my ex-lawyers). But I was hoping it would all be over soon and I had Kieran by my side, supporting me all the way.

He is the perfect husband! When he's at work he texts me throughout the day, telling me how much he loves me and making me feel so good. There is no game-playing between us whatsoever, no reason for me to feel insecure. I don't have any worries about him cheating on me. A lot of my friends tell me that they couldn't put up with him being a stripper, but I have no problem with it at all. As I've said, I've seen the show and I loved it. Yes, other women are looking at my man naked, and there are even times when they can touch him, though he holds their hands and controls where they can put them, but it's all part of the performance. Kieran actually said that he wanted to give up stripping because he was now part of a family and we're having a baby together, but I said, 'You don't need to stop. Look at me. In the past I got my tits out with my glamour modelling. Carry on, don't worry about it!'

In fact, I want him to carry on doing it because I think it's a great ego boost for him every weekend. Any man loves receiving attention from women because it gives them a buzz, and what better way of getting it than by stripping off in a packed club full of women, who are all watching and admiring your every move and probably wishing they could smuggle you home with them. I'd rather that than he went off clubbing and ended up flirting with other women.

* * *

I had suffered from morning sickness with all of my pregnancies and this one was no different. Ugh! I hated that feeling of nausea which seemed to last throughout the day, and was worse if I had to go anywhere in the car. I tried to eat what I could, when I could, because not eating made the nausea even worse. I can't say that I had any cravings, but I could always manage a jacket potato, a comforting plateful of carbs!

But this pregnancy was different in the way it made me far more tired and showed really early on. I was definitely bigger than I was with the others. And whereas before I didn't seem to gain weight anywhere else apart from my bump, this time every time I looked in the mirror I seemed even bigger. And, bloody hell, I noticed that my arse had really dropped! I wanted to start doing some gentle exercise at the gym, but just didn't have the energy.

I asked my obstetrician, Dr Gibb, why I was showing so soon and he replied that because it was my fourth child my body knew exactly what to do. Dr Gibb had delivered Junior and Princess, and as soon as I knew I was pregnant I decided I wanted him to deliver this baby too. I trusted him completely. Because I'd already had two caesarians I was going to have a C-section with this baby too. I did ask him if I could have a natural delivery, but he said no. I suppose I was relieved that I didn't have to go through labour again, because, believe me, ten years on I can still remember how painful it was giving birth to Harvey naturally. And when I watch *One Born Every Minute*, I always think, I can't believe I went through natural birth! Thank God I don't have to any more. But it also meant that I would probably only be able to have two more children because the more caesarians you've had, the more scar tissue you have on your womb and the higher the risks of complications during pregnancy. Once Dr Gibb told me that, I was thinking, Right! I'd better roll them out! And Kieran wants more children too.

At one of my ante-natal checks it was discovered that I was anaemic, which explained why I was feeling so exhausted all the time and out of breath. I had to take strong iron tablets, which I hate doing as they make me feel sick. I also had very low blood pressure and a low platelet count. Platelets are cells in your blood which help it to clot. Because of the low count I was going to be monitored very carefully. It might mean that I would need a transfusion of platelets, because if the count continued to be too low I wouldn't be able to have a C-section or an epidural. I was worried about that, but knew I was in the best possible hands with my doctor.

But even without the anxiety about the low platelet count, I was definitely more anxious with this pregnancy, constantly worrying about everything. The miscarriage I'd suffered in 2009 had devastated me; I couldn't lose this baby.

As with all my pregnancies I was obsessed with checking the different stages of development, even though I know them all practically off by heart! And the brilliant thing about technology today is that you can follow all the stages online, watch videos, see images. Honestly, I spend hours looking at them all! I have shown some to Kieran, but as I've said before I don't think the whole pregnancy thing sinks in with men until they can feel the baby kicking, or even until they are presented with their son or daughter. And I didn't want to keep going on about it. I've never been one of those mumsy mums, and I didn't want to feel that I was constantly saying, 'Look at this! Our baby now has their own unique set of fingerprints!' Or, 'Our baby can frown!' And driving him mad.

Anyway, Kieran said that he couldn't wait to see the baby. But you know what it's like when your hormones are all over the place; I was probably being paranoid, worrying about how he was feeling. I didn't know what exactly I wanted him to say. He was hardly going to be exclaiming 'OMG!' every day about the latest developments. No man would be like that, and nor would I want Kieran to be. He came to all the scans with me and was as thrilled as I was to see images of our baby. Hilariously, at one scan the baby seemed to be giving us the finger! So s/he is a feisty one! But what else do you expect with me as their mum? We found out the sex very early on, but decided to keep it a secret, hard as it was, because that is the question people always, *always* ask.

I tried to keep my bump under wraps whenever I went out. I didn't want to be papped while I was pregnant. I felt that I wanted to do everything differently from before, when I was pregnant with Junior and Princess and did interviews and photo shoots for *OK!* Though, at the end of May, when I was five months pregnant, I ended up posing for a shot for the *Sun.* I didn't want to, but I didn't think I could get away with not being papped for much longer and I knew it would really piss me off if a pap sneaked his money shot.

I told Kieran and his mum about the crippling post-natal depression I suffered from after I had Junior. And I told them about how I had felt that Pete's family hadn't given me the space to bond with my son, and that I was convinced that had been one of the triggers of my depression. Even now, I can clearly remember the surge of anger I felt whenever his mum and dad went near Junior while he was a baby, and then Princess. And I'll never forget how, just a few days after I'd had her, when I was lying in bed, still recovering from the caesarian, I overheard Pete on the phone to his brother saying that his dad was his first priority and, as if that wasn't hurtful enough: 'I don't really care what *that* thinks.'

I remember it felt as if I'd been hit. My then husband was calling me *that*. His dad was unwell at the time, and Pete was planning to bring his parents to our house, even though he knew I didn't want any visitors because I was so anxious about getting post-natal depression again. In fact, Pete and our two families had been expressly told by the doctors to give me all the space I needed and not crowd me. But with that phone call my husband had made me feel worthless; I could never forget that comment. It was downhill all the way in our marriage from there, and we split up a year and a half later. Even writing about it here, six years later, brings all those feelings of anger back.

But, deep breath, I am sure that things will be different with Kieran's family. Already I feel close and comfortable with them, in a way I never did with past partners' families. I've told his mum that I want her to come up to the hospital so she can see the baby as soon as I come out of surgery. But even as I said it, I still felt a bit funny and couldn't help thinking about when I was taken back to my room, wondering if everyone would be there, wanting to hold the baby? Already I could feel stress and anxiety bubbling up inside me. *I* wanted to be the one holding the baby! No one else but me. So I tried to calm myself down, and say to myself, Kate, just relax! Of course his family want to see the baby, it's natural, but they're not going to take it away from you. I guess post-natal depression leaves its mark for ever...

I've already mentioned that I had to start taking anti-depressants again in September 2012. As soon as I found out I was pregnant, I talked to my doctor and started coming off them – you have to do it gradually otherwise it can make you feel very unwell. There was still the stress of the court case ahead, especially when we found out that my ex-husband Alex Reid was also getting involved – though that is a whole different story.

But overall everything about the pregnancy felt very positive even though it had happened so early in my relationship with Kieran. He had hardly ever known me not to be pregnant! And he hasn't really seen me out socialising. I'm always a home girl at heart, but even more so at the moment. On Saturday nights, when he's got a show on, I'm tucked up at home on the sofa watching TV! I've not been in the mood to go out. I wouldn't know what to wear and don't want the pressure of the media speculating about when the baby's due. They can guess all they like, but they won't be told.

I say to Kieran, 'Do you think I'm boring because all I want to do is stay at home?'

Fortunately it doesn't bother him at all, and when he's not working he's perfectly happy to be at home with me, socialising with our friends and family. I know that when I was single I went nuts, wanted to go out clubbing and drinking, didn't want to stay at home on my own every night. I met Kieran while I was in my going out phase, but as soon as we were in a relationship I stopped wanting to go out. I was happy to stay in. I know myself, and I'm calmer and happier when I'm in a relationship. Luckily that home girl is the one Kieran loves.

Ironically, I had been quiet work-wise at the beginning of 2013, but then from June 2013, when I was six months pregnant, it was suddenly work, work, work, as I had my latest novel, *He's The One*, out; then my new perfume Kissable in July; I had a range of shoes to promote in July in LA and Australia, and my wedding range in August and September. This book came out in October, just over a month after I was due to have the baby! Talk about a packed schedule! But all the time I felt completely supported by Kieran, who planned to take a month off work so he could come on the book tour with the baby and me.

The only downside (and it's really only a small one) is that my lovely new pert, high up, stuck on boobs were ruined by the pregnancy! They dropped dramatically. I might just as well never have had them done at all. And they were so good! I only had them done because I had no idea that I was going to meet someone, fall in love, get married and have a baby, three months after the surgery. But that's life. All I really cared about was that my baby was healthy. I hoped that my body would snap back into shape as it had done after my last three children, but I think that might be too optimistic nowadays. I'm pretty sure that this time I will need to hit the gym, and work out to get back into shape – good genes can only do so much. I'm looking forward to having the energy to do it.

I know I want to have more kids with Kieran so I definitely won't rush into having another boob job after this baby is born. I'll wait until hopefully we've had another child together. Then that will be it! I'll go back to Belgium again for another boob job and this time no one will be ruining them!

CHAPTER 23

MY BIG FAT WILLY WONKA WEDDING!

Many people spend ages planning their wedding, two years, a year . . . many people but not me. I had barely two months to plan a blessing ceremony and reception for nearly two hundred guests. But I had a vision. Junior, Princess and I have always loved the film of *Charlie and the Chocolate Factory* and I thought it would be brilliant to have a Willy Wonka-themed party in a world of sweets, though I thought it was unlikely we'd be able to book Oompa-Loompas at such short notice . . . I wanted it to be a spectacle and I wanted it to be fun!

Kieran was completely up for the theme as well. I'm not criticising anyone else's wedding but they can all seem very similar and blur into one with their subtle light colours, tasteful toning table decorations, you know the kind of thing. I feel that once you've seen one, you've seen them all. Because this was my third marriage, I think I was especially keen to make it different and special. I wanted it to be a fitting celebration of our relationship and to show how committed Kieran and I were to each other.

Initially we wanted to have the blessing at a nearby stately home, but unfortunately they would only allow us to have ninety guests and that simply wasn't enough. Then I looked into having a marquee in the grounds of my house, but the quote the company gave us seemed excessive and my mum thought a marquee was a bad idea.

'You need to get married away from the house! Knowing you, if you have it here, halfway through the ceremony you'll nip back into the house and change into your PJs and then go back when you feel more comfortable.'

She was right, of course. I probably would end up doing exactly that.

I didn't want to stress about this blessing at all, but suddenly time seemed to be on fast-forward and we still hadn't settled on a venue, though we had the date: Saturday 30 March. Then my manager introduced me to a friend of his called Ian, who had just bought a stately home outside Ipswich and wanted to make it into a wedding venue. That sounded promising...However, when we went to see it, although the driveway and the exterior of the house were impressive, the inside needed a lot of work. And there wasn't one room that was large enough to seat all our guests for dinner, they would have to be spread over three rooms and that didn't seem ideal. Ian was convinced that he would be able to accommodate everyone and put on the theme that I wanted, but I was starting to have doubts. It seemed a lot to do, in a short space of time, and I felt uneasy about leaving it all to him.

Meanwhile I was busy thinking about my dress. I asked Kieran what kind of dress he would like me to wear, and he suggested something lacey, in a style that I hadn't worn to my other weddings...Men! What do they know! There was no way I was going to wear a little dress, I'd already worn one of those for our beach wedding, it had to be the big white number, nothing else would do. I found a dress which I thought would be perfect, and as the style was called Katie it seemed like a very good sign. It was a beautiful cream colour, with lace. But naturally I needed it to be blinged up and requested that they sew on more crystals.

We went ahead and sent out the invitations with only two weeks to go, giving the venue as the stately home. But then one of my guests leaked the details to the press...Here we go again, I thought. I really didn't want to have our big day ruined because of the paps. I didn't know what else to do since time was so tight. And then we had a meeting with Ian, near his home in Weston-super-Mare, and it turned out that he owned Rookery Manor, a hotel and spa which specialised in putting on weddings. He showed us round the venue and instantly I thought it would be brilliant for our wedding. Everything was there already; it would make life so much easier. Also, if we held it there, the press wouldn't know. When I asked Ian, he said it would be possible, except he already had a wedding booked for 30 March; ours would have to be 29 March. I knew that might mean some people couldn't make it, which was a pity, but I also knew that this venue was the right one for us.

Ian also owned two wedding boutiques and before the visit I'd taken a look at the website and seen an absolutely gorgeous dress. It was a striking creation with an ostrich-feather bodice. I had already chosen my dress, and no doubt it had been blinged up to my liking by now, but there was no harm in looking at another one, was there? During our hotel visit we went into the bridal boutique and I asked if they had the ostrich-feather dress there. In fact it was at the other store and they had to send off for it. We waited an hour or so but it was so worth it because when I saw the dress I loved it. And when I tried it on, I knew this was the one for me. But I wasn't keen on the ruched skirt so I said, 'I'd love it with a plain silk skirt, with tulle dotted with' (yes, you've guessed it) 'crystals. Would it be possible to change it?'

The look on everyone's faces was priceless. 'But, Kate!' my mum exclaimed. 'You're getting married in a week and a half and now you want to change the dress!'

I'm sure my reply wasn't what they wanted to hear: 'Yes!' And when they had made the changes to the dress I absolutely loved it.

Of course I had to wear a tiara. And not just any old tiara, it had to be made to my specifications and that meant it was going to be a whopper! I asked the designer to bring her biggest samples to my house and I tried three of them on at once.

'Right, I want to go to this height, plus a little bit more!' I declared as I looked in the mirror. The designer replied that she had never made one like that before...but there you go, that's me.

Now we had the venue, I could see my ideas for the wedding working perfectly. There were two large reception suites, decorated with ivory drapes, chandeliers and LED starlit ceilings. Very me. One suite was going to be converted into a kind of chapel of love, with white flower arrangements and roses studded with crystals. I had booked a gospel choir as I love gospel singing. Funnily enough, the choir ended up on *Britain's Got Talent* a few weeks later.

We were going to take our wedding vows under an ornate white canopy with pillars, cascades of crystals, and garlands of white flowers. These canopies, called *mandaps*, are often used in Asian weddings. This was my idea and I thought it would really add to the spectacle to take our vows like that, make it really magical, rather than simply standing in front of the guests. Oh, and we were having two gold thrones. Maybe that was going a bit Posh and Becks circa 1999 but, hey, what the hell!

The second reception room was going to be for the sit-down wedding breakfast and that was going to be where we let rip with the Willy Wonka theme. It was going to be a treat for the senses with bright-coloured drapes on the walls and ceiling, more twinkling LED lights, giant lollipops, packets of love hearts and candy sticks decorating the walls. Instead of flower decorations, each table was going to have a tree made of sweets, mini-chocolate eggs, love hearts, that kind of thing. There was going to be fake grass, sweet stalls, popcorn stalls and a chocolate fountain. The only downside to having the wedding here was that because the venue was booked for other weddings before and after ours, the wedding planners hardly had any time to set up and all the many props that I wanted for the theme could only be delivered the night before. I had wanted to have a purple bridge with a chocolate river flowing underneath it, exactly like you see in the film, but there simply wasn't the time to set it up. Maybe that was a good thing; imagine if someone had taken a tumble in it, after downing too many glasses of bubbly.

While we were eating, the chapel of love where we took our vows would be transformed into the entertainment area, with a dance floor, a DJ and stage. Here I decided to keep the look simple with candle-lit tables and arrangements of white flowers. I knew that by the evening our guests would have had a drink, or two; besides they would already have experienced the wow factor with the Willy Wonka-themed suite. But I wasn't just having a disco, I wanted entertainment! I didn't want anyone to be bored so I booked a Kylie impersonator and a Michael Jackson impersonator, we were going to have fireworks outside, and finally at midnight we were having a nineties tribute band – and I was sure if people hadn't yet hit the dance floor, they definitely would then.

As for food, I wanted everything to be simple, nothing fancy, so we went for bangers and mash for dinner, with a trio of real old-school puddings: a chocolate one, rice pudding, and sticky toffee. Later, there would be bacon butties to keep everyone going.

When it came to my bridesmaids there was nothing so simple. I was having thirteen. There were supposed to be fourteen but just before the wedding one of my friends let me down. I had so many bridesmaids because they are all good friends and I felt if I simply asked a few the others would be offended, and I hate to upset anyone. They were wearing long red silk off-the-shoulder dresses, which we had specially made, and delicate diamante tiaras, about a quarter of the size of mine. Oh, and in true Pricey style I arranged to have hairpieces made for all of them by Annabelle's Hair, and they had their hair styled by my hairdresser Mikey. Princess and Ruby, the daughter of my friend Jane, were going to be flower girls, and Junior, Harvey and George, Jane's son, were going to be page boys.

I took my mum and Kieran's shopping to buy their wedding outfits. My mum is turning into a hippy and put her foot down about wearing the fitted dress I picked out for her in Karen Millen. We came to a compromise over a pretty floral dress from Ted Baker. Kieran's mum Wendy had never worn pink and I said, 'I'm going to transform you!' and found her a long baby pink silk maxi dress which she wore with a fake-fur shrug and a fascinator. She looked stunning!

Kieran had our initials and a love heart tattooed on his ring finger, and no doubt when I've had the baby I'll get his name tattooed somewhere. There's still plenty of room.

Typically, I didn't make life easy for myself in the run up to the celebrations when, just four days before the blessing, I held a press call to celebrate the fifth anniversary of KP Equestrian and to launch our new range of show jumps and show jackets. That was when I dressed up as a pantomime My Little Pony. And as if I didn't have enough to do, I suddenly had the idea that I wanted to record a song for Kieran. When I was introduced to someone who owns a recording studio in Worthing, which is just down the road from me, it seemed too good an opportunity to miss. I love singing (as you probably know), and the chance to sing something for Kieran seemed very romantic. We didn't have a song that we could say was ours, so I decided to record Vanessa Williams's romantic ballad 'Save the Best', which summed up my feelings for him. He is the best, and he is the last, of my husbands.

Anyway, I wanted it to be a surprise so two nights before the wedding I pretended that I had to pick up the wedding tiaras. As I'd just had a spray tan and was in trackies and flip-flops it certainly looked as if I wasn't planning on going anywhere special. I dashed to the studio and told the man who was recording me that I only had thirty minutes, and even then I had Kieran texting me halfway through asking me where I was. Ah, pressure! I have to say that I was really pleased with the results when I heard the recording and it made me think that I wanted to concentrate on my singing again. In fact, after the festivities I booked up lessons with the singing coach from *X Factor* and *Britain's Got Talent,* and Junior had lessons with her as well.

*   *   *

Friday 29 March was the day of the blessing. I have to say that I felt very relaxed. There was no stress, nothing to worry about, everything was in hand. It was such a good feeling! The night before Kieran and I slept in separate hotel rooms. I had Princess and Harvey with me and he had Junior. And we kept the tradition of the bride not seeing the groom all the way until I went downstairs to have breakfast and Kieran was there! So we ended up sitting together and said that we might as well have spent the night together too. After breakfast we all had a quick run through so everyone knew what they needed to do, and where they had to stand. That all went smoothly. Then we had the chance to check out the two suites and...wow! We were all so impressed! The chapel of love was so pretty and romantic. The Willy Wonka-themed room was just brilliant! Exactly how I had imagined it. Crazy, funny, cute. I loved the bright colours of the drapes and the chairs and tables.

There were giant toadstools dotted here and there, giant cupcakes, stripy candy sticks, colourful giant lollipops, slabs of chocolate, giant tubes of love hearts, sherbet fountains, and the table centrepieces made of sweets were fab. I thought that the wedding planners and organisers had done an amazing job, given that they'd only had a week and a half to get things together, and had only been able to set them up the night before.

I had arranged for make-up artists to do the brides-maids' make up, and my mum's and Kieran's mum's. I felt so relaxed that I let everyone go ahead of me to get theirs done. I'd intended to have a make-up artist do my make up as well, but in the end I actually did my own and don't think I made a bad job either. There was such a good atmosphere as we all got ready and Princess was dancing around, full of excitement and looking beautiful in her long white dress. Harvey was with us as well, relaxed and happy, while Junior was hanging out with the boys and no doubt rehearsing the song he planned to sing later. But even on my wedding day, my morning sickness wasn't going to go away. I had to lie down on the bed, getting up every now and then to dash to the loo to be sick.

Then it was time for me to go. I took one last look in the mirror. The dress was perfect. The new skirt they'd had made for me was exactly what I wanted. I know I'd been here before in the big dress, waiting to say my vows and get married, but I can honestly say that this felt special and right. I couldn't wait to see Kieran!

The gospel choir sang 'I Will Always Love You' as

I walked up the aisle, on the arms of my dad and my step-dad. As I walked past my guests I thought, I want to remember every single minute of this. Kieran looked so handsome in his classic grey tail suit: masculine, handsome and clean-cut. My husband, and the father of my baby. It didn't get better than this. He had tears in his eyes when he saw me, and I felt very emotional as well.

We had gone for traditional vows again, and even though we had said them before at our Bahamas wedding, it still felt good to say them out loud in front of family and friends. Kieran's sister Leanne did a reading and got all emotional as she did, which touched everyone. Then my brother made a speech. Typically he made a joke about it being my third wedding as he pulled one piece of paper out of his pocket and said, 'Oops, that was a speech from 2005,' and then pulled out another piece, adding, 'And that was 2010!' But I didn't mind, I'd expected it to be honest. Then he became more serious as he read out some of my all-time favourite lines from Whitney Houston's love songs, ending with the lines from a Jermaine Stewart number: 'We don't have to take our clothes off to have a good time'. He, and all our family and friends, could see how happy Kieran makes me.

And then it was champagne all round and on to the wedding breakfast. I think everyone was impressed by the Willy Wonka theme. It gave the room such a happy, family feel, which was exactly what I'd wanted because this was meant to be a family celebration. My kids absolutely loved it and that was important to me.

Naturally there were more speeches, but everyone kept it short. Kieran's two best men gave a great one, as did my best friend Jane. Paul gave a really good one where he said it was clear to everyone how happy I was with Kieran, how nice he was, and that they all hoped we would grow old together. Everyone was looking forward to the new arrival. Kieran's speech was very romantic and emotional, though he did joke about how there was now a Kevin in our lives…that is, Kevin the puppy! Then, at the end, he ad libbed and kept saying, 'I love her! I just love her!' I felt exactly the same. I thanked everyone and said it was third time lucky, there were definitely going to be no more weddings for me, and that I'd saved the best till last.

My song for Kieran started the night of entertainment. He was so touched that I had recorded it especially for him. We took to the dance floor on our own and danced in each other's arms, a truly special, romantic moment. Then it was party central with non-stop music and acts. We didn't want to miss any of it. I danced with Kieran, with my children and friends. Junior took to the stage and sang 'Let Me Entertain You'. He absolutely loves performing and was brilliant. Princess danced all night. And Harvey, who I thought would hate the noise, loved it. He was up on that dance floor, grooving away with me and our friends. He was so happy to be there and didn't go to bed until half-past one.

At the end of the night, tired but very happy, Kieran and I went off to our honeymoon suite. His friends said they would bring up his bag from the room he'd stayed in the night before, and we collapsed on the bed together, waiting for them. We both fell asleep! I woke up at four a.m. fully clothed with the lights still on! I snuggled up to Kieran and went back to sleep, my mind full of images of our perfect day. There was no doubt that our big day had been exactly like it should be, and had been exactly the celebration I had always wanted.

*   *   *

Only one thing happened to upset me that day, and it was when I found out that a really close friend of mine had been caught on the phone to the *Mirror* telling them all about the blessing, and his other half tried to sell a picture of me in my white dress to the *Mirror*, which they didn't buy because it wasn't clear enough. Now I know I have to keep my distance from the pair of them, which is so sad because we have been friends a very long time. I suppose I'm used to this kind of thing happening, but it still hurts and I never imagined in a million years that these two trusted friends would sell out on me.

I didn't do a deal with a newspaper but because I'm a columnist with the *Sun* I said they could have a few pictures. It ended up being a double page pull-out in the paper, exactly like you get for Royal weddings, which was a nice surprise! Kieran and I took a week off, but we decided that the honeymoon would have to wait. Hopefully we'll go to the Maldives soon. For now we are back to our normal, happy, family life.

IT'S A WRAP...
FOR NOW, MAY 2013

It was just as well our honeymoon was postponed because I felt exhausted by my pregnancy. I had a scare in April when I didn't think the baby had moved for a while. I can't tell you how relieved I was when Kieran tracked down my foetal heart monitor and we heard our baby's heartbeat. Stay safe, little one, we both love you so much and can't wait to meet you!

As I said at the beginning of this book, there's always drama with me, but right now I'm hoping for a little less of it! I feel as if I'm moving into a new era in my life when I can concentrate properly on my family and career. I feel very content and happy, in my marriage and with my family, which is a brilliant feeling. I chose to take a step back from the public eye in 2009 because of the sort of press attention I was getting. That has calmed down, though there are still some magazines I am wary of. When I split with Pete I carried on at full tilt for a while with my career when I think I should have taken some time out instead. I'm only human after all. I think the journalists realised they'd pushed me to the very edge, but luckily I've stayed sane and grounded despite them. I weathered the storm. So what does the future hold for the Pricey? I still have ambitions to model. I haven't done any shoots for ages and am itching to get my kit off again. I miss the buzz I used to get from doing the shoots and working the camera. Of course I want to bring out more products, books, and my reality series on YouTube. I want to push myself with my riding, and get better at show jumping and dressage. There are so many things I want to do!

So I'll sign off now. I've got four months to go before we meet our new baby, and I'm praying that everything goes well. It looks like Kieran will be a fantastic dad, really caring, patient and loving. He's great with my kids and such a genuine, lovely man. I love him so much. I really have saved the best for last.